This book is dedicated to the memory of my father-in-law,
the late DR. JAMES HOWARD MAXWELL,
who by his generous friendship and wise counsel
played an indispensable role in my preparation for pastoral ministry.
By growing in the grace of the gospel and by living according to
God's law, he spread the fragrance of the knowledge
of Christ everywhere.

2 Corinthians 2:14b

# CONTENTS

# PREFACE

"He who knows how to distinguish Gospel from Law should thank God and know that he is a theologian." This statement from Martin Luther always gives me pause because I'm not sure that I can make such a claim. Few things are more difficult to master than the biblical teaching about the law in its relationship to the gospel. Yet my prayer is that as you read this book you will gain clearer insight into both what God demands in his law and gives in his gospel.

Good teaching on the law and the gospel has never been more badly needed than it is today. We are living in lawless times, when disrespect for authority has led to widespread disdain for God's commandments. People are behaving badly, even in church. Part of the problem is that most people don't know what God requires. Even among Christians there is an appalling lack of familiarity with the perfect standard of God's law, and of course the situation is worse in the culture at large. This ignorance undoubtedly contributes to the general lowering of moral standards in these post-Christian times, but it does as much damage to our theology. People who are ignorant of God's law never see their need for the gospel. As John Bunyan explained it, "The man who does not know the nature of the law cannot know the nature of sin. And he who does not know the nature of sin cannot know the nature of the Savior."

This book is about God's law—specifically, the Ten Commandments—but it is also intended to help people understand the gospel. The law is what shows us our need for the saving work of Jesus Christ. Then, once we come to Christ by believing in the gospel of his cross and empty tomb, it shows us how to live for his glory. In the pages that follow I have tried to be practical, showing what the Ten Commandments mean for daily life. By way of illustration, I have chosen a Bible story that shows what happens when each commandment gets broken. I have also tried to be Christ-centered, constantly explaining how the law of God relates to the person and work of Jesus Christ.

Like most of the books I have written, this one began in the pulpit of Philadelphia's Tenth Presbyterian Church. I owe a great debt of gratitude to Tenth's session and congregation for their prayers, their encouragement, and in this case their many requests to publish this material in book form. By all accounts, the preaching of the Ten Commandments was a blessing to our church, and our sincere hope is that it will be a blessing to you as well.

Several more thank yous need to be offered. One goes to my friends at P&R Publishing for helping this book find its way back into print. Another thank you goes to my sister Nancy Taylor for her hard work in preparing the questions at the end of each chapter. I am also grateful to my friends Randall Grossman, Jonathan Rockey, and David Skeel for their improvements to my manuscript; to Pat Russell and Danny Bombaro for helping prepare the indexes; and to David Madder for first suggesting the title *Written in Stone*. But the biggest thanks go to my wife, Lisa, for her partnership in ministry, and especially for the way she organizes our household so that my writing is not a sacrifice for our children.

*Philip Graham Ryken*
Philadelphia, Pennsylvania

# 1

# Written in Stone

*And God spoke all these words, saying, "I am the LORD your God, who brought you out of the land of Egypt, out of the house of slavery."*

EXODUS 20:1-2

In their book *The Day America Told the Truth*, James Patterson and Peter Kim lay down the law for postmodern times. They observe that today there is "absolutely no moral consensus at all. . . . Everyone is making up their own personal moral codes—their own Ten Commandments." Patterson and Kim proceed to list what they call the "ten real commandments," the rules that according to their surveys people actually live by. These rules include the following:

— I don't see the point in observing the Sabbath;
— I will steal from those who won't really miss it;
— I will lie when it suits me, so long as it doesn't cause any real damage;
— I will cheat on my spouse—after all, given the chance, he or she will do the same;
— I will procrastinate at work and do absolutely nothing about one full day in every five.[1]

These new commandments are based on moral relativism, the belief that we are free to make up our own rules, based on our own personal preferences. The law is not something that comes from God, but something we come up with on our own. And our laws usually conflict with God's laws. It is not surprising that what Patterson and Kim call the "ten real commandments" generally violate the laws that God gave to Moses: remember the Sabbath, do all your work in six days, you shall not commit adultery, you shall not steal, you shall not bear false witness, and so forth. We have become a law unto ourselves.

One would hope to find that the situation is somewhat better in the church. Surely God's own people honor the permanent, objective standard of God's law! Yet the church is full of worshipers who do not even know the Ten Commandments, let alone know how to keep them. This problem was documented in a recent report from The Princeton Religion Research Center. The headline read, "Religion Is Gaining Ground, but Morality Is Losing Ground," and the report showed how recent increases in church attendance and Bible reading have been offset by a simultaneous decline in morality.[2]

How is this possible? How can people be more interested in God and at the same time less willing to do what he says? The only explanation is that people do not know the God of the Bible, because if they did, they would recognize the absolute authority of his law. Respect for God always demands respect for his law. And whenever people have a low regard for God's law, as they do in our culture, it is ultimately because they have a low regard for God.

## THE LORD YOUR GOD

If the law comes from God, then the best place to begin understanding the law is with God himself. This is precisely where the book of Exodus begins its presentation of the Ten Commandments, also known as the Decalogue, meaning "ten words": "And God spoke all these words" (Exod. 20:1).

To get a sense of who God is, it helps to remember the setting. God was speaking to the Israelites as they were gathered at the foot of Mount Sinai. Exodus 19 described how God descended on the mountain in great power and glory, with thunder and lightning, fire and smoke. The Israelites were forbidden to come any closer, upon the pain of death. They had come into the presence of the awesome and Almighty God, who lives in unapproachable holiness. Obviously, whatever such a God has to say demands our fullest and most careful attention. What we received from Mount Sinai was not simply the law of Moses, but the law of *God*, spoken in the revelation of his glory. As Isaiah was later to write, "The LORD was pleased, for his righteousness' sake, to magnify his law and make it glorious" (Isa. 42:21).

Although God revealed his glory in the fire and smoke on the mountain, he made a fuller disclosure of his deity when he began to speak. He said, "I am the LORD your God, who brought you out of the land of Egypt, out of the house of slavery" (Exod. 20:2). This verse is sometimes called the preface or prologue to the Ten Commandments. In it God defends his authority as the lawgiver. What gives God the right to tell people what to do? In the words of the Westminster Shorter Catechism, "The preface to the ten commandments teaches us, That because God is the Lord, and our God, and Redeemer, therefore we are bound to keep all his commandments" (A. 44).

God is the Lord. Here he uses his special covenant name *Yahweh*. He is the great I AM, the sovereign and Almighty Lord. He is the supreme, self-existent, eternal, and unchangeable God, who bound himself to Abraham, Isaac, and Jacob with the unbreakable promise of his covenant. Furthermore, he is our very own God. "I am the LORD *your* God," he says. Somewhat surprisingly, he uses the second person singular, thus indicating that he has a personal relationship with each and every one of his people.[3] That personal relationship is also a saving relationship, for as God goes on to say, "I am the LORD your God, who brought you out of the land of Egypt, out of the house of slavery" (Exod. 20:2b). This was a summary of everything that had happened so far in Exodus. God was reminding the Israelites that he was not only their Lord and their God, but also their Redeemer. And it was on this basis that he laid down his law for their lives. It was Israel's unique privilege to receive the law straight from God.

What God said to Israel is essentially the same thing he says to every believer in Christ: "I am the Lord your God, who brought you out of the Egypt of your sin, out of your slavery to Satan." Through the saving work of Jesus Christ, crucified and risen, God is our sovereign Lord and very own Savior, and thus he has the right to claim legal authority over us. The law comes from God, who is our Savior and our Lord.

## GOD AND HIS LAW

If the law comes from God, then it must reflect his divine character. This is true of rules and regulations in general: They reveal something about the rule-maker. To give just one example, consider the extensive federal regulations that govern handicapped access to public buildings. What do these laws tell us about the society that made them? They tell us that Americans want to include the disabled in the ordinary events of public life.

The law always reveals the character of the lawgiver. This was especially true at Mount Sinai, where every one of the Ten Commandments was stamped with the being and attributes of Almighty God. So what does each law tell us about the God who gave it?

The *first* commandment is, "You shall have no other gods before me" (Exod. 20:3). Obviously the God who gave this command is jealous; he will not share his glory with any other god. And rightly so, because he is the one and only true God. All the others are impostors. The first commandment announces the unique sovereignty of the God who alone is able to say, "I am the LORD, and there is no other" (Isa. 45:18b). It also indicates his omnipresence, because it tells us not to have any other gods "before him," meaning "in his presence" (this point is developed in Chapter 4).

The *second* commandment is, "You shall not make for yourself a carved image, or any likeness of anything that is in heaven above, or that is in the earth beneath, or that is in the water under the earth" (Exod. 20:4). This commandment is about worshiping the right God in the right way. God refuses to be worshiped by means of images. This shows that he is spirit, that he does not have a physical form. The mention of the heavens and the earth also shows that he is the Creator. One problem with idols is that they confuse the Creator with his creation. The commandment goes on to speak of God's mercy and justice: "You shall not bow down to them or serve them; for I the LORD your God am a jealous God, visiting the iniquity of the fathers on the children to the third and the fourth generation of those who hate me, but showing steadfast love to thousands of those who love me and keep my commandments" (Exod. 20:5-6). The God who gave the law is a God who makes absolute moral distinctions. He punishes sinners while at the same time showing his love to generation after generation of the people he has chosen to save.

The *third* commandment is about honoring God's name: "You shall not take the name of the LORD your God in vain, for the LORD will not hold him guiltless who takes his name in vain" (Exod. 20:7). The threat attached to this commandment shows that God expects to be obeyed. Those who break his law will be charged with guilt. The commandment itself shows that God is honorable, and that therefore he deserves to be treated with respect. Even his name is holy.

The *fourth* commandment is, "Remember the Sabbath day, to keep it holy. Six days you shall labor and do all your work, but the seventh day is a Sabbath to the LORD your God" (Exod. 20:8-10a). This commandment shows that God is sovereign over all the events of daily life. He is Lord every day of the week. It also makes an explicit connection between what is commanded and the one who commands it, between God and his law: "For in six days the LORD made heaven and earth, the sea, and all that is in them, and rested the seventh day. Therefore the LORD blessed the Sabbath day and made it holy" (Exod. 20:11). We are commanded to work and rest because we serve a working, resting God.

The first four commandments govern our relationship to God; the last six concern our relationships with one another. But even these commandments rest on various divine attributes. The *fifth* commandment is about respecting authority: "Honor your father and your mother, that your days may be long in the land that the LORD your God is giving you" (Exod. 20:12). What stands behind this commandment is God's own authority as our Father. This is also the first command with a promise—the promise of long life in a good land, which shows how generous God is to provide for his people.

The *sixth* commandment is, "You shall not murder" (Exod. 20:13). This reminds us that God is the Lord and giver of life. He forbids the taking of innocent life because he is a life-giving God. Furthermore, this commandment preserves his sovereignty over life's end. He is Lord over death as well as life.

The *seventh* commandment is the one that everyone knows: "You shall not commit adultery" (Exod. 20:14). What does this tell us about God? It tells us that he is a God of purity and faithfulness, a God who expects covenants to be kept. It also tells us that he is a God of joy, because this command preserves sex for the fellowship of marriage.

The *eighth* commandment is, "You shall not steal" (Exod. 20:15). The God who gave this commandment is our Creator and Provider. To keep it is to recognize that ultimately everything belongs to him, and that therefore we do not have the right to take what he has given to someone else.

The *ninth* commandment is to tell the truth: "You shall not bear false witness against your neighbor" (Exod. 20:16). This commandment comes from the God of truth, who is true in all he is, says, and does. As the Scripture says, "The Glory of Israel will not lie" (1 Sam. 15:29a).

The *tenth* commandment is about contentment: "You shall not covet" (Exod. 20:17a). Covetousness comes from a desire to possess what God has not given us. Like the eighth commandment, keeping this commandment requires faith in God's providence. God commands us not to covet because he can be trusted to give us everything we truly need. He is our provider.

One further divine attribute is revealed by the Ten Commandments as a whole, and that attribute is love. When Jesus summarized God's law he said, "'You shall love the Lord your God with all your heart and with all your soul and with all your mind.' This is the great and first commandment. And a second is like it: 'You shall love your neighbor as yourself'" (Matt. 22:37-38; cf. Deut. 6:5; Lev. 19:18; Rom. 13:9). In other words, the Ten Commandments can be reduced to two commandments: love God and love your neighbor. So they are all about love. We love God by worshiping him and using his name properly. We love our parents by honoring them. We love our spouses by being faithful to them. We love our neighbors by protecting their lives, respecting their property, and telling them the truth.

The God who gave these commandments is a God of love, who wants us to love him and to share his love with others. As Jesus said, "Whoever has my commands and keeps them, he it is who loves me" (John 14:21a; cf. 1 John 5:3a). If that is true, then we cannot separate God's law from God's love.

To summarize, the Ten Commandments display the character of God. They reveal his sovereignty, jealousy, justice, holiness, honor, faithfulness, providence, truthfulness, and love.

When we see how God has poured himself into his law, it becomes obvious that he could not have given us any other commandments than the ones he gave. The Ten Commandments express God's will for our lives because they are based on his character. This helps answer an ancient dilemma, one that Plato posed in one of his famous dialogues: Does God command the law because the law is good, or is the law good because God commands it?[4] The answer is, both! The law, with all its goodness, springs from the goodness of God's character. The law is good because God is good, and his goodness penetrates every aspect of his law.

### IT WILL NEVER PASS AWAY

The fact that God's law expresses God's character has many implications. One is that when we break God's law we are making a direct assault on God himself. To worship another god is to deny God's sovereignty; to misuse his name is to deny his honor; to steal is to deny his providence; to lie is to deny his truthfulness; and so forth. Every violation of the law is an offense against God's holy character.

Another implication of the relationship between our Lord and his law is that the law is perpetually binding, that it remains in force for all persons in all places and at all times. Sovereignty, justice, faithfulness, truthfulness, love—these are God's eternal attributes. He would have to un-God himself to set them aside. We should expect, therefore, that the law that expresses his eternal attributes has eternal validity.

This perhaps explains why God set the Ten Commandments in stone, writing them out with his own finger (Exod. 31:18; 32:16). A. W. Pink comments:

Their uniqueness appears first in that this revelation of God at Sinai—which was to serve for all coming ages as the grand expression of His holiness and the summation of man's duty—was attended with such awe-inspiring phenomena that the very manner of their publication plainly showed that God Himself assigned to the Decalogue peculiar importance. The Ten Commandments were uttered by God in an audible voice, with the fearful adjuncts of clouds and darkness, thunders and lightnings and the sound of a trumpet, and they were the only parts of Divine Revelation so spoken—none of the ceremonial or civil precepts were thus distinguished. Those Ten Words, and they alone, were written by the finger of God upon tables of stone, and they alone were deposited in the holy ark for safe keeping. Thus, in the unique honor conferred upon the Decalogue itself we may perceive its paramount importance in the Divine government.[5]

The Ten Commandments were written in stone because they would remain in effect for as long as time endured. When would it ever be permissible to worship another god, to misuse God's name, to lie, murder, or steal? Never, because these things are contrary to God's very nature.

One way to prove that God's law is eternal is to show that it was in effect even before God wrote it down. Exodus 20 is sometimes described as "the giving of the law." However, these laws had already been given! The commandments God gave to Moses at Mount Sinai were not new; in fact, they were as old as the human race. We know this from the stories of the Bible, in which God often rebuked and punished people for breaking these very laws.

There are clear examples of commandment-breaking earlier in Exodus. The ten plagues God visited on Pharaoh were a direct punishment for Egypt's idolatry, which violated the first and second commandments (Num. 33:4). Moses' own personal exodus was occasioned by his violation of the sixth commandment (Exod. 2:11-15). At the burning bush God taught his prophet to honor his name (Exod. 3:1-15), very much in keeping with the third commandment. God revealed the Sabbath principle of the fourth commandment by giving manna six days out of seven, and those who failed to follow the appropriate instructions suffered for their disobedience (Exod. 16). So at various points the exodus presupposed the existence of God's law, even before the Israelites reached Mount Sinai.

We find the same principle at work in the book of Genesis, which contains many stories about people breaking God's law. Noah's son Ham was cursed for dishonoring his father (Gen. 9:18-28). Cain was condemned as a murderer (Gen. 4:10-12), the Sodomites as adulterers (Gen. 19:24-25), Rachel as a thief (Gen. 31:19-32), Abraham as a liar (Gen. 20), and Lot's wife as a covetous woman (Gen. 19). God had always dealt with people on the basis of his law. Certain commandments had been revealed to them, and if they were written nowhere else, they were written on the tablets of their hearts (see Rom. 2:14-15).

God's moral law went all the way back to the Garden of Eden, where (in addition to various other commands concerning sexuality, rest, and work), God told Adam and Eve not to eat from the tree of the knowledge of good and evil. Theologians argue about whether or not our first parents also knew any of the Ten Commandments. The Bible simply doesn't say. But whether or not God revealed any of its specific commands, Adam and Eve were ruled by its basic principles: love for God and love for one another. They were obligated to honor one another, to preserve life, and to tell the truth—the kind of conduct later mandated on Mount Sinai. And in their first sin, Adam and Eve managed to violate nearly all ten of God's basic rules. Taking the forbidden fruit was a theft, stimulated by a covetous desire, based on a lie about God's character. Eating it was a way of having another god. It was also tantamount to murder because it led to the death of the entire human race. From the beginning our first parents were bound by the basic principles of what theologians call "the law of creation" or "the law of nature."

So to summarize, God's law was in effect in various ways long before the Israelites ever reached Mount Sinai. What, then, were the Ten Commandments? Think of them as a fresh copy. They were a republication, in summary form, of God's will for humanity. As Peter Enns comments, "The 'giving' of the law at Sinai is not the first time Israel hears of God's laws, but is the codification and explicit promulgation of those laws."[6] This makes perfect sense when we remember that the Ten Commandments express the character of God, who does not change.

## THE LAW OF CHRIST

Is the law still binding today? This is a vital question. Do the Ten Commandments have any abiding relevance for Christians and the culture in which we live? Once we understand the relationship between our Lord and his law, this question is easy to answer: Yes, God's law is still binding today! His standard has not changed, any more than his character has changed. As ABC's Ted Koppel said in his now famous commencement address at Duke University, "What Moses brought down from Mount Sinai were not the Ten Suggestions . . . they are commandments. *Are*, not were."[7]

Some people deny that God's law is still in effect today. This denial is obviously made by many non-Christians, who act as a law unto themselves. But even many people in the church pay little attention to God's law. This is partly because of the lawlessness of our surrounding culture, but it also comes from the way some Christians read the Bible. After all, the New Testament makes a number of statements that seem to set aside the Old Testament law. For example, according to John, "The law was given through Moses; grace and truth came through Jesus Christ" (John 1:17). Likewise, the apostle Paul wrote, "You are not under law but under grace" (Rom. 6:14), and "Now that faith has come, we are no longer under a guardian [the law]" (Gal. 3:25; cf. 5:18). These and similar statements would seem to suggest that God's law has been superseded. On the other hand, the New Testament also seems to claim that the law remains in effect. It claims that we are "under the law of Christ" (1 Cor. 9:21), for example, or even that "It is easier for heaven and earth to pass away than for one dot of the Law to become void" (Luke 16:17).

This is not the place to give a full exposition of everything the Bible says about God's law. But it is vitally important to understand that one reason the New Testament talks about the law in several different ways is because there are several different kinds of law. Here we should at least make a distinction between three types of law: the moral, the civil, and the ceremonial. These were all given in the Old Testament, sometimes interspersed. But in order to make sense of the law—and ultimately of the gospel—they must be carefully distinguished, as we see them through the clear lens of the person and work of Jesus Christ. "It is of the utmost importance," writes Ernest Reisinger, "to discern the differences between the ceremonial law, which pertained to the worship of Israel and prefigured Christ; the civil or judicial laws, which detailed the duties to Israel as a nation (having their roots in the moral law, particularly in the second table); and the moral law, by which the Creator governs the moral conduct of *all* creatures for *all* times."[8]

The *moral law* is summarized in the Ten Commandments. It is the righteous and eternal standard for our relationship with God and with others. The *civil law* consisted of the laws that governed Israel as a nation under God. These included guidelines for waging war, restrictions on land use, regulations for debt, and penalties for specific violations of Israel's legal code. The *ceremonial law* consisted of regulations for celebrating various religious festivals (e.g., Exod. 23:14-19) and for worshiping God in his sanctuary (e.g., Exod. 25—30). It included laws for clean and unclean foods, instructions for ritual purity, guidelines for the conduct of priests, and especially instructions for offering sacrifices—the whole sacrificial system (see Leviticus). God gave detailed regulations that covered specifics like who was supposed to cut which animal's throat, and how, and what was to be done with the blood.

The ceremonial law is no longer in effect; it has been abrogated. This is because all its regulations pointed forward to Jesus Christ. Concerning the Old Testament ceremonies, the Scripture says, "These are a shadow of the things to come, but the substance belongs to Christ" (Col. 2:17; cf. Heb. 10:1). This is most obviously true of the sacrifices. Now that Christ has offered himself as the once-and-for-all atonement for sin, no further sacrifice is needed. To continue to follow the old ceremonies would be to deny the sufficiency of his work on the cross. One of the errors of the theological perspective known as dispensationalism is to imagine that the old ceremonies and sacrifices will be reinstated in Israel.[9] But the sacrificial system has been superseded by Christ, and the only two ceremonies still in effect—the sacraments of baptism and the Lord's Supper—both look back to his cross.

The civil law has also expired, but for a slightly different reason: The church is not a state. We do have a king (namely, Christ), but his kingdom is spiritual. Therefore, although the civil laws of the Old Testament contain principles that are useful for governing nations today, God's people are no longer bound by their specific regulations. The basic error of the theological perspective known as theonomy (or "Christian reconstruction") is to imagine that civil laws from the time of Moses should still be enforced in America today. This is what some people mean when they talk about restoring a "Christian America." But as Calvin recognized, this approach to politics is "perilous and seditious" because like the ceremonial law, the civil law has been superseded by Christ.[10] Today the people of God are governed instead by church discipline, which is based on the moral law, and which has spiritual rather than civil consequences.

The distinction between these three kinds of law—the moral, the civil, and the ceremonial—helps us understand what the New Testament teaches about God's law. The ceremonial law and the civil law were types and figures pointing forward to the cross and kingdom of Christ. Now that he has come, they have been set aside, which is why the New Testament sometimes seems so dismissive of the law. As we have seen, what are now in effect are the sacraments and discipline of the church, which echo the ceremonial and the civil law respectively. The New Testament also completely rejects the idea that we can be justified by keeping the law. It is in this sense especially that we are no longer "under law" (Rom. 6:14; Gal. 5:18). Our salvation does not depend on our ability to keep the law. As we shall learn in the next chapter, we are unable to keep it, and therefore we cannot be declared righteous by it (Rom. 3:20). But since our natural inclination is to think that we *can* be saved by our own obedience, the Bible condemns any and every attempt to use the keeping of God's law as a way of justifying ourselves.

What the New Testament never does, however, is to declare an end to God's moral law as the standard for our lives. It is still, in the words of the Westminster Confession of Faith, "a perfect rule of righteousness" (19.1), or as Calvin termed it, the "true and eternal rule of righteousness."[11] Similarly, Ernest Reisinger describes the moral law as "the eternal standard of right moral conduct—a fixed, objective standard of righteousness."[12] This makes sense when we remember the close relationship between the moral law and the character of the Lord who gave it. The moral law is as eternal as God is.

Furthermore, the character of God is also the character of his Son Jesus Christ. The Bible teaches, "He is the radiance of the glory of God and the exact imprint of his nature" (Heb. 1:3a). Jesus is one and the same as the God who revealed his law to Moses; the law expresses the character of the Son as well as of the Father. Therefore, to try and separate the God who gave the law from the God who has shown his grace in the gospel would practically be to divide the Trinity. The Son is every bit as sovereign, jealous, life-giving, faithful, truthful, and loving as the Father revealed himself to be in the Ten Commandments.

Given the close relationship between God and his law, and between the Father and the Son, it is not surprising that Jesus warned us, "Do not think that I have come to abolish the Law or the Prophets; I have not come to abolish them but to fulfill them. For truly, I say to you, until heaven and earth pass away, not an iota, not a dot, will pass from the Law until all is accomplished" (Matt. 5:17-18). Clearly Jesus was speaking about the moral law, at least in part, because he went on to say, "Whoever relaxes one of the least of these commandments and teaches others to do the same will be called least in the kingdom of heaven, but whoever does them and teaches them will be called great in the kingdom of heaven" (Matt. 5:19). The law of Moses is not simply the law of God; it is also the law of Christ.

## THE RIGHT WAY TO LIVE

Our focus throughout the rest of this book will be on God's moral law. One way to prove that this law is still binding is to show how, in one way or another, all ten of the original commandments are repeated in the New Testament, either by Jesus himself or in the teaching of his apostles.

When the New Testament lists the sins that lead to condemnation, or the acts of obedience that are pleasing to God, it sometimes follows the outline of the Ten Commandments (e.g. Matt. 15:19; 19:17-19; Rom. 7:8-10; 1 Cor. 6:9-10; 1 Tim. 1:9-11; Rev. 21:8). But the commandments are also treated individually. The *first* commandment tells us to have no other gods. Jesus made essentially the same claim about himself: "I am the way, and the truth, and the life. No one comes to the Father except through me" (John 14:6; cf. Acts 4:12). The *second* commandment forbids idolatry. John said, "Little children, keep yourselves from idols" (1 John 5:21). The *third* commandment tells us to honor God's name, which is exactly the way Jesus taught us to pray: "Hallowed be your name" (Matt. 6:9). The *fourth* commandment is about working and resting. As believers in Jesus Christ we are told that whatever we do, we should work at it with all our hearts (Col. 3:23). We are also told that Jesus is Lord of the Sabbath (Matt. 12:8), and that there remains "a Sabbath rest for the people of God" (Heb. 4:9).

The first four commands are about loving God, but what about loving our neighbor? In the *fifth* commandment we are bound to honor our parents. This command is repeated by the apostle Paul: "Children, obey your parents in the Lord, for this is right. 'Honor your father and mother'" (Eph. 6:1-2a). Next, without in any way changing the *sixth* commandment, Jesus clarified its true spiritual purpose when he said, "You have heard that it was said to those of old, 'You shall not murder' . . . But I say to you that everyone who is angry with his brother will be liable to judgment" (Matt. 5:21-22a). Jesus did the same thing with the *seventh* commandment: "I say to you that everyone who looks at a woman with lustful intent has already committed adultery with her in his heart" (Matt. 5:28). As for the *eighth* commandment, the New Testament says, "Let the thief no longer steal, but rather let him labor" (Eph. 4:28a). And with regard to the *ninth* commandment, the Scripture says, "Do not lie to one other" (Col. 3:9a). Finally, the *tenth* commandment forbids coveting, which the apostle James condemns by saying, "You ask and do not receive, because you ask wrongly, to spend it on your passions" (James 4:3).

Is the law still binding today? Of course it is! As the Bible demonstrates all the way through, the Ten Commandments show us the right way to live. They are based on the righteousness of God, which explains why even the New Testament has so many positive things to say about God's law. "Do we then overthrow the law?" asks the apostle Paul. "By no means! On the contrary, we uphold the law" (Rom. 3:31). Later he goes on to describe the commandments as "holy and righteous and good" (Rom. 7:12) and to insist that he is "not . . . outside the law of God" but remains "under the law of Christ" (1 Cor. 9:21).

So much for the law. But what about the gospel? We will attempt to give a fuller answer to this question in the coming chapters. But the answer basically goes like this: It is our breaking of the law that helps us see our need for the gospel. The more clearly we see what God's law requires, the more obvious it becomes that we cannot keep its commands, which is exactly why we need the gospel. We cannot be saved by our own keeping of the law because we do not keep it. But Jesus did! He kept the whole law on our behalf. Perfectly. More than that, in his death on the cross he suffered the penalty we deserve for our failure to keep God's law. Now everyone who believes in Jesus Christ will be saved by his keeping of the law and by his suffering of its curse.

As believers in Jesus Christ, do we need still need to keep God's law? Yes. The moral law expresses God's perfect and righteous will for our lives. So Jesus commands us to keep it, not as a way of getting right with God, but as a way of pleasing the God who has made us right with him.

## STUDY QUESTIONS

1. How many of the Ten Commandments can you list (without peeking!)?
2. What does the prologue "I am the LORD your God" tell us about God and his relationship with his people?
3. What do the first four commandments tell us about God's character?
4. Look at each of the Ten Commandments and discuss how each one relates to the law of loving God and our neighbor.
5. How do we know that God's laws are eternal—binding before and ever since he gave them?
6. Some Christians use the New Testament to argue that they no longer need to obey the Ten Commandments. Why are these arguments ineffective?

7. Can we be justified by the law? Why or why not?
8. What are the purposes of the law?
9. In what ways does Jesus fulfill the whole law of God?
10. "Whenever people have a low regard for God's law . . . it is ultimately because they have a low regard for God." What are some areas in your life where your actions and attitudes show a high regard for God and his law—specifically, the Ten Commandments? What are some areas that need some work?

# 2

# A MULTI-USE ITEM

*We know that the law is good, if one uses it lawfully.*
1 TIMOTHY 1:8

American consumers have a fascination with multi-use items. Consider the extraordinary success of the Swiss army knife. In addition to an ordinary knife blade, this handy gadget comes with a toothpick, a tweezer, a pair of scissors, a couple of screwdrivers, a file, a saw blade, and a corkscrew. The tool is a knife, but it is also much more: an indispensable tool to perform seemingly any task.

Like an all-in-one tool, the law of God is a multi-use item. This important truth helps explain why the Bible talks about the law in so many different ways. God has more than one purpose for his law, and the important thing is to know how to use it. As the apostle Paul observed, "the law is good, if one uses it lawfully" (1 Tim. 1:8). In this chapter we consider three ways to use God's law: First, the law teaches God's redeemed people how to live for God's glory; second, the law restrains sin in society; and third, the law shows sinners their need of a Savior. To say the same thing in a slightly different way, the law is a map (it guides our conduct), a muzzle (it keeps us from doing wrong), and a mirror (it shows us our sin).[1]

## TEACHING US HOW TO LIVE

It may be surprising to discover that the Ten Commandments do not begin with the law, but with the gospel: "And God spoke all these words, saying, 'I am the LORD your God, who brought you out of the land of Egypt, out of the house of slavery'" (Exod. 20:1-2). As we have seen, these verses teach that the law comes from God—the great God of the covenant who revealed his glory on the mountain. And this great God is a God who saves!

At the beginning of chapter 20 God summarizes the whole epic adventure of the exodus in two short phrases: "who brought you out of the land of Egypt, [and] out of the house of slavery." God was reminding his people of the good news of their salvation. For centuries they had languished in the prison house of Pharaoh. But by sending ten terrible plagues, by holding back the sea, by saving them through the blood of a lamb, and by providing bread in the wilderness, God delivered his people. Their liberation was *the* great saving event of the Old Testament.

Almost immediately after he set his people free, God gave them his law. The order is significant: first the gospel, then the law. As the Dutch theologian Jochem Douma writes in his masterful exposition of Exodus 20, "The commandments follow the gospel of undeserved deliverance."[2]

Many Christians think that the law is somehow opposed to the gospel. They assume that in the Old Testament salvation came by law, whereas in the New Testament salvation comes by grace. But the truth is that salvation has always come by grace, and the law and the gospel work together for salvation in *both* testaments. The grace of the gospel has never been opposed to the proper use of the law.

We see the law and the gospel working together in Exodus, which contains both the Old Testament's clearest example of salvation by grace and its fullest presentation of God's law. Significantly, God did not give Israel the Ten Commandments until chapter 20. Chapters 1—19 come first, and they tell the story of salvation by grace—God fulfilling his covenant promise by bringing Israel out of Egypt. Then comes chapter 20, in which God gives his people a law to live by.

This law was for those who had *already* been redeemed. The overarching theme of Exodus is that God's people are saved for God's glory. The problem with Pharaoh and the Egyptians was not simply that it was wrong for them to hold slaves, but that they were preventing the

Israelites from serving their God. With the exodus came a change of masters. God's people were released from their bondage to Pharaoh in order to serve the true and living God—not as captured slaves, but as liberated sons and daughters. The law that God gave them at the time of their emancipation was not a new form of bondage, therefore, but a freedom charter. It was just because God's people had been saved by grace that they were now free to live by the law of his covenant community. They had been redeemed; *therefore*, they were not to have any other gods, make any idols, and so on. God did not set his people free so that they could do whatever they wanted, but so that they could live for him. This was the whole point of the exodus. Moses kept saying to Pharaoh, "Let my people go, so that they may serve me" (e.g., Exod. 7:16). And this is one of the law's most important uses: to teach people who have been redeemed how to live for the glory of their God.

God's people always need to remember this connection between God's grace and God's law. In the book of Deuteronomy God gave Israel's parents these instructions:

> When your son asks you in time to come, "What is the meaning of the testimonies and statutes and the rules that the LORD our God has commanded you?" then you shall say to your son, "We were Pharaoh's slaves in Egypt. And the LORD brought us out of Egypt with a mighty hand. The LORD showed signs and wonders, great and grievous, against Egypt and against Pharaoh and all his household, before our eyes. And he brought us out from there, that he might bring us in and give us the land that he swore to give to our fathers. And the LORD commanded us to do all these statutes, to fear the LORD our God, for our good always, that he might preserve us alive, as we are this day."—6:20-24

When the children of Israel asked why they had to keep God's law, their parents were supposed to tell them a story. The only way they could understand the meaning of the law was by knowing its context, which was the experience of the exodus—the story of their salvation. First the gospel, then the law.

The relationship between law and gospel in the exodus sets the pattern for (or "typifies") one purpose of the law in the Christian life: The law teaches God's redeemed people how to live. We too have a story to tell—the story of our redemption in Jesus Christ. The story begins with our slavery to sin. We were in such spiritual bondage that there was no way for us to escape. But God set us free from sin and from Satan through the saving work of Jesus Christ. His death and resurrection were our great exodus, our emancipation.

Now that we have received God's grace in the gospel, what comes next? Are we free to live as we please? Can we be saved and still lead a sinful life? Of course not! What we are free to do is to live in a way that is pleasing to God. Martin Luther once explained this principle to one of his students. Luther had been talking about God's free grace for sinners, how our salvation does not rest upon our own good works, but upon the saving work of Jesus Christ. "If what you're saying is true," the student objected, "then we may live as we want!" Luther replied, "Yes. Now what do you want?"[3]

What Luther said to his student was fully in keeping with Scripture. The apostle Peter said, "Live as people who are free, not using your freedom as a cover-up for evil, but living as servants of God" (1 Pet. 2:16). It is just because we have been set free by God's grace that we are obligated to love and obey God. The apostle Paul adds that we are also obligated to love our neighbor: "You were called to freedom, brothers. Only do not use your freedom as an opportunity for the flesh, but through love serve one another" (Gal. 5:13). Notice what Peter and Paul are doing in these verses: They are telling us to love God and to love our neighbor, which is what the Ten Commandments are all about. Paul makes this connection explicit when he goes on to say, "The whole law is fulfilled in one word: 'You shall love your neighbor as yourself'" (Gal. 5:14). But of course Peter and Paul were simply repeating what Jesus said when he summarized the law in two Great Commandments: Love God and love your neighbor (see Matt. 22:37-40). Jesus also said, "If you love me, you will keep my commandments" (John 14:15). The gospel of Jesus Christ obligates us to keep the law of God.

As believers in Christ, we are called to live in a way that is pleasing to God, which means living according to his perfect standard. God's standard has not changed, as if somehow his grace has redefined his righteousness. On the contrary, as we saw in the previous chapter, the moral law expresses the very character of Christ. Now, under the skillful direction of the Holy Spirit, it is still our teacher and our guide. The Puritan Thomas Watson wrote, "The moral law is the copy of God's will, our spiritual directory; it shows us what sins to avoid, what duties to pursue."[4] Writing in a similar vein, the Anglican bishop J. C. Ryle argued, "There is no greater mistake than to suppose that a Christian has nothing to do with the law and the Ten Commandments, because he cannot be justified by keeping them. The same Holy Ghost who convinces the believer of sin by the law, and leads him to Christ for justification, will always lead him to a spiritual use of the law, as a friendly guide, in the pursuit of sanctification."[5] The law is useful for instructing us in righteousness. It helps us to know what is pleasing to God. It shows us how to live.

## RESTRAINING SIN IN SOCIETY

There is a second use of the law that is also mentioned in Exodus 20. God uses his law to restrain sin in human society. The commandments of the law, with their accusation of guilt and threat of punishment, discourage people from sinning against God. The law does not keep people from sinning entirely, of course, because it cannot change our sinful nature. But to a certain extent the law does serve to restrain our sin.

God intended his law to have this restraining effect on Israel. Once the people had received the Ten Commandments, they responded with fear and trembling. They were overawed by God and by the commanding power of his voice. But Moses assured them that God's law was ultimately for their benefit. He said, "Do not fear, for God has come to test you, that the fear of him may be before you, that you may not sin" (Exod. 20:20). The law was partly a deterrent. It had the preventive purpose of keeping God's people away from sin. The threat of the law's penalty held their depravity in check. Calvin compared this use of the law to the bridle that controls an unruly horse:

> The second office of the Law is, by means of its fearful denunciations and the consequent dread of punishment, to curb those who,

unless forced, have no regard for rectitude and justice. Such persons
are curbed, not because their mind is inwardly moved and affected,
but because, as if a bridle were laid upon them, they refrain their
hands from external acts, and internally check the depravity which
would otherwise petulantly burst forth.[6]

The reason the law is able to keep people from sinning is because, as we
saw in the last chapter, it expresses many of the divine attributes of
Almighty God, such as his sovereignty and justice. Therefore the law
has the power to encourage the fear of God, and at the same time to discourage any desire to sin against him. The law teaches that there is a
great and mighty God who punishes people for their sins. This
inevitably has the effect of warning us not to sin against him.

The law continues to have this restraining effect today, which is
why many Christians are in favor of posting the Ten Commandments
in the classroom and the courtroom. We live in an increasingly lawless
society. The effects of this are seen at school, where teachers almost
always deal with misbehavior and often with the real threat of violence.
The effects are also seen at court, where juries are confronted with
unspeakable crimes and judges struggle to know what justice requires.
We need moral guidance, and what better guide than God's commandments, written in stone?

There are some reasons to be skeptical about how much good this
will do. There is always the risk that putting God's law on a public
building will trivialize it—much the way that God is trivialized when
his name is plastered on American currency. Will simply posting the Ten
Commandments make people respect God and his law? To some extent
it will, but what people really need is not simply the law, but the gospel.
What good will it do for people to know what God requires unless the
Holy Spirit makes them able to do it? Furthermore, as we shall see in a
moment, one of the law's main purposes is to prove that we are *not* able
to keep it. Rather than keeping us from sin, therefore, what hanging the
Ten Commandments on the wall mainly does is to show us how sinful
we really are!

Nevertheless, and apart from any constitutional questions concerning the separation of church and state, posting the Ten

Commandments is a good and godly idea. The commandments come from God's Word, which never fails to fulfill its purpose (Isa. 55:11). Furthermore, it is good for people to be confronted with an objective standard of right and wrong, given by a God of truth and justice. The very existence of the Ten Commandments declares that we are accountable to God for what we do, and for what we fail to do.

This no doubt explains why today there is so much opposition to posting the Ten Commandments. People feel uncomfortable having God tell them what to do; so they try to have his commandments taken down, and often they are successful. In *Stone v. Graham*, the United States Supreme Court rejected the idea that the Ten Commandments have any place in secular education. The Court reasoned:

> The preeminent purpose for posting the Ten Commandments on schoolroom walls is plainly religious in nature. The Ten Commandments is undeniably a sacred text . . . and no legislative recitation of a supposed secular purpose can blind us to that fact. The commandments do not confine themselves to arguably secular matters, such as honoring one's parents, killing or murder, adultery, stealing, false witness, and covetousness. Rather, the first part of the commandments concerns the religious duties of believers: Worshipping the Lord God alone, avoiding idolatry, not using the Lord's name in vain, and observing the sabbath day.[7]

Whether the justices reached the right decision on the constitutional question or not, they were exactly right about what the Ten Commandments do: They confront us with our duty to God as well as to our neighbor. And it is good for people to be confronted because God's law has the ability to restrain sin in society. Christians who want to post the Ten Commandments have the right instinct. Although by itself the law cannot save, it does help to promote a just society. God's law informs the conscience, so that someone who reads the Ten Commandments has a heightened sense of what God requires and what God forbids. This knowledge of God and his law can keep people from sin. And as God's law—with all its threats and punishments—works its way into the law of the land, it deters people from committing especially destructive sins.

## Revealing Our Need for a Savior

So far we have considered what the law is able to do. It teaches God's redeemed people how to live for God's glory, and it restrains sin in society. But there is one thing the law is not able to do, and that is to bring full and final salvation. The law is powerless in this regard because it is weakened by the sinful nature (see Rom. 8:3). Yet even in its powerlessness the law turns out to be useful, because it proves that we need someone else to save us. This is perhaps the most important use of the law: to show sinners their need of a Savior.

To see how the law does this, it is necessary to understand that Israel was obligated to keep the law perfectly. There are several indications of this in Exodus. One comes in chapter 24, where the Israelites promise to obey God's law. After Moses read the Book of the Covenant, the people said, "All that the LORD has spoken, we will do" (v. 7). The Israelites were bound by their own promise to keep the whole law of God. Another way to say this is that they were required to keep God's covenant. Moses later told them, "He [God] declared to you his covenant, which he commanded you to perform, that is, the Ten Commandments, and he wrote them on two tablets of stone" (Deut. 4:13).

The Israelites were bound to keep God's law, not simply because that is what they promised, but because that is what their salvation required: perfect obedience to the revealed will of God. In one sense, of course, the Israelites were already saved. They had been delivered from Egypt. However, that was not their full and final salvation. It was only an earthly deliverance, and God was planning for them to spend an eternity with him in heaven. But in order for them to reach that destiny, they had to fully meet the righteous requirements of God's law. As Moses later reminded them, "The LORD commanded us to obey all these statutes. . . . And it will be righteousness for us, if we are careful to do all this commandment before the LORD our God, as he has commanded us" (Deut. 6:24a-25). Or again God said to them, "Keep my statutes and my rules; if a person does them, he shall live by them" (Lev. 18:5). Jesus later made much the same claim: "If you would enter life, keep the commandments" (Matt. 19:17b). To be righteous before God, the Israelites had to keep his law; and if they did that, they would be saved forever.

The trouble was, they couldn't keep it! In fact, no sooner had God told them not to have any other gods or make any idols than they made a golden calf (Exod. 32). This shows that for all its usefulness in teaching us how to live, the law does not have the power to transform our sinful nature. Instead, like a mirror that shows every spot on someone's face, it shows how sinful we truly are.

Even worse, the law has a way of actually provoking our sin. The apostle Paul discussed this in Romans 7. First he made the point that we have just been making, namely, that the law reveals our sin. He said, "If it had not been for the law, I would not have known sin" (Rom. 7:7b). Then, using the tenth commandment as an example, he went on to explain that in some ways the law actually serves to stimulate sin: "I would not have known what it is to covet if the law had not said, 'You shall not covet.' But sin, seizing an opportunity through the commandment, produced in me all kinds of covetousness" (vv. 7c-8a).

It is bad enough that the law provokes sin, but the situation gets even worse, because sin leads to death. Paul continued: "Apart from the law, sin lies dead. I was once alive apart from the law, but when the commandment came, sin came alive and I died. The very commandment that promised life proved to be death to me. For sin, seizing an opportunity through the commandment, deceived me and through it killed me" (vv. 8b-11). Breaking the law leads to death. That would be bad enough, but believe it or not, the situation gets even worse, because those who sin and die are under God's curse. As the Scripture says, "Cursed be everyone who does not abide by all things written in the Book of the Law" (Gal. 3:10).

So here was the situation: God's people were bound to keep a law that they could not obey. Rather than bringing them full and final salvation, therefore, the law exposed their sin, subjecting them to death and finally to the wrath and curse of God. John Calvin wrote that while the law "shows God's righteousness, that is, the righteousness alone acceptable to God, it warns, informs, convicts, and lastly condemns, every man of his own unrighteousness."[8]

So why did God give his people the law? Why did he give them something that would not simply command them, but also condemn them? The answer is that he gave them his law so that they would believe his gospel. All the great theologians have understood this. Augustine said, "The usefulness of the law lies in convicting man of his infirmity and moving him to call upon the remedy of grace which is in Christ."[9] Martin Luther explained it like this: "Therefore we do not abolish the Law; but we show its true function and use, namely, that it is a most useful servant impelling us to Christ. After the Law has humbled, terrified, and completely crushed you, so that you are on the brink of despair, then see to it that you know how to use the Law correctly; for its function and use is not only to disclose the sin and wrath of God but also to drive us to Christ."[10] John Calvin put it more simply, saying, "Moses had no other intention than to invite all men to go straight to Christ."[11] And Charles Spurgeon said, "As the sharp needle prepares the way for the thread, so the piercing law makes a way for the bright silver thread of divine grace."[12]

God's plan was to send his people a Savior. But first he gave them the law in the form of a covenant of works—a covenant they could not keep. By revealing their sin, this law showed them that they needed an everlasting Savior, and thus it made them long for the coming of Christ. Like us, the Israelites were saved by grace through faith. The primary difference is that their faith was in the Savior to come, whereas ours is in the Savior God has already sent. But how would the Israelites ever have seen their need of a Savior unless their sin was first exposed and cursed by the law of God? This is why they needed the law. They needed it to help them believe in the gospel, and in this way God's law ultimately served to glorify God's grace. Paul explained it like this: "Now the law came in to increase the trespass, but where sin increased, grace abounded all the more, so that, as sin reigned in death, grace also might reign through righteousness leading to eternal life through Jesus Christ our Lord" (Rom. 5:20-21).

## USING THE LAW TODAY

As a multi-use item, God's law is as useful now as ever. It shows God's redeemed people how to live for God's glory, and it restrains sin in society. But there is one thing the law cannot do, and that is to make us right with God. We cannot be justified by our own keeping of the law.

If we were able to keep God's law perfectly, then it *would* be able to save us. According to God's own Word, the person who obeys the commandments will live by them (Rom. 10:5; Gal. 3:12). The trouble is, we can't keep them. As the Scripture says, "no one living is righteous before [God]" (Ps. 143:2b). And what proves that we are unrighteous is the law of God: "For by works of the law no human being will be justified in his sight, since through the law comes knowledge of sin" (Rom. 3:20). And because sin leads to judgment, the law therefore shows us that we are condemned by God, and that apart from his grace we will be lost forever.

In one of his many Exodus-related drawings, the cartoonist Baloo depicts Moses giving Israel the Ten Commandments. With a look of dismay, the people say, "We were hoping to be accepted as we are."[13] That is what we always hope, that God will let us come "as we are." But because God is holy, he cannot accept us as we are, and we need to know that. It is absolutely essential for us to know. We need to see ourselves as we really are, which is why we still need God's law—not to save us, but to show us how much we need a Savior. According to Martin Luther, "The true function and the chief and proper use of the Law is to reveal to man his sin, blindness, misery, wickedness, ignorance, hate and contempt of God, death, hell, judgment, and the well-deserved wrath of God."[14]

The law shows us these things so that we will start looking for a Savior. Donald Grey Barnhouse explained it like this: "The law of God is like a mirror. Now the purpose of a mirror is to reveal to you that your face is dirty, but the purpose of a mirror is not to wash your face. When you look in a mirror and find that your face is dirty, you do not then reach to take the mirror off the wall and attempt to rub it on your face as a cleansing agent. The purpose of the mirror is to drive you to the water."[15] This is how the law helps us: not by saving us, but by showing us our need for a Savior. And it does this for Christians as much as for non-Christians. The law shows us our sin to remind us to praise God for saving us through Christ.

Sadly, God's law has fallen out of favor in the contemporary church. It is no longer preached as the eternal standard of God's righteousness or applied in its full relationship to the gospel. No doubt this is because the law is not very seeker-friendly. In fact, sometimes it makes people mad. However, preaching the law is absolutely essential for reaching the lost. It is only by hearing God's law that sinners are convicted of their sin, and thus see their need for the gospel. One minister who understood this was Archibald Alexander, one of the founding professors of Princeton Seminary. When Dr. Alexander's son was ordained to the pastoral ministry, he gave him this advice: "Let the law be faithfully proclaimed, as binding on every creature, and as cursing every impenitent sinner, and let the utter inability of man to satisfy its demands be clearly set forth, not as an excuse, but as a fault; and then let the riches of grace in Christ Jesus be fully exhibited and freely offered, and let all—however great their guilt—be urged to accept of unmerited pardon, and complete salvation."[16]

This is the right place to end this chapter on the right use of the law, with the riches of grace that God offers in Jesus Christ. The more we look into the mirror of God's law, the more clearly we see that we are sinners who need a Savior. Once we see that, we need to look to Jesus, who has fully met the requirements of God's law and has suffered the penalty that we deserve for our sin. There is pardon for every lawbreaker and forgiveness for every sinner who trusts in Jesus Christ.

### STUDY QUESTIONS

1. What is one multi-use item you have bought in the last year? Was it a good purchase or one you regretted?
2. Which of the three uses of the law—teaching God's redeemed people how to live for God's glory, restraining sin in society, and showing sinners their need of a Savior—is most often emphasized in your church? Where do you see it being taught?
3. Give some examples of grace working with the law to save people in the Old Testament.
4. If the law is for those who have already been redeemed, should we desire or expect unbelievers to follow any of God's laws? Explain your answer.

5. What is the relationship between our freedom from sin and our obedience to God's law?
6. How have you seen the connection between freedom and obedience demonstrated in your own life?
7. The Israelites responded with fear and trembling when they heard God's law. What is your customary response when you hear or think about God's law?
8. Defend a proposal to post the Ten Commandments in schools and courtrooms. What will it accomplish?
9. How does the law lead us to Christ?
10. Share some ways God has used the law in your life.

# 3

# INTERPRETING
# GOD'S LAW

*This Book of the Law shall not depart from your mouth, but you
shall meditate on it day and night, so that you may be careful to
do according to all that is written in it. For then you will make
your way prosperous, and then you will have good success.*

JOSHUA 1:8

One cartoon depicts Moses standing on top of God's mountain,
holding the two tablets of the Ten Commandments. The prophet
is beaming. "Hey, these are great," he says enthusiastically. "From now
on, nobody will have trouble distinguishing right from wrong."[1]

What makes the cartoon funny is that obviously we still *do* have
trouble distinguishing right from wrong, the Ten Commandments
notwithstanding. The problem is not the commandments themselves.
As we have seen, God's law provides an objective moral standard that
clearly distinguishes between good and evil. The problem is with us. In
our fallen condition, sin often deceives us into thinking that what is
wrong is right, and that what is right is wrong. We also live in a fallen
world. Sin has such a corrupting influence on human society that we
don't always know the right thing to do. As sinful people living in a sinful world, we face real moral dilemmas that make it hard for us to distinguish right from wrong. The Ten Commandments do not clarify
everything.

There is another reason why the Ten Commandments don't

immediately answer all our ethical questions: They are not as simple as they look. At first they seem thoroughly straightforward. There are only ten of them—one for each finger—so they are relatively easy to remember. They are not very long either. It takes only a minute or so to recite them. They are so simple, in fact, that the Bible refers to them as "the ten words" (Exod. 34:28, literal translation). God has given us ten short rules that apply to all people in all places. What could be simpler?

When these apparently simple commandments are studied carefully, however, they turn out to have amazing depth. The Ten Commandments are profound in what they reveal about God and about living for his glory. The commandments are also broad. When they are properly understood, they turn out to be relevant for any and every situation—one law for all of life. To make full and proper use of this law, therefore, we need to know how to apply it. And if there is any doubt as to the importance of having the right interpretation, one need only think of the Pharisees, who despite all their efforts to keep God's law often violated it. This was partly because they did not know how to interpret the Decalogue according to its true intention and proper application.

## In All the Scriptures

The first rule of interpretation is *the biblical rule*: Every commandment must be understood in the context of the entire Bible. This is simply the Reformation principle that Scripture interprets Scripture. The way to know the full and true meaning of any Bible passage is to know what the rest of the Bible says on the same theme. And this is true of the Ten Commandments. To understand the full implications of each commandment, we need to know what the whole Bible teaches about it, including the teaching of Jesus and his apostles.

To take just one example, consider the second commandment, which says, "You shall not make for yourself a carved image, or any likeness of anything that is in heaven above, or that is in the earth beneath, or that is in the water under the earth. You shall not bow down to them or serve them" (Exod. 20:4-5a). This command sounds so simple that further explanation hardly seems necessary. Yet our understanding of the second commandment is greatly expanded when we know what the rest of the Bible says about worship in general and about idolatry in particular. We need to know what the prophet Isaiah said about the folly of making images with our own hands and then bowing down to worship them (Isa. 44:6-23), what Jesus said about worshiping God in spirit and in truth (John 4:24), and what the apostle Paul said about greed as a form of idolatry (see Eph. 5:5; Col. 3:5). In addition to studying the second commandment on its own terms, we need to study what is taught on the subject elsewhere in the Scripture.

What makes this method of interpretation valid is that everything in the Bible comes from the mind of God, as breathed out by his Holy Spirit. What God says in one place agrees with what he says somewhere else because God cannot disagree with himself! Furthermore, all the prophets and apostles accepted the abiding authority of God's moral law. They did not set it aside, but in various ways interpreted and explained it. And because their teaching is also authoritative, whatever they have to say about the law also applies to us.

The same is true of what Jesus Christ said about the law. Some people refer to Jesus as the new Moses who gave God's people a new law. It is not hard to understand why. Like Moses, Jesus went up the mountain to teach God's people how to live. There he addressed some of the same issues that God dealt with in the Ten Commandments. Jesus said, "You have heard that it was said to those of old, 'You shall not murder, and whoever murders will be liable to judgment.' But I say to you that everyone who is angry with his brother will be liable to judgment" (Matt. 5:21-22a). Jesus said something similar about adultery. It almost sounded as if he were giving a whole new law.

That is not what Jesus was doing, however. When he said, "You have heard that it was said," he was not correcting Moses, but was contradicting the Pharisees for their false interpretation of Moses. As John Calvin explained, rather than adding to the law, Christ "only restored it to its integrity, in that he freed and cleansed it when it had been obscured by falsehood." Calvin thus referred to Jesus as the law's "best interpreter."[2] Similarly, the great Swiss theologian Francis Turretin said, "[Jesus] does not act as a new lawgiver, but only as an interpreter and vindicator of the law given by Moses."[3] If we want to understand the Ten Commandments properly, therefore, we need to know how Jesus interpreted them. This is in keeping with our first rule of interpretation, namely, that the law must be understood in the context of the whole Bible.

## INSIDE AND OUT

The second rule is *the inside/outside rule*: The Ten Commandments are internal as well as external. They demand inward integrity as well as outward conformity. Another way to say this is the way the apostle Paul said it: "the law is spiritual" (Rom. 7:14). In other words, it deals with our souls as well as our bodies. This distinguishes God's law from any human law. According to an old Puritan proverb, "Man's law binds the hands only, God's law binds the heart."[4]

This guideline for interpretation is in keeping with the being and character of God. God himself is spirit. He is omniscient and omnipresent. Nothing escapes his attention. He is immediately aware of everything we think as well as everything we say or do. He knows our inward intentions as well as our outward actions. As the Scripture says, "Man looks on the outward appearance, but the LORD looks on the heart" (1 Sam. 16:7b). Therefore, God holds us accountable not only for the sins we commit with our bodies, but also for the sins we commit in the privacy of our own hearts, minds, and wills. Remember too that each of the Ten Commandments was given in the second person singular. When God holds us accountable to keep his law, he holds us personally accountable—inside as well as out.

The spirituality of God's law is made most explicit by the tenth commandment. On the surface at least, the first nine commandments only deal with outward conduct. They govern observable actions like bowing down before idols, cursing, killing, and stealing. But the tenth commandment deals exclusively with the heart: "You shall not covet your neighbor's house; you shall not covet your neighbor's wife, or his male servant, or his female servant, or his ox, or his donkey, or anything that is your neighbor's" (Exod. 20:17).

The tenth commandment does not address an action at all, but only an affection. According to the Jewish scholar Umberto Cassuto, this kind of commandment was completely unprecedented in the ancient world.[5] All the other legal codes governed outward sins like stealing. But only Israel's God presumed to rule a person's thoughts and desires.

What was made explicit in the tenth commandment is equally true of all the others. The Ten Commandments are spiritual; they require inward as well as outward obedience. This is one of the things that Jesus clarified in his Sermon on the Mount. One might think that the seventh commandment—which outlaws adultery—only deals with how we use our bodies. But Jesus said, "I say to you that everyone who looks at a woman with lustful intent has already committed adultery with her in his heart" (Matt. 5:28). What the seventh commandment forbids is not just inappropriate sexual activity, but also sinful desires. Jesus handled the sixth commandment the same way, teaching that it condemned anger and hatred as well as murder (Matt. 5:21-22; cf. 1 John 3:15a). For as Jesus later said, "out of the heart come evil thoughts, murder, adultery, sexual immorality, theft, false witness, slander" (Matt. 15:19).

Now we begin to see how demanding God is, and how thoroughly his law exposes our sin. If we thought that somehow we could get by on good behavior, we were mistaken. Since the law is spiritual, we must apply the Ten Commandments to our inward affections as well as to our outward actions. And now we can sympathize with the tribal chieftain who said, "I would rather have the 7777 commandments and prohibitions of the Torajda Adat than the Ten Commandments of the Christians, for the Ten Commandments demand my whole heart, whereas the 7777 ancestral commands and prohibitions leave room for a lot of freedom."[6]

## BOTH SIDES OF THE LAW

Like the second rule, the third rule of interpretation widens our application of the Ten Commandments. It is *the two-sided rule*. It could also be called the law of opposites, the law of contraries, or the law of contrapositives. Whatever it is called, what it means is very simple: Every commandment is both positive and negative. Where a sin is forbidden, the corresponding duty is required; and where a duty is required, the corresponding sin is forbidden.

People usually think of the Ten Commandments as a list of don'ts: don't make other gods, don't steal, don't lie, and so forth. It is true that most of the commandments are worded as don'ts rather than dos. Perhaps this is because we have such a strong propensity to do what is displeasing to God, and thus we need to be told to stop. The only completely positive commandment is the fifth: "Honor your father and your mother" (Exod. 20:12). Even the fourth commandment, which tells us to "Remember the Sabbath day," also tells us not to work (Exod. 20:8-10).

All these "thou shalt nots" can sound rather negative. However, when we interpret the Ten Commandments properly, we find that they are both positive and negative. There is a flip side to every commandment. Each one condemns a particular vice, while at the same time it commands a particular virtue. For example, the third commandment forbids the misuse of God's name. We may not dishonor God by abusing his name. However, by sheer force of logic, this command also requires us to use God's name honorably and reverently. As Joy Davidman (later C. S. Lewis's wife) pointed out, the third commandment means, "Thou shalt take the name of the Lord your God in earnest!"[7] To give another example, the commandment that forbids murder simultaneously requires the preservation of life. Similarly, while the eighth commandment rules out theft, it also demands that we give generously to people in need. The true intent of each commandment is to tell us what *to* do as well as what *not* to do.

The commandments that are stated positively need to be interpreted the same way. Where a duty is commanded, the corresponding sin is forbidden. Consider the fourth commandment, which reads in part, "Six days you shall labor, and do all your work" (Exod. 20:9). The command to work promotes the virtue of industry. At the same time, it forbids all the sins that hinder our work, such as time-wasting and other forms of laziness. The same commandment also tells us to "remember the Sabbath day." That very positive command also forbids us to do something—namely, to break the Sabbath.

Every commandment is both positive and negative. This "law of opposites" helps to keep us from following the letter of the law while avoiding its full application. We can't just say, "Well, at least I don't shoplift," while failing to give to the poor, and still think that we are really keeping the eighth commandment. This rule also makes the Ten Commandments at least twice as hard to keep as most people think! In order to keep the first commandment, for example, we must not only stay away from false religions, but we must enthrone the one and only true God as our supreme Lord. And in order to keep the ninth commandment, it is not enough simply to avoid telling any lies; we must also use our words to encourage and to bless. As we shall see, these principles make the Ten Commandments much more impossible to obey than most people have ever imagined.

## CATEGORIES

When the Ten Commandments are interpreted properly, they are comprehensive. They deal with areas of sin that are discussed all through the Scriptures. They command both the body and the soul. They not only forbid disobedience, but they also require obedience. To those guidelines we can now add a fourth, *the rule of categories*: Each commandment stands for a whole category of sins. It governs not only the specific sin that is mentioned, but all the sins that lead up to it, and all the supposedly lesser sins of the same kind. The Westminster Larger Catechism states this rule formally: "That under one sin or duty, all of the same kind are forbidden or commanded; together with all the causes, means, occasions, and appearances thereof, and provocations thereunto" (A. 99.6).

The easiest way to explain what this means is to give some examples. Consider the sixth commandment: "You shall not murder." Taken literally, this is a commandment that relatively few people break (although as Jesus explained, since the law is spiritual, it also condemns very common sins such as hatred). But in addition to outright murder, the sixth commandment forbids any form of physical violence. It even condemns fistfights, bodily injury, and domestic violence. It condemns neglecting our personal health. It also includes everything that leads up to these sins, such as fits of anger, reckless driving, or even playing violent video games. What God forbids is not simply murder, but everything that harms the body, threatens physical well-being, or inures us to the dangers of violence.

To take another example, consider the seventh commandment, which forbids adultery. In its most literal sense, what the seventh commandment forbids is extramarital intercourse. If that is the only sin it covers, then it is a (relatively) easy law to keep. However, according to our fourth rule of interpretation, each commandment stands for a whole category of sin. So the seventh commandment includes not simply the act of adultery, but every form of sexual misconduct. Premarital sex, the use of pornography, self-stimulation—all of these sins are forbidden. Also forbidden are all the sins that lead up to adultery. God calls husbands and wives to nurture their fellowship with one another. It is unlawful for a couple to grow apart from one another physically, spiritually, emotionally, or sexually. It is also wrong for a husband or wife to have intimate relationships with other men or women, even if those relationships are not sexual (at least not yet)—adultery begins long before two people get in bed together. These are only a few examples of the many sins included under the category of the seventh commandment.

These examples help us understand that the Ten Commandments generally forbid the most extreme example of a particular kind of sin. Bowing down in front of an idol is the worst form of false worship; misusing God's sacred divine name is the worst form of blasphemy; murder is the worst form of violence; adultery is the most destructive act of sexual sin; and so forth. But this approach is not intended to make us think that the big sins are the only ones that matter. Rather, it shows us that God considers every sin in that category to be as sinful as the most heinous form of that particular sin. So, for example, every kind of poor stewardship is as culpable as stealing; every kind of dishonesty is as reprehensible as lying under legal oath; and so on.

The rule of categories also warns us not to commit lesser sins that by their very nature are bound to lead us into greater sins. People generally do not start out with grand larceny; they start with petty theft.

Similarly, it is by telling little white lies that people learn how to pull off grand deceptions. But God rules out the little sins so as to help prevent the big ones. Turretin explained the principle this way: "What are most base and capital in each species of sin are forbidden, under which all the others are included, either because they flow thence or because they lead at length to it; or because what appear the smallest to men are in the most accurate judgment of God rated more severely. This is not done, therefore, to excuse or exclude lesser sins, but that a greater detestation of sin may be impressed upon our minds."[8]

## MY BROTHER'S KEEPER

It was Cain who asked the famous question: "Am I my brother's keeper?" (Gen. 4:9b). The next guideline for interpreting and applying God's law answers in the affirmative. In addition to keeping the Ten Commandments ourselves, we are required to help others keep them. According to *the brother's keeper rule*, we are not allowed to encourage someone else to do what God has told us not to do. To put it more positively, we must do everything in our power to help other people keep God's law. Ernest Reisinger writes, "Whatever is forbidden or commanded of us, we are bound, according to our position, to discourage or encourage in others according to the duty of their positions."[9]

Reisinger uses the word "position" because our station in life often gives us spiritual influence over others. Parents shape their children's morals, both for evil and for good. The Ten Commandments thus require fathers and mothers to teach their children how to put God first, how to keep the Sabbath, how to tell the truth, and so on. The same principle applies to the classroom, and also to the workplace. Employers set the moral standard for their employees. They have a responsibility not only to keep God's law, but also to create an environment in which their workers are encouraged to keep God's law, too.

If we fail to help others keep God's law—or worse, if we fail to hinder them from breaking it—then in some way we share in the guilt of their sin. In his commentary on the Ten Commandments, the Puritan Thomas Watson listed some of the many ways we can become an accessory to someone else's sin.[10] One is by telling people to do something that God forbids, like when Aaron told the Israelites to give him their jewelry to make a golden calf (Exod. 32). Few Christians actually tell other people to sin the way that Aaron did. But that is not the only way to share in the guilt of others. Another way to participate in their iniquity is by encouraging them to sin. The Bible says, "Woe to him who makes his neighbors drink—you pour out your wrath and make them drunk" (Hab. 2:15). Anyone who has ever been to school knows that some kids have a way of coming up with the ideas that get other kids in trouble without ever getting caught themselves. But according to God's law, they are still guilty.

Then there are the sins we help cause by setting a bad example. Our own failure to keep God's law has a way of encouraging others to break it too. This is an area where spiritual leaders need to be especially careful. As Jesus said to his disciples, "Temptations to sin are sure to come, but woe to the one through whom they come. It would be better for him if a millstone were hung around his neck and he were cast into the sea than that he should cause one of these little ones to sin. Pay attention to yourselves!" (Luke 17:1-3a).

A more subtle way to promote sin is by failing to prevent it. The failure to stop a sin, when it lies within our power to do so, is as culpable as committing the sin itself. This is one of the ways that parents often share in the sins of their children. By failing to rebuke and punish them, they actually condone their disobedience. This is why God judged Eli so harshly. He said, "I declare to him that I am about to punish his house forever, for the iniquity that he knew, because his sons were blaspheming God, and he did not restrain them" (1 Sam. 3:13). Like Eli, those who fail to punish offenders share in their offense.

Yet another way to become an accessory to sin is by endorsing someone else's violation of the law. A clear biblical example is what Saul did at the stoning of Stephen. The Bible says that the people who carried out this murderous act "laid down their garments at the feet of a young man named Saul" (Acts 7:58). Saul didn't even lift a stone; all he did was run the coat check! Yet by agreeing with his heart, he too had a hand in Stephen's death. The Bible thus condemns him with these words: "And Saul approved of his execution" (Acts 8:1). As far as God is concerned, we are as guilty for the sins that have our consent as we are for the sins that we commit.

There are many ways to share in someone else's sin. In their widest application, what the Ten Commandments require is not merely our own obedience, but also our refusal to participate in the sins of others. More than that, we are called to do everything we can to help others respect and obey God's law.

## THE CURSE OF THE LAW

These are some of the rules for interpreting God's moral law. There are others. One is *the law of the tables*, which states that the first table of the law always takes precedence over the second. In other words, our duty to God in the first four commandments always governs our duty to one another in the last six commandments; our love for our neighbor is subject to our love for God. So if a parent tells a child to worship a false god, the child is bound by the first commandment ("no other gods") rather than the fifth commandment ("Honor your father and mother"). This is the principle Peter was applying when he said to the Sanhedrin, "We must obey God rather than men" (Acts 5:29).

There is also *the all-at-once rule*. Obviously, we cannot perform every positive duty simultaneously. So the Westminster Larger Catechism teaches "That what God forbids, is at no time to be done; what he commands, is always our duty; and yet every particular duty is not to be done at all times" (A. 99.5). Then there is *the rule of love*, which states that the purpose of every commandment is to show love, especially love for God. As the Scripture says, "love is the fulfilling of the law" (Rom. 13:10). Even the commandments that require love for our neighbor promote love for God. We do not love and serve our neighbor simply for the sake of our neighbor, but ultimately for the sake of God.[11]

In the chapters that follow, we will use these rules both implicitly and explicitly to interpret and apply the Ten Commandments. As we begin to do so, we will quickly discover that these laws are not so simple after all. They cover everything. They rule us inside as well as outside. They are positive as well as negative. Each of them governs a whole category of sins and duties. They apply not only to our own conduct, but also to our influence over the conduct of others.

Using these principles, even the simplest commandment places overwhelming demands on our obedience. To take just one example, consider the ninth commandment: "You shall not bear false witness against your neighbor" (Exod. 20:16). In other words, "Don't lie." This sounds simple enough, until we understand the full implications of the commandment, as explained in the Westminster Larger Catechism:

> The sins forbidden in the ninth commandment are, all prejudicing the truth, and the good name of our neighbours, as well as our own, especially in public judicature; giving false evidence, suborning false witnesses, wittingly appearing and pleading for an evil cause, out-facing and over-bearing the truth; passing unjust sentence, calling evil good, and good evil; rewarding the wicked according to the work of the righteous, and the righteous according to the work of the wicked; forgery, concealing the truth, undue silence in a just cause, and holding our peace when iniquity calleth for either a reproof from ourselves, or complaint to others; speaking the truth unseasonably, or maliciously to a wrong end, or perverting it to a wrong meaning, or in doubtful or equivocal expressions, to the prejudice of truth or justice, speaking untruth, lying, slandering, backbiting, detracting, tale-bearing, whispering, scoffing, reviling, rash, harsh, and partial censuring; misconstructing intentions, words, and actions; flattering, vain-glorious boasting, thinking or speaking too highly or too meanly of ourselves or others; denying the gifts and graces of God; aggravating smaller faults; hiding, excusing, or extenuating of sins, when called to a free confession; unnecessary discovering of infirmities; raising false rumours, receiving and countenancing evil reports, and stopping our ears against just defence; evil suspicion; envying or grieving at the deserved credit of any, endeavouring or desiring to impair it, rejoicing in their disgrace and infamy; scornful contempt, fond admiration; breach of lawful promises; neglecting such things as are of good report, and practising, or not avoiding ourselves, or not hindering what we can in others, such things as procure an ill name (A. 145).

And that is only what is *forbidden*! The catechism also explains what the ninth commandment *requires* in similar detail. Now we see that if somehow we thought we were not guilty of breaking the ninth commandment, it was only because we didn't have much idea what it required. The truth is that we are liars.

This is bad news, because God requires perfect obedience. To quote again from the Larger Catechism, "The law is perfect, and bindeth every one to full conformity in the whole man unto the righteousness thereof, and unto entire obedience for ever; so as to require the utmost perfection of every duty, and to forbid the least degree of every sin" (A. 99.1). And if we break even one commandment we are guilty before God. As the apostle James wrote, "whoever keeps the whole law but fails in one point has become accountable for all of it" (James 2:10). Even worse, everyone who breaks the law is subject to the wrath and curse of God.

## THE CURSE OF THE LAW

Some people—including some Christians—might think that interpreting the law too carefully is legalistic. We have enough trouble keeping the easy commandments. So what is the point of looking at God's law in exhaustive detail? Isn't that legalistic?

On the contrary, it is when we have a limited understanding of the law that we are most tempted to legalism, because then we think that we can keep it. If all God commanded us to do was to avoid murdering someone, we might be able to obey him. But we need to interpret the sixth commandment in the context of the whole Bible, with everything it says about murderous intentions. Since the law is spiritual, it condemns anger as well as murder. Since it is positive as well as negative, it requires the active preservation of life. And since it represents a whole category of sins, we are forbidden to harm people in any way, or to allow others to do so.

Is this a legalistic way of thinking? Not at all. This kind of biblical reasoning rescues us from legalism by preventing us from lowering God's standard. God's standard is only maintained when we recognize what his righteousness truly requires. And when we know what God requires, in all its fullness, we also see the full extent of our sin. It is only a full understanding of God's law that reveals our full need for the gospel. In the words of J. Gresham Machen, "a low view of law always brings legalism in religion; a high view of law makes a man a seeker after grace."[12]

Here we need to recall how to use God's law. As we have seen, the Ten Commandments are a multi-use item. One of their primary purposes is to show us our sin, so that we will see our need for a Savior. The law points us to Jesus Christ, whom the Scriptures identify as "the end of the law" (Rom. 10:4), meaning that he is the goal or true purpose of the law. The more clearly and thoroughly we understand what God's law requires, the more clearly and thoroughly we understand the grace that God has provided for us in Jesus Christ.

What does the moral law, summarized in the Ten Commandments and rightly interpreted, reveal about the person and work of Jesus Christ? It reveals the full extent of his perfect obedience. The Bible assures us that although Jesus was "born under the law" (Gal. 4:4), he "fulfill[ed] all righteousness" (Matt. 3:15) and "committed no sin" (1 Pet. 2:22). This was no small accomplishment! The law of God searches to the very soul. It is utterly exhaustive in the righteousness it requires. We are not capable of keeping even a single commandment with perfect integrity. But Jesus kept them all, down to the last detail, and he did it on our behalf. If we are joined to him by faith, then God regards us as if we had kept his whole law perfectly. For Christ was crucified "in order that the righteous requirements of the law might be fulfilled in us" (Rom. 8:4a). Therefore, the law shows us what perfect righteousness we have in Christ. To put this in more technical terms, when we know what the law requires, we can understand the doctrine of justification.

The moral law also reveals the full extent of Christ's atonement. The Bible teaches that Jesus Christ died on the cross for our sins. If we have a narrow understanding of God's law, we might imagine that we did not have very many sins to die for. But a full interpretation of the Ten Commandments reveals the full extent of our sin, and thus it reveals the full extent of the atonement. Christ died for all our sins. He died for our sins against God and our sins against humanity. He died for our idolatry, profanity, and adultery. He died for our lying, stealing, and murder. He died for our sins both inside and out. He died for all the sins we commit in every category of God's command. He even died for all the sins we committed by sharing in the sins of others. Christ died for *all our sins*, suffering the full penalty that our guilt deserved. The more thoroughly we understand the implications of God's law, the more truly grateful we are for the grace of God in the atoning death of Jesus Christ. When we know what the law requires, we can understand the cross.

Finally, for those who have put their faith in Jesus Christ, the moral law reveals the full duty of the Christian life. This is another use of God's law. It shows God's redeemed people how to live for God's glory. When we give the law its full interpretation, we gain a better grasp of God's righteous standard in all its perfection, and thus we have a better idea how to please him. To put this in theological terms, when we know what the law requires, we can understand the doctrine of sanctification. This is why we study God's law: to understand our great need for Christ and his gospel, and to learn how many ways we can glorify God for his grace.

## STUDY QUESTIONS

1. Can you think of a time when you have had a misunderstanding with someone—with humorous or disastrous results?
2. How does sin confuse us about right and wrong?
3. Why was Jesus known as the second Moses? What was similar about the two men?
4. Why is it important to interpret Scripture in the context of the rest of Scripture? What are the dangers if we fail to do this?
5. What attributes of God compel us to obey his law with inward integrity as well as outward conformity?
6. Does thinking about both the positive and negative sides of each commandment change how you view the Ten Commandments? In what way(s)?
7. Explain how to apply "the rule of categories" to a few of the Ten Commandments.
8. Discuss examples of how someone could lead someone else to sin in each of the ways offered in the book (encouraging someone to sin,

setting a bad example, failing to prevent sin, endorsing a violation of God's law).

9. How does understanding the depth of each of the Ten Commandments guard against legalism? How have you seen this principle at work in your own life?

10. As you take a closer look at each commandment in the weeks ahead, what is your prayer for how God will change you?

# 4

# THE FIRST COMMANDMENT:
## NO OTHER GODS

*You shall have no other gods before me.*
EXODUS 20:3

One of the first lessons parents try to teach their children is how to share. Fathers and mothers are forever reminding their sons and daughters to share their space, share their toys, and share their food. "You have to share," they say.

As important as it is to learn how to share, it is also important to realize that some things are not meant to be shared. A bite-sized candy bar, for example. Or a unicycle. Or a piece of confidential information, like the answers to a test. Or, to take an even more serious example, the sexual love between a husband and wife. These things were never intended to be shared with someone else. In order to be used properly at all, they have to be kept exclusive.

If some things were never meant to be shared, then it is not surprising to learn that there are times when even God refuses to share. He is a loving and merciful God who loves to pour out his mercy and grace on his people. But there are some things that he will not share. This is especially true when it comes to the prerogatives of his deity. God will not share his glory with any other god. So he has given us this command: "You shall have no other gods before me" (Exod. 20:3).

This is the fundamental commandment, the one that comes before all the others and lays the foundation for them. Before we learn anything else about what God demands, we need to know who he is, and who we are in relationship to him. "Now get this straight," God is saying, "I am the one and only God. And since I am the only God, I refuse to share my worship with anyone or anything else." God will not share the stage with any other performers. He refuses to have any colleagues. He will not even acknowledge that he has any genuine rivals. God does not simply lay claim to one part of our life and worship; he demands that we dedicate all we are and all we have to his service and praise. Thus the Ten Commandments begin by asserting the great theological principle of *soli Deo gloria*: glory to God alone.

## THE GODS OF EGYPT

In order to understand the first commandment, it helps to know the context in which it was given. The Israelites had just come out of Egypt, where they had lived in one of the most polytheistic cultures ever. *Polytheism* is simply the worship of many gods, and in this the Egyptians were unsurpassed. They worshiped the gods of fields and rivers, light and darkness, sun and storm. Swearing their allegiance to the gods and goddesses of love and war, they bowed down to worship idols in the form of men and beasts.

The Israelites worshiped these gods, too. Over the long centuries of their captivity, they had gradually given in to the temptation to worship strange gods. God told them, "Cast away the detestable things your eyes feast on, every one of you, and do not defile yourselves with the idols of Egypt; I am the LORD your God." "But," he lamented, "they rebelled against me and were not willing to listen to me. None of them cast away the detestable things their eyes feasted on, nor did they forsake the idols of Egypt" (Ezek. 20:7-8a). Like the Egyptians, the Israelites worshiped many gods.

As for God, he has always been a monotheist; he has only ever believed in one God. So in the first commandment he took his stand against the gods of Egypt and against every other false deity—past, present, and future. He said, "You shall have no other gods before me" (Exod. 20:3). In other words, "I am to be your one and only God." This command was without precedent. None of the other nations in the

ancient world prohibited the worship of other gods. They simply
assumed that every nation would serve its own deities. But on this issue
the God of Israel was completely intolerant. He refused to acknowledge
the legitimacy of any other god.

What gives God the right to make this kind of demand? He's God!
Remember how the first commandment is introduced. God said, "I am
the LORD your God, who brought you out of the land of Egypt, out of
the house of slavery. You shall have no other gods before me" (Exod.
20:2-3). What God commanded was based on who he was and what he
had done. God had saved his people for his glory, and now he was saying to them, "As the sovereign Lord of heaven and earth, it is my right
to rule over you. But more than that, I am your very own God. We are
bound together by my covenant promise. And I have redeemed you. I
have released you from your bondage to Pharaoh. With ten mighty
plagues I have defeated all the deities of Egypt, showing that I am the
one and only true God. And now I claim my right to all your worship
and all your praise. Because of who I am and on the basis of what I have
done, I will not share my glory with any other god."

If God is the only God, then why does he speak of "other gods" as
if they had any real existence? The Bible insists that there is only one
God and that every other deity is a fraud. As God said through his
prophet Isaiah, "there is no other God besides me, a righteous God and
a Savior; there is none besides me" (Isa. 45:21). "We know that 'an idol
has no real existence,'" wrote the apostle Paul, "and that 'there is no God
but one'" (1 Cor. 8:4b). If that is true, then what is the point in telling
us not to have any other gods? If there aren't any other gods to begin
with, then how *could* we have another one?

The answer is that even false gods hold a kind of spiritual power
over their worshipers: "People worship powerful forces within creation
as if these were deities. They are not gods, but only so-called gods; still,
they are very real powers, able to enslave a person totally."[1] As Paul
reminded the Galatians, "Formerly, when you did not know God, you
were enslaved to those that by nature are not gods" (Gal. 4:8). The reason false gods have this enslaving power is ultimately because demonic
forces use them to gain mastery over their worshipers. Thus the gods

of Egypt held real spiritual power over the minds and hearts of the Egyptians, and also the Israelites. That is why God took the trouble to defeat them, one by one. It was to break their spiritual influence, and thereby to show that he alone was worthy of worship.

## BEFORE MY FACE

The first commandment comes from the God who is our Lord and Savior. But what about the commandment itself? What can we learn from the way it is worded—specifically from its last phrase? God said, "You shall have no other gods *before me*" (Exod. 20:3). This does not mean that it is permissible to worship other deities, so long as we put God first. When God says "before me," he is not trying to tell us where he falls in the rankings! But what is he trying to say?

The words "before me" mean "before my face." Sometimes they are used in a spatial sense. In that case, the commandment would mean something like this: "You shall have no other gods 'in front of me,' or 'in my presence.'" Taken literally, that would forbid people from bringing foreign idols into the place where God is worshiped. But since God is everywhere, it really forbids us from worshiping false gods anywhere. Any time we serve any other god, we are doing it in the presence of God. The word "before" can also be used to describe two things that are in opposition to one another. In that case, the commandment would read, "You shall not have any gods over against me." Here the picture is one of putting something in someone's face. In other words, setting up a false deity is like insulting God to his face.[2] Obviously "before" is a flexible word, and although it is hard to decide how it is used here, both of the possible meanings are biblically correct. No matter where we do it, we are not allowed to serve anyone or anything besides God. To do such a thing is to set ourselves against him and against his commandment.

The point is that when it comes to worshiping God, it is all or nothing. This is the way it has always been. It was this way on Mount Sinai, when God first gave Moses the law. It was this way when Joshua renewed the covenant and said, "Put away the gods that your fathers served . . . in Egypt, and serve the LORD. . . . [C]hoose this day whom you will serve" (Josh. 24:14-15a). This is the way it was on Mount

Carmel when Elijah liberated the Israelites from their bondage to Baal. He said, "If the LORD is God, follow him; but if Baal, then follow him" (1 Kings 18:21). And it is the same way with Jesus Christ, who says, "No one can serve two masters. . . . You cannot serve God and money" (Matt. 6:24). God's people have always faced a choice. Religious pluralism is not a recent development. There have always been plenty of other gods clamoring for our attention, and God has always demanded our exclusive loyalty.

When God commands us to reject false gods, he is also commanding us to choose him as the true God, enthroning him as our only Lord. John Calvin said that the first commandment requires us "to contemplate, fear and worship his majesty; to participate in his blessings; to seek his help at all times; to recognize, and by praises to celebrate, the greatness of his works—as the only goal of all the activities of life."[3] So the command tells us whom to worship as well as whom not to worship. It is positive as well as negative. For its positive statement, consider the creed that most Israelites recited every day: "Hear, O Israel: The LORD our God, the LORD is one. You shall love the LORD your God with all your heart and with all your soul and with all your strength" (Deut. 6:4-5).

"Love" is the right word to use because the first commandment solidifies the covenant relationship between God and his people. Notice that in this commandment God speaks to us in the singular. God says, "*You* [individually] shall have no other gods before *me* [personally]." We do not worship *a* god, but *the* God, who wants to have an exclusive love relationship with each one of his people. Obviously, in order for this relationship to work, it is essential for us not to share our love with any other god. We must be faithful to the only true God. We must give him our total allegiance—honoring, adoring, and revering him as our Lord and Savior.

## A ROYAL FOLLY

The first commandment is, "You shall have no other gods before me." What happens when we break it? There is a story about violating the first commandment in the Bible. It is the story of the tragic downfall of a great king. He was one of the greatest kings in the ancient world. He was powerful, the most powerful king his nation had ever seen. He had horses and chariots by the thousands. He crushed his enemies, expanding his kingdom until it stretched from the mountains to the sea. He was also the wealthiest king his nation had ever seen. His palace was filled with gold, but not with silver, which during his reign was considered too common for royal use. The name of this rich and powerful king was Solomon.

The most remarkable thing about Solomon was that he possessed true spiritual wisdom. In the early days of his reign, God appeared to him in a dream and said, "Ask what I shall give you" (1 Kings 3:5). It was the opportunity of a lifetime! The king could ask for anything he wanted. His answer would reveal what god he wanted to serve: If he served riches, he would ask for gold; if he served power, he would ask for death to his enemies; if he served pleasure, he would ask for beautiful women. But Solomon wanted to serve the one and only true God; so he asked for the wisdom to rule his people in righteousness.

God granted the king's request. Solomon was recognized as the wisest man in the ancient world. People came from all over to test his knowledge. The Bible tells how he judged between right and wrong, and how he served as a counselor to kings and queens. In his wisdom Solomon did many great things for God. He was generous; he built a temple in God's honor. He was also a man of prayer. The magnificent prayer he offered at the dedication of the temple could only have come from a man who knew the Scriptures and understood the character of God (2 Chron. 6). And God answered Solomon's prayer by descending on his temple in power and glory. There has never been a man more greatly blessed than King Solomon. He had everything a person could possibly want, including the opportunity to do great things for God.

If only Solomon had kept the first commandment! God said to him, "As for you, if you will walk before me, as David your father walked, with integrity of heart and uprightness, doing according to all that I have commanded you, and keeping my statutes and my rules, then I will establish your royal throne over Israel forever. . . . But if you turn aside from following me . . . and do not keep my commandments and my statutes that I have set before you, but go and serve other gods and worship them, then I will cut off Israel from the land that I have given them, and the house that I have consecrated for my name I will cast out of my sight" (1 Kings 9:4-7a). It was very simple: All Solomon had to do was give God the glory. In particular, he had to obey the first commandment by refusing to serve any other gods.

Sadly, Solomon failed to keep God's law: He served other gods. The Scripture tells how "Solomon went after Ashtoreth the goddess of the Sidonians, and after Milcom the abomination of the Ammonites" (1 Kings 11:5). It also tells how God responded: "The LORD was angry with Solomon, because his heart had turned away from the LORD, the God of Israel, who had appeared to him twice, and had commanded him concerning this thing, that he should not go after other gods. But he did not keep what the LORD commanded. Therefore the LORD said to Solomon, 'Since this has been your practice and you have not kept my covenant and my statutes that I have commanded you, I will certainly tear the kingdom from you'" (1 Kings 11:9-11). King Solomon was condemned specifically for violating the first commandment.

## A REAL TRAGEDY

Most people are surprised by what happened to Solomon. The collapse of his kingdom comes as a real shock. How could a man who was so wise be so stupid! Yet if we look at Solomon's life carefully, we see that his heart started to turn away from God long before he ever bowed down in front of any idols. Solomon started well, but gradually he drifted away until finally he was worshiping completely different deities. The same thing happens to many Christians. Although we never intend to break the first commandment, our hearts are lured away by the temptation to follow other gods.

What is so tragic about King Solomon is that he ended up serving the very gods that he had once rejected. He did not ask God for gold; yet in time he started serving the god of wealth. The best example of this comes in 1 Kings 7, which describes how he built his palace. Chapter 6 tells how Solomon built a house for God and ends by saying that he spent "seven years in building it" (1 Kings 6:38b). Then the king built a house for himself. Chapter 7 begins with words that can only be interpreted as a reproach: "Solomon was building his own house thirteen years, and he finished his entire house" (1 Kings 7:1). Once the king had done something for God he decided it was time to do something for himself, and he took almost twice as long doing it! This shows how dangerous it is to be rich. Money brings many temptations, and even if we resist them at the beginning, they may come back to destroy us in the end.

Solomon also began to worship power. Again, this was not something he asked for, but in time he started serving the god of military strength. God had specifically forbidden the Israelites to build up a cavalry (see Deut. 17:16); yet Solomon amassed an entire army of horses and chariots (1 Kings 10:26-29).

He made the same mistake when it came to women. God said, "[The king] must not take many wives, or his heart will be led astray" (Deut. 17:17a). Sadly, Solomon failed to heed God's warning. Although at the beginning he did not ask for pleasure, he started serving the goddess of sex, and this was his downfall. King Solomon "loved many foreign women, along with the daughter of Pharaoh: Moabite, Ammonite, Edomite, Sidonian, and Hittite women, from the nations concerning which the LORD had said to the people of Israel, 'You shall not enter into marriage with them, neither shall they with you, for surely they will turn away your heart after their gods.' Solomon clung to these in love. He had 700 wives, princesses, and 300 concubines. And his wives turned away his heart" (1 Kings 11:1-3). Some of these wives were acquired to satisfy his political ambitions; they helped him form strategic alliances. But most of them were acquired to satisfy his sexual addiction. Solomon had the wealth and power to pursue pleasure to its limits. All the while, he was following after other gods, until finally he suffered the ultimate spiritual degradation: He bowed down to blocks of wood and stone.

God punished Solomon by tearing apart his kingdom, but that was not the real tragedy. The real tragedy was not the punishment, but the sin itself—the sin of breaking the first commandment. Solomon discovered to his own dismay how empty life is for those who follow other gods. Later, when he looked back on what he had done, he wrote, "I said in my heart, 'Come now, I will test you with pleasure; enjoy yourself'" (Eccles. 2:1a). Then he described his royal projects: "I built houses and planted vineyards for myself. I made myself gardens and parks, and planted in them all kinds of fruit trees. I made myself pools from which to water the forests of growing trees. I bought male and female slaves and had slaves who were born in my house. I also had great possessions of herds and flocks, more than any who had been before me in Jerusalem. I also gathered for myself silver and gold and the treasure of kings and provinces. I got singers, both men and women, and many concubines, the delight of the children of man" (Eccles. 2:4-8). Solomon had it all.

This was Solomon's grand experiment: the pursuit of other gods. He summed it all up by saying, "Whatever my eyes desired I did not keep from them; I kept my heart from no pleasure" (Eccles. 2:10a). What was the result? Was he satisfied? Did he get what he wanted? Was it worth it? No; his pursuit of power, pleasure, and prosperity led him into emptiness and despair. He said, "Then I considered all that my hands had done and the toil I had expended in doing it, and behold, all was vanity and a striving after wind, there was nothing to be gained under the sun. . . . So I hated life, because what is done under the sun was grievous to me" (Eccles. 2:11, 17a).

This is what happens to everyone who breaks the first commandment. In the end, of course, those who follow other gods will be judged for their sins, as Solomon was. But long before judgment there is emptiness and despair. The desire to have more and more is insatiable. But the shiny new products and exciting new experiences cannot quiet the nagging doubt. Is this all there is? Isn't there something more to life? When we break the first commandment we discover that other gods do not satisfy and cannot save. "How weak the gods of this world are," wrote Elizabeth Barrett Browning in a poem called "Idols"—"And weaker yet their worship made me!"

## Two Tests for Idolatry

The story of Solomon is a warning to everyone who has made a decision to follow God but is gradually coming under the influence of other gods.

Many people assume that idolatry is a thing of the past. Who would ever bow down to a figure made of wood or stone? It sounds so primitive! But the truth is that the spirit of Solomon is alive and well today. We may not worship Ashtoreth anymore or Molech (also known as Milcom), but we do worship other deities. And in many cases we serve exactly the same gods that Solomon served: money, sex, and power.

How can we identify our own private idolatries? There are two tests that we can use to determine which gods we are tempted to worship. One is *the love test*: What do we love? Writing sometime in the third century, Origen observed that the first commandment has to do with what we love. He wrote, "What each one honors before all else, what before all things he admires and loves, this for him is God." It only makes sense: We are called to love God with all our hearts and all our minds, but if instead we give our love to someone or something else, then we are serving some other god.

So what do you love? Or to ask the same question a different way, what do you desire? When your mind is free to roam, what do you think about? How do you spend your money? What do you get excited about? A false god can be any good thing that we focus on to the exclusion of God. It could be a sport or recreation. It could be a hobby or personal interest. It could be an appetite for the finer things in life. It could be a career ambition. It could be personal health and fitness. It could even be a ministry in the church. Certainly we are allowed to enjoy the good things in life, but we must not allow them to replace God as the object of our affections.

Another test is *the trust test*: What do you trust? Where do you turn in times of trouble? Martin Luther said, "Whatever thy heart clings to and relies upon, that is properly thy God."[4] Similarly, the Puritan Thomas Watson said, "To trust in any thing more than God, is to make it a god."[5] This makes sense, too. We are called to trust in God alone for our salvation, but if we put our trust in someone or something else, we are serving some other god.

So what do you trust? Some people trust their addictions. When they are in trouble—when they are lonely or discouraged—they count on drugs and alcohol or sex or shopping or some other obsession to pull them through. Other people trust things that are good in themselves, but that nevertheless have a way of replacing our confidence in God. Some trust their jobs, their insurance policies, or their pension plans for their security. Some put their faith in the government and its control of the economy. Some trust their families or their social position. Some people trust science and medicine. God can use all of these things to care and provide for us, but we are to place our ultimate confidence in him alone.

The truth is that we are tempted to love and to trust many things other than God. The Puritan Matthew Henry said, "Pride makes a god of self, covetousness makes a god of money, sensuality makes a god of the belly; whatever is esteemed or loved, feared or served, delighted in or depended on, more than God, that (whatever it is) we do in effect make a god of."[6] There are many examples of this kind of reasoning in the Bible. Job said, "If I have made gold my trust or called fine gold my confidence . . . this also would have been an iniquity to be punished by the judges, for I would have been false to God above" (Job 31:24, 28). The prophet Habakkuk described God's enemies as people "whose own might is their god" (Hab. 1:11). The apostle Paul was even more blunt, saying of the enemies of Christ, "their god is their belly" (Phil. 3:19). Whether it's money, power, or even your own belly, the world is full of God-substitutes and God-additives—things that take the place of God in daily life. The reason we have trouble recognizing our own private idolatries is not because we don't have false gods anymore, but because we have so many!

Behind all the lesser idols we serve is the god or goddess of self, the supreme deity of these postmodern times. In his famous study of American religion, Robert Bellah recounted an interview with a woman named Sheila Larson. Sheila was the ultimate individualist. She said, "I believe in God. I'm not a religious fanatic. I can't remember the last time I went to church. My faith has carried me a long way. It's Sheilaism. Just my own little voice." Bellah comments, "This suggests the logical possibility of over 220 million American religions, one for each of us."[7] What do we love? We are infatuated with ourselves. Whom do we trust? We believe in ourselves.

Christians are as prone to this kind of false worship as anyone else. We say that we want to serve God, but we spend most of our time thinking about our own needs, plans, problems, and desires. We have discovered, as Oscar Wilde famously wrote, that to "love oneself is the beginning of a life-long romance."[8]

## NO GOD BUT CHRIST

What can deliver us from the worship of self and all the other gods we are tempted to serve? *Rolling Stone* magazine asked this question back in December 1992. "Thou shalt not worship false idols," the editors wrote, slightly misquoting the Scripture, "but who else is there?"

The only answer is to fall passionately and deeply in love with God, specifically by trusting in his Son, Jesus Christ. The only thing that can tear our hearts away from all our other affections is true love for God. And the only thing that can replace all the other things we trust is a total faith commitment to the Lord Jesus Christ.

The Bible teaches that there is one God in three persons—Father, Son, and Holy Spirit. Jesus is God the Son, and since there is only one God, he is one with the Father (John 10:30), "God over all" (Rom. 9:5). Therefore, to worship Jesus is not to worship some other god, but to worship God, "the only Son from the Father" (John 1:14). Jesus makes the same claim on us that God has always made: "I am the LORD; that is my name; my glory I give to no other" (Isa. 42:8); "You know no God but me, and besides me there is no savior" (Hos. 13:4b). And Jesus calls us to turn away from everything else we are tempted to worship and give glory to him alone.

It is becoming increasingly common for people to claim that there are many ways to God. Pluralism has come to America, where there are now more than six hundred non-Christian religions. With so many options, people say it doesn't really matter which religion we choose, as long as our faith is right for us. It is fine to follow Christ, but only if we recognize that he is not the only god. Even in the church there are some people who say that Jesus is *a* Savior but not *the* Savior.

This pluralistic approach to religion is a direct attack on the first commandment, in which we are commanded to worship God alone.

God is as intolerant today as ever. To deny that Jesus is the only way is to say that there are other gods. But there are no other gods! This false theology must be rejected both for the honor of Christ and for the keeping of the first commandment. Jesus claims exclusive rights to our worship. He is not simply one among many prophets. He is the only way, the only truth, and the only life (John 14:6). He is the only incarnate Son of God. He alone kept the whole law for God's people, offered a perfect sacrifice for our sins, and was raised from the dead to open the way to eternal life. So he alone deserves our praise.

It is not simply our duty to worship Christ as the only God, but also our privilege. He alone is our Savior and our Lord. So we make it our aim to please him in all our work and play, in all we do. We worship him and adore him; we trust him and thank him. For he says to us, "I am the Lord your God, who brought you out of your bondage to sin, out of your slavery to Satan. You shall have no other gods before me."

## STUDY QUESTIONS

1. What is one thing you love to share? What is one thing you would rather keep for yourself?
2. How would you counter the argument that the first commandment either makes God out to be selfish or Christians to be narrow-minded and intolerant?
3. Why do you think God made this the first commandment?
4. What powers do false gods have? What is the source of their power?
5. What is the positive duty implied in this commandment? Read 1 Kings 3:5-15; 9:4-9; 11:9-11.
6. If God gave you the choice he gave Solomon—to have whatever you wanted—what would you ask for?
7. After reading 1 Kings 3:5-15, what would you expect Solomon's rule to be like?
8. Read 1 Kings 6:38 and 7:1; 1 Kings 10:26-29 and 11:1-3; and Ecclesiastes 2:10-11, 17. What were the idols that led to Solomon's downfall?
9. Using the "love" and "trust" tests, what are some potential idols—God-substitutes or God-additives—in your life?
10. How can you prevent these things from becoming idols that lure you away from wholehearted devotion to God? Make some specific goals and limits for yourself, and find someone who can keep you accountable.

# THE SECOND COMMANDMENT:
# THE RIGHT GOD, THE RIGHT WAY

*You shall not make for yourself a carved image, or any likeness of anything that is in heaven above, or that is in the earth beneath, or that is in the water under the earth. You shall not bow down to them or serve them, for I the LORD your God am a jealous God, visiting the iniquity of the fathers on the children to the third and the fourth generation of those who hate me, but showing steadfast love to thousands of those who love me and keep my commandments.*

EXODUS 20:4-6

Whenever I have a chance to show Roman Catholics the interior of Tenth Presbyterian Church in Philadelphia, I ask them what's missing. "Do you notice anything strange about this sanctuary?" I ask. "Yes," they invariably reply, "there's no crucifix! Why not? Where is it?"

My standard answer is that the cross is in our message. Every week we preach that Jesus Christ was crucified for sinners. This is something that we announce from the Scriptures, but it is not something that we hang on our walls. There is an important biblical and theological reason for this: A visual representation of Christ on the cross can easily become an object of worship and thus violate the second commandment.

## Two Different Commandments

One reason most Roman Catholics have trouble accepting this is that they divide the Ten Commandments differently. According to Catholics, and also to Lutherans, Exodus 20:3-6 is a single commandment. The prohibition against making idols is part of the commandment not to have any other gods (the way they make up the difference is by dividing coveting into two commandments).

This raises an important question: Are Reformed Protestants correct in recognizing Exodus 20:4 as the beginning of a new commandment? The answer is yes. Having other gods and not making idols are two different regulations. The first commandment has to do with worshiping the right God. We must reject every false god in order to worship the true God, who alone is our Lord and Savior. The second commandment has to do with worshiping the right God in the right way. We may not worship him in the form of any man-made idol. Whereas the first commandment forbids us to worship false gods, the second commandment forbids us to worship the true God falsely. *How* we worship matters nearly as much to God as *whom* we worship. We may not worship him any way we like, but only the way that he has commanded. In the words of the Westminster Shorter Catechism, "The second commandment forbiddeth the worshipping of God by images, or any other way not appointed in his word" (A. 51).

A good illustration of the difference between the first and second commandments comes from the life of King Jehu. The Bible praises Jehu for eliminating Baal worship from Israel, which he did by putting the wicked queen Jezebel to death (2 Kings 9:30-37) and by destroying the ministers of Baal (2 Kings 10:18-27). The account of Jehu's victory ends with this commendation: "Thus Jehu wiped out Baal from Israel" (2 Kings 10:28).

So far, so good. Jehu refused to worship other gods. But the Bible goes on to say, "Jehu did not turn away from the sins of Jeroboam the son of Nebat, which he made Israel to sin—that is, the golden calves that were in Bethel and in Dan" (2 Kings 10:29). If Jehu got rid of Baal worship, then what were these sacred cows still doing in Israel? The answer is that although Jehu enforced the first commandment, he allowed his people to break the second commandment. The golden calves did not represent other gods; they were intended to represent the God of Israel. But that is precisely what the second commandment forbids: worshiping God with an idol. Whereas the first commandment forbids false gods, the second forbids false worship.

## IDOLATRY EXPLAINED

The second commandment is one of the longest: "You shall not make for yourself a carved image, or any likeness of anything that is in heaven above, or that is in the earth beneath, or that is in the water under the earth. You shall not bow down to them or serve them, for I the LORD your God am a jealous God, visiting the iniquity of the fathers on the children to the third and the fourth generation of those who hate me, but showing steadfast love to thousands of those who love me and keep my commandments" (Exod. 20:4-6).

There are four parts to this commandment: the rule, the reason, the warning, and the promise. *The rule* is very simple: Don't make any idols (Exod. 20:4a), or as the King James Version refers to them, "graven images" (ESV, "carved image"; see also Lev. 26:1). This translation comes close to the original meaning. An idol was something crafted by a tool. Whether it was carved out of wood, chiseled out of stone, or engraved in metal, it was cut and shaped by human hands. It was a man-made representation of some divine being.

This did not mean that the Israelites were forbidden to use tools. Nor did it mean that they were not allowed to produce artwork. Later, when it was time to build the tabernacle, God sent the Israelites his Spirit "to devise artistic designs, to work in gold, silver and bronze, in cutting stones for setting, and in carving wood, to work in every craft" (Exod. 31:4-5). So what the second commandment ruled out was not making things, but making things to serve as objects of worship. This is clarified in the second part of the rule: "You shall not bow down to them or serve them" (Exod. 20:5a). The Israelites were strictly forbidden to make images of God to use in worship. Although God appreciates artistry, he will not tolerate idolatry.

This rule is clarified with a list of the kinds of idols God forbids:

"You shall not make for yourself a carved image, or any likeness of anything that is in heaven above, or that is in the earth beneath, or that is in the water under the earth" (Exod. 20:4). That pretty much covers it: nothing in the sky, nothing on the ground, and nothing in the sea! In other words, the Israelites were not allowed to represent God in the form of anything in all creation. Remember that the Israelites had been living with the Egyptians, who worshiped many gods, nearly all of which they represented in the form of animals. The god Horus had the head of a falcon, the god Anubis had the head of a jackal, and so on. When it came to the Egyptians and their idols, any animal was fair game! But the God of Israel refused to be represented in the image of any of his creatures.

There are many good reasons for this rule, but the one God specifically mentions is his love: "You shall not make for yourself a carved image . . . for I the LORD your God am a jealous God" (Exod. 20:4–5). This is *the reason* for the rule. God forbids idolatry because of his jealousy. To use a more positive and also a more accurate word, it is because of his zeal—the burning passion of his love.

Jealousy doesn't get very much positive publicity these days. When people talk about it, they generally mean something more like envy, the desire to get something that does not belong to you. However, when something really does belong to you, there are times when it needs to be protected. A holy jealousy is one that guards someone's rightful possession. The most obvious example is the love between a husband and wife. No husband who truly loves his wife could possibly endure seeing her in the arms of another man. It would make him intensely jealous, and rightly so!

God feels the same way about his people. His commitment to us is total. His love is exclusive, passionate, intense—in a word, jealous. As one commentator explains, "Godly jealousy is not the insecure, insane, and possessive human jealousy that we often interpret this word to mean. Rather, it is an intensely caring devotion to the objects of His love, like a mother's jealous protection of her children, a father's jealous guarding of his home."[1]

If that is what jealousy means, then God *has* to be jealous. He loves us too much not to be! In fact, jealousy is one of his divine perfections.

As Christopher Wright has written: "A God who was not jealous . . . would be as contemptible as a husband who didn't care whether or not his wife was faithful to him. Part of our problem with this profound covenantal reality is that we have come to regard religion, like everything else, as a matter of 'consumer choice.' . . . . We resent monopolies. But the unique and incomparable, only living God makes necessarily exclusive claims and has the right to a monopoly on our love. . . . Jealousy is God's love protecting itself."[2]

What God so jealously protects in the second commandment is the honor of his love. God not only loves us, but he also wants us to love him in return. Among other things, that means worshiping him in a way that is worthy of his honor. God has the right to tell us how he wants to be worshiped, and he has commanded us not to spurn his love by turning him into an idol.

## THE SINS OF THE FATHERS

God's jealousy explains why the second commandment ends with a warning ("visiting the iniquity of the fathers on the children to the third and the fourth generation of those who hate me," Exod. 20:5b) and a promise ("but showing steadfast love to thousands of those who love me and keep my commandments," Exod. 20:6). God shows his zeal to be glorified in our worship by cursing those who break the second commandment and blessing those who keep it.

*The warning* is that children will be punished for the sins of their fathers. The word translated "iniquity" refers to something twisted. It suggests that idolatry is a kind of perversion, a turning against God. It may seem very religious to worship idols, but since God hates idolatry (Deut. 16:22), it is really a way of showing hatred for him, and it is not at all surprising that God threatens to punish those who do such a hateful thing. What some people wonder, however, is whether God's curse is just. How can God judge a person for someone else's sin? Is it really fair to punish children for the sins of their fathers?

Many scholars do not think that it is fair; so they try to find some other way to explain this verse. Some interpret it sociologically. They point out that a father's sin has consequences that can last for generations. They also point out that because children imitate their parents, sin tends to run in the family. One generation sets the spiritual tone for the next. So perhaps the second commandment is based on universal truths about family relationships.

The commandment says something more, however. It says that God punishes children for the sin of their fathers. What a father passes on to his children is not simply a bad example, but the guilt of his sin. The principle here is covenant solidarity: God holds families responsible for their conduct as families. The Israelites were in covenant with God, and when the covenant head of any family sinned against God, his whole family was judged. To give just one example, all seventy of Ahab's sons were killed for their father's idolatry (2 Kings 10:1-17).

This is not to deny individual responsibility. God holds each one of us accountable for our own sin. The Bible says, "The soul who sins shall die. The son shall not suffer for the iniquity of the father, nor the father suffer for the iniquity of the son" (Ezek. 18:20a). God never condemns the innocent, but only the guilty. Here it is important to notice something in the second commandment that is often overlooked, namely, how the threat ends. God says that he will punish three or four generations "of those who hate me" (Exod. 20:5). It is not just the fathers who hate God, but also their children. People who struggle with the fairness of this commandment usually assume that although the father is guilty, his children are innocent. But the children hate God as much as their father did (which, given the way they were raised, is not surprising). Therefore, it is fair and just for God to punish them for their sin and for their father's sin.

God also promises to show mercy to those who love him and keep his commandment not to serve idols. *The promise* is more powerful than the warning because its blessing lasts not just for three or four generations, but for a thousand; in other words, it will last forever. This was God's promise going all the way back to Abraham: "I will establish my covenant between me and you and your offspring after you throughout their generations for an everlasting covenant, to be God to you and your offspring after you" (Gen. 17:7). All we have to do is respond to the God who loves us by loving him in return.

God's threat in the second commandment may seem discouraging to someone who comes from a family that does not honor God, but God's blessing triumphs over God's curse, and God often intervenes in the history of a family to turn their hatred into love and worship. He does what he did for Abraham: He calls a family to leave its idols behind and follow him. And when God does that, he establishes a lasting legacy. His grace rests on a family from one generation to the next. This is not some kind of automatic guarantee, because children are free to turn away from the God of their fathers and mothers. But it is a promise to receive by faith.

What is God doing in your family? As parents plan for the future they should be more concerned about the second commandment than they are about their financial portfolio. This commandment contains a solemn warning for fathers. When a man refuses to love God passionately and to worship God properly, the consequences of his sin will last for generations. The guilt of a man who treasures idols in his heart will corrupt his entire family, and in the end they will all be punished. But a man who loves God supremely—a man who bows before him in genuine worship and serves him with true praise—will see the blessing of God rest on his household forever. What kind of life are you leading? What kind of worship are you giving? What kind of legacy will you leave?

## IDOLATRY ILLUSTRATED

There is a story in the Bible that shows what's wrong with idols. It is set in Athens—the story of Paul and the philosophers. Athens was a great city in those days, the intellectual capital of the world. High on the Acropolis stood the Parthenon, the showpiece of Greek architecture. The streets bustled with commerce. There was also a great deal of traffic in the marketplace of ideas. As the Scripture reports, "Now all the Athenians and the foreigners who lived there would spend their time doing nothing except hearing or telling something new" (Acts 17:21).

Athens was also full of idols. There were images of all shapes and sizes, made of wood and stone, gold and silver. They represented all the gods and goddesses in the Greek pantheon. There were so many idols that one Roman writer joked that it was easier to find a god in Athens than a man![3] And towering over them all was the great goddess Athena, whose statue could be seen forty miles away.[4] Athens held perhaps the most spectacular display of idols that the world has ever seen.

When the apostle Paul saw all these graven images, he was provoked almost to anger. The Bible says that he was "provoked within him as he saw that the city was full of idols" (Acts 17:16). He was disheartened and dismayed to see so many people worshiping so many idols, and thus denying God his glory. For days he reasoned with the Athenians, trying to persuade them to turn away from all their false gods in order to worship the one and only true and living God. He preached the gospel, the good news about Jesus and the resurrection.

Eventually Paul came into contact with members of the Areopagus, the famous philosophical society that met on Mars Hill. These men were the censors who controlled the religious lectures given in Athens. Their society also served as a kind of think tank, something like the Brookings Institution or the American Enterprise Institute. The Areopagus included some of the most learned men of the ancient world, men who loved to argue about philosophy and religion. Wanting to learn more about what Paul was saying, they invited him to address their assembly.

One might have expected Paul to tell the philosophers that they were worshiping the wrong gods. All of their idols represented false deities; so he might have said, "You shall have no other gods," addressing them on the basis of the first commandment. That is not what Paul said, however. It was one of the implications of what he said, but it is not where he placed his emphasis. Instead, he addressed them on the basis of the *second* commandment. He told them that God cannot be worshiped by way of idols. Their problem was not simply that they were serving the wrong gods, but that they were worshiping the wrong way altogether.

Paul began by establishing a point of contact. He stood up and said, "Men of Athens, I perceive that in every way you are very religious. For as I passed along and observed the objects of your worship, I found also an altar with this inscription, 'To the unknown god.' What therefore you worship as unknown, this I proclaim to you" (Acts 17:22b-23). This was a clever rhetorical strategy. By making an idol to an unknown god, the Athenians were trying to cover all their bases. But they were also admitting that there was at least one thing about religion that they didn't know. So the apostle told them that he was there to explain it.

Next Paul said that the Creator God is a living spirit who cannot be put in a box: "The God who made the world and everything in it, being Lord of heaven and earth, does not live in temples made by man, nor is he served by human hands, as though he needed anything, since he himself gives to all mankind life and breath and everything" (Acts 17:24-25). Paul was clarifying the relationship between the Creator and the creature. We do not make God; he made us. We do not give life to God; he gives life to us. To strengthen this point, Paul proceeded to quote from one of their own Greek poets, who said, "For we are indeed his offspring" (Acts 17:28b).

This brief doctrine of God had one very obvious implication. If God is the Creator and Giver of Life, then he cannot be squeezed into some man-made idol. How could the transcendent God possibly be reduced to a mere object? Hence Paul's conclusion: "Being then God's offspring, we ought not to think that the divine being is like gold or silver or stone, an image formed by the art and imagination of man. The times of ignorance God overlooked, but now he commands all people everywhere to repent" (Acts 17:29-30). Paul was saying something very important about the second commandment. He was saying that when we use idols we are not worshiping the true God, but are constructing a false god—a god made in our own image. As Paul later explained to the Romans, "They exchanged the truth of God for a lie and worshiped and served the creature rather than the Creator" (Rom. 1:25).

This was the problem with idolatry all along: It created a false image of God that was inadequate to his deity and unworthy of his majesty. God is infinite and invisible. He is omnipotent and omnipresent. He is a living spirit. Therefore, to carve him into a piece of wood or stone is to deny his attributes, the essential characteristics of his divine being. An idol makes the infinite God finite, the invisible God visible, the omnipotent God impotent, the all-present God local, the living God dead, and the spiritual God material. In short, it makes him the exact opposite of what he actually is. Thus the whole idea of idolatry rests on the absurdity of human beings trying to make a true image of God. An idol is not the truth, but a lie. It is a god who cannot see, know, act, love, or save.

## IDOLATRY APPLIED

It is tempting to think of idol worship as a thing of the past. Unless we go overseas to serve as missionaries, the only place we are likely to see traditional idols is in a museum. We certainly don't have any idols in the church, do we?

Maybe not, if an idol is only something we can see and touch. But like the rest of God's law, the second commandment is spiritual: It applies to the heart. And in our hearts we are always busy fashioning God in our image. John Calvin said the human heart is "a perpetual factory of idols."[5] Rather than worshiping God "in spirit and truth" (John 4:24), we reshape and remake him until he is safely under our control. What are some of the ways we manufacture our own gods?

We make an idol whenever we worship an image rather than listening to the Word. One of the problems with physical images of God is that they hinder us from hearing God's voice. This is why God did not reveal himself in a physical form on Mount Sinai. Moses said to the Israelites, "Since you saw no form on the day that the LORD spoke to you at Horeb out of the midst of the fire, beware lest you act corruptly by making a carved image for yourselves" (Deut. 4:15-16a). The way God revealed himself at Mount Sinai was not through a visible image, but through an audible word. This tells us something about the way he wants to be worshiped. He does not want us to look, but to listen.

We are living in a visual age. Everywhere we go we see images flickering across the screen. Some Christian leaders say that the church needs to adapt by becoming more visual in its presentation of the gospel. Instead of simply talking about God, we need to *show* people something. But that impulse is idolatrous. In his influential book *Amusing Ourselves to Death*, Neil Postman writes:

In studying the Bible as a young man, I found intimations of the idea that forms of media favor particular kinds of content and therefore are capable of taking command of a culture. I refer specifically to the Decalogue, the Second Commandment of which prohibits the Israelites from making concrete images of anything. . . . The God of the Jews was to exist in the Word and through the Word, an unprecedented conception requiring the highest order of abstract thinking. Iconography thus became blasphemy so that a new kind of God could enter a culture. People like ourselves who are in the process of converting their culture from word-centered to image-centered might profit by reflecting on this Mosaic injunction.[6]

Indeed. What the image always wants to do in worship is to distract us from hearing the Word. The crucifix, the icon, the drama, and the dance—these things are not aids to worship, but make true worship all but impossible. In a visual age, we need to be all the more careful not to look at the image, but to listen to the Word.

We also make an idol whenever we turn God into something that we can manipulate. This was the whole point of pagan idolatry. The Egyptians did not think that the gods actually lived in their idols, but they did think that idols gave them the kind of spiritual contact that would enable them to control their gods. So much contemporary spirituality tries to do the same thing. People are always looking for a more user-friendly god, a god who can be adapted to suit their purposes. They say, "If I do this, then God will do that." If I touch the minister, then I will be healed. If I fulfill my vow, then God will make me rich. If I say the right prayer every day, I will have the key to unlock God's blessing. If I follow the right parenting method, then my kids will grow up to be godly. As long as we approach God the right way, we will get what we want. But God will not be manipulated. When he commands us not to make idols, he is saying that he "will not be captured, contained, assigned or managed by anyone or anything, for any purpose."[7] God wants us to trust him and obey him, not use him.

We also make an idol whenever we choose to worship God for some of his attributes, but not others. The old liberal church wanted a

God of love without justice; so they denied fundamental doctrines like the wrath of God and the substitutionary atonement. Now many evangelicals are downplaying the same doctrines. Nearly half of the students at evangelical colleges and seminaries say that talking about divine judgment is bad manners.[8] Feminist theologians deny the Fatherhood of God. They prefer a god more in the image of woman. Open theists deny the foreknowledge of God. Although they say that God knows some things about the future, since he does not know what human beings will decide to do, he does not know everything. In effect, these theologians are advocating a deity who thinks more the way they do, a god who is trying to figure things out as he goes along. But all these new theologies are really forms of idolatry. When people say, "I like to think of God as . . ." they are usually remaking God in their image.

We too are tempted to worship God the way we want him to be, rather than the way he actually is. We tend to emphasize the things about God that we like and minimize the rest. We place a higher priority on knowing the Bible than on loving God. We think that God is more concerned with private morality than with social justice. And since we are legalists at heart, we are motivated more by a sense of duty than by a deep gratitude for God's grace. When we do all this, we end up with a deity without the love, compassion, or grace of God.

How can we worship God the right way? What can save us from our own private idolatries? The answer is very simple: Rather than remaking God into *our* image, we need to be remade into *his* image. God does that by bringing us into a personal saving relationship with his Son Jesus Christ.

Here is a deep mystery. When God first created the world, he made men and women in his image (Gen. 1:26-27). We were made to be like God, to reflect his glory. And this is another reason why God tells us not to make images. He already has an image! *We* are created according to God's image. As Calvin said, "God cannot be represented by a picture or sculpture, since He has intended His likeness to appear in us."[9] Or as Christopher Wright has written: "The only legitimate image of God . . . is the image of God created in his own likeness—the living, thinking, working, speaking, breathing, relating human being (not even a statue will do, but only the human person)."[10] We are not allowed to make God's image, but only to *be* God's image.

Our ability to do that was badly damaged by our fall into sin. The image of God in us has been defaced, like so much graffiti on a mirror. In our fallen and sinful condition, we are no longer able to reflect God's glory as he intended. But God has sent his Son Jesus Christ into the world to repair his image in us. Jesus is the true image, "the image of the invisible God" (Col. 1:15; cf. 2 Cor. 4:4), "the exact imprint of his nature" (Heb. 1:3). This is why Jesus could say that anyone who sees him has seen God (John 14:9). He is the point of contact. In order to come to God in true worship, we don't need to make some kind of idol; all we need to do is come to him through Jesus Christ. And when we come to Christ, then God lives in us by his Holy Spirit. He works in us to repair his image, so that we can live for his glory.

## STUDY QUESTIONS

1. Give an example of a time when you tried to do the right thing but did it the wrong way. What were the results?
2. What is the relationship between the first and second commandments? In other words, how are they different, and how do they inform one another?
3. What does it mean—and not mean—that God is jealous?
4. Why does God punish children for their fathers' sin? Is this fair? Why or why not?
5. As you think of your own family or other families you know well, how does the threat contained in the second commandment affect the way you view family difficulties and the legacy that parents are leaving for their children?
6. Read Acts 17:16-34. Outline the main points in Paul's rhetorical argument. Why was this an effective approach to reach his audience?
7. How might this passage serve as a model for us today as we introduce others to Jesus?
8. What does Paul say in this passage about the nature and attributes of God?
9. What makes idols so appealing? What are some ways in which Christians in general, and you in particular, are tempted to worship idols?
10. How can you guard against idolatry in your church and in your own life?

# 6

## THE THIRD COMMANDMENT:
# NAME ABOVE ALL NAMES

*You shall not take the name of the LORD your God in vain, for the LORD will not hold him guiltless who takes his name in vain.*
EXODUS 20:7

One of the first duties of parents is to name their children. This can be a difficult task. The parents make lists. They read baby name books and field suggestions from family members. They try various combinations and say them out loud to see how they sound. They consider all the possible nicknames, and then they check to see what the initials spell. Even after all of that, however, they may still end up at the hospital not having reached agreement about what to call the child!

The one thing that is certain in all of this is that the parents will do the naming. Human beings do not name themselves. Our full names are given, not chosen, which shows that naming is an act of authority. I remember holding each of my newborn children in my arms, calling them by name, and telling them that I was their daddy. Naming a child is the first way that parents exercise their God-given authority.

By contrast, one of the remarkable things about God is that no one ever named him. Admittedly, from time to time people have come up with various false names for God. But God's true name is chosen and revealed by God himself. We do not tell God who he is; he tells us. God has his own naming rights, and this is a sign of his sovereign authority. God's name comes before all other names.

## WHAT'S IN A NAME?

The third commandment defends the honor of God's great name: "You shall not take the name of the LORD your God in vain, for the LORD will not hold him guiltless who takes his name in vain" (Exod. 20:7). Unlike the first two commandments, here God refers to himself in the third person. There is a special reason for this. First God said, "You shall have no other gods before me" (Exod. 20:3), speaking in the first person. But in the third commandment he refers to himself more indirectly. Rather than saying, "You shall not take my name in vain," he says, "You shall not take the name of the LORD your God in vain." He does this to call attention to his special covenant name Yahweh, or Lord.

This was a name that God revealed long before the Israelites even reached Mount Sinai. Back at the burning bush Moses asked for God's name, and because of his great love for his people, God gave it to him:

> God said to Moses, "I AM WHO I AM. This is what you are to say to the Israelites: 'I AM has sent me to you.'" God also said to Moses, "Say this to the people of Israel, 'The LORD, the God of your fathers, the God of Abraham, the God of Isaac and the God of Jacob, has sent me to you.' This is my name forever, and thus I am to be remembered throughout all generations."—Exod. 3:14-15

The name that God revealed was his personal name Yahweh, sometimes called the *tetragrammaton* because in Hebrew it consists of four letters: YHWH. Literally, God's name means "I am who I am," or "I will be who I will be." It speaks of God's self-existence, self-sufficiency, and supreme sovereignty. As the events of the exodus unfolded, it also testified to his saving power. The Israelites learned from their deliverance that the God who revealed his name to Moses is a God who saves.

As we start unpacking the meaning of God's name, it quickly becomes obvious that "Yahweh," or "LORD," is much more than a name. It is God's identity. This was the whole Hebrew understanding of names. For us a name is a label; it is something we have, not something we are. But for the Hebrews the name was inseparable from the person. It expressed a person's inward identity. When we use the name of God, therefore, we are referring to the essence of his divine being.

His supreme name was simply Yahweh, the Lord God. This name is much more than a convenient way to address God. It represents God's entire reputation. The literary term for this manner of speech, in which one part stands for the whole, is *synecdoche*. For example, when someone says, "There were a lot of new faces at the meeting," this does not imply that their faces were somehow disconnected from the rest of their bodies. A face is part of a whole, and thus it can stand for the entire person. Similarly, God's name represents his whole identity.

God's name is also used this way elsewhere in the Old Testament. David sang, "O LORD, our Lord, how majestic is your name in all the earth!" (Ps. 8:1a). He was praising God not simply for his name, but for being the God who made all things for his own glory. God has made a name for himself in creation, and also in redemption. This was the whole point of the exodus. God was saving a people for his glory. Or as the psalmist put it, referring specifically to the rescue at the Red Sea, "he saved them for his name's sake, that he might make known his mighty power" (Ps. 106:8; cf. Ps. 111:9). God brought Israel out of Egypt for the honor of his name. Therefore, by the time the Israelites reached Mount Sinai, they should have known that God's name was much more than a name. It communicated God's glory in creation and redemption, and thus it deserved as much reverence and respect as God himself.

## MISUSING GOD'S NAME

Like the rest of God's moral law, the third commandment is both negative and positive. In its negative form it forbids the misuse of God's name: "You shall not take the name of the LORD your God in vain" (Exod. 20:7a). Or to give a more literal translation, "You shall not lift up the name of the Lord your God for nothingness."[1]

What does it mean to "lift up" God's name? This term had a fairly technical meaning. It was used in legal situations to refer to the taking of an oath.[2] When witnesses needed to confirm their testimony, instead of swearing on a Bible, they lifted a hand and swore by God's name. However, the term was also used more broadly for other situations when people took God's name on their lips. His name was "lifted up" in worship and whenever else people talked about him.

God's people were not forbidden to use God's name. Many orthodox Jews take this commandment more strictly than God intended, refusing to use God's special divine name at all, for fear of misusing it. But God *wants* us to use his name! This is proven by the Old Testament, where God's sacred divine name is used all over the place—almost seven thousand occurrences in all. God gave us his name so that we would be able to address him personally. Calling him by name strengthens our love relationship with him.

What God forbids is not the use of his name, then, but its *misuse*. To be specific, we are not to use it in a vain or empty way. The specific misuse that God has in mind is speaking about him carelessly, thoughtlessly, or even flippantly, as if he didn't matter or really didn't exist at all. God's name has deep spiritual significance; so to treat it like something worthless is profanity in the truest sense of the word: It is to treat something holy and sacred as common and secular. To dishonor God's name in any way is to denigrate his holiness. It is a way of saying that God himself is worthless.

In his careful study of the Ten Commandments, the Dutch scholar Jochem Douma mentions three ways that God's name was commonly profaned in Old Testament times: in sorcery, in false prophecy, and in the taking of false oaths.[3]

Sorcery has to do with the occult. In the ancient world many people believed that they could gain access to supernatural power by using divine names in magical incantations. They called upon their gods to heal their bodies, to tell the future, and to give them victory in battle. The Egyptians specialized in this kind of thing. But God refuses to be manipulated; so he commanded his people not to use his name for the casting of spells. Later he said, "There shall not be found among you anyone . . . who practices divination or tells fortunes or interprets omens, or a sorcerer or a charmer or a medium or a wizard or a necromancer, for whoever does these things is an abomination to the LORD" (Deut. 18:10-12a).

God's name was also misused in connection with false prophecy.

The prophets always said, "Thus saith the Lord." However, when a false prophet tried to quote God this way, it was a lie, and therefore an abuse of God's holy name. As God said on one occasion, "The prophets are prophesying lies in my name. . . . Therefore thus says the LORD concerning the prophets who prophesy in my name although I did not send them . . ." (Jer. 14:14a–15a). False prophecy was an attempt to use God's special divine name to advance a prophet's own agenda. There are many examples of this from church history. People often try to boost their own credibility by claiming that God is on their side. His name has been used to endorse everything from the Crusades to the slave trade, from political parties to social causes, and the results are almost always disastrous.

The third common misuse of God's name was in swearing false oaths. To persuade others that they were telling the truth—in court, for example, or in connection with a business deal—people often said something like, "As the LORD lives" (Jer. 5:2). By lifting up God's name they were trying to prove that what they were saying was true. In effect they were calling God as their witness. The problem came when people took an oath in God's name and then proceeded to lie. This was perjury—a direct violation of the third commandment. It was using God's name to confirm what was false rather than what was true. So God said, "You shall not swear by my name falsely, and so profane the name of your God: I am the LORD" (Lev. 19:12).

These are some of the ways that God's sacred name was misused in Old Testament times. In each case, people tried to use his name for their own advantage. But God said, "You shall not take the name of the LORD your God in vain" (Exod. 20:7a).

He also said that anyone who breaks the third commandment will be held accountable: "the LORD will not hold him guiltless who takes his name in vain" (Exod. 20:7b). The precise punishment is left unspecified. In fact, the threat seems almost understated: The lawbreaker simply is said not to be without guilt. However, this expression is what grammarians call a *meiosis*, in which less is said, but much more is intended.[4] For example, when people in authority say, "I wouldn't do that if I were you," they are not simply offering a casual opinion, but are issuing a stern warning. So when God says that he will not hold us guiltless, what he means is that he will condemn us. We will not be innocent, but guilty—reckoned unrighteous by Almighty God.

The reason God will condemn us is because misusing his name is a very great sin. It is a direct attack on his honor and glory, and anyone who makes such an attack deserves to be condemned. Here God's justice can be defended by means of an analogy:

> One way for a modern American to begin to understand this commandment is to treat God's name as a trademarked property. In order to gain widespread distribution for His copyrighted repair manual—the Bible—and also to capture greater market share for His authorized franchise—the Church—God has graciously licensed the use of His name to anyone who will use it according to His written instructions. It needs to be understood, however, that God's name has not been released into the public domain. God retains legal control over His name and threatens serious penalties against the unauthorized misuse of this supremely valuable property. All trademark violations will be prosecuted to the full limits of the law. The prosecutor, judge, jury, and enforcer is God.[5]

When people break the third or any other commandment, they are guilty before God, and ultimately they will be judged for their sins. There are many examples in the Bible. Perhaps the most shocking occurs in Leviticus 24. A dispute broke out between two Israelites, one of whom was part Egyptian. As they fought, the man of mixed descent blurted out a curse against God. The Scripture says that he "blasphemed the Name, and cursed" (Lev. 24:11a). The bystanders were appalled at what the man said; so they seized him and brought him to stand trial before Moses.

The Lord did not hold the man guiltless, but he said, "Bring out of the camp the one who cursed, and let all who heard him lay their hands on his head, and let all the congregation stone him. And speak to the people of Israel, saying, 'Whoever curses his God shall bear his sin. Whoever blasphemes the name of the LORD shall surely be put to death'" (Lev. 24:13-16a). When God says that anyone who misuses his name will be held responsible, we should take him at his word!

## His Name Is Wonderful

Like the rest of the moral law, the third commandment is positive as well as negative. At the same time that it forbids the misuse of God's name, threatening us with guilt, it also commands us to use his name properly. Instead of taking his name in vain, we should take it in all seriousness. According to John Calvin:

> The purpose of this commandment is: God wills that we hallow the majesty of his name. Therefore, it means in brief that we are not to profane his name by treating it contemptuously and irreverently. To this prohibition duly corresponds the commandment that we should be zealous and careful to honor his name with godly reverence. Therefore we ought to be so disposed in mind and speech that we neither think nor say anything concerning God and his mysteries, without reverence and much soberness; that in estimating his works we conceive nothing but what is honorable to him.[6]

Calvin's use of the word "hallow" brings to mind the first petition of the Lord's prayer: "Hallowed be your name" (Matt. 6:9b). To hallow is to consecrate, to set apart for a sacred purpose. And that is what God wants us to do with his name: to preserve it for the purpose of worship and praise.

There are many ways to use God's name properly. His name can be praised, honored, blessed, and celebrated. It can be lifted on high and exalted. It can be worshiped and adored. To honor God's name, wrote Martin Luther, is to "use that very name in every time of need to call on, pray to, praise, and give thanks to God."[7] But one of the best places to learn the proper use of God's name is the book of Psalms. Many of the biblical psalms show us how to honor God's name: "Ascribe to the LORD the glory due his name" (Ps. 29:2a; 96:8a); "Sing the glory of his name; give to him glorious praise" (Ps. 66:2); "Blessed be his glorious name forever" (Ps. 72:19a); "Bless the LORD, O my soul, and all that is within me, bless his holy name!" (Ps. 103:1). Elsewhere the Bible instructs us to "call on the name of the LORD" (Gen. 4:26), to prophesy in the name of the Lord (Deut. 18:19), to "trust in the name of the LORD" (Isa. 50:10), and in every way to "fear this glorious and awesome name, the LORD your God" (Deut. 28:58).

By telling us to honor God's name, the third commandment helps us honor God himself, giving him the same reverence and respect that we give to his holy name. The apostle Paul gave perhaps the fullest, most positive statement of this command in his letter to the Colossians: "And whatever you do, in word or deed, do everything in the name of the Lord Jesus, giving thanks to God the Father through him" (Col. 3:17).

## A Terrible Beating

Mentioning "the name of the Lord Jesus" brings to mind a Bible story about breaking and keeping the third commandment. It is the story of the seven sons of Sceva, whom the apostle Paul met on his first mission to Ephesus. It had been an extraordinary visit. Shortly after arriving, Paul baptized some of the Ephesians, and they received the Holy Spirit. He then spent three months in the synagogue, arguing with the Jews about the kingdom of God. After this he preached to the Greeks daily for two years at the public lecture hall. During these years he performed many signs and wonders: "God was doing extraordinary miracles by the hands of Paul, so that even handkerchiefs or aprons that had touched his skin were carried away to the sick, and their diseases left them and the evil spirits came out of them" (Acts 19:11-12).

Now there was one group of men who were watching Paul's ministry very carefully, and they noticed that whenever he performed a miracle, he always did it in the name of Jesus. Paul did everything in Jesus' name. Baptizing, preaching, healing—it was all in the name of Jesus. Eventually they realized that there was something powerful about this name, and they reasoned that if this fellow Paul could use it, they could use it too. They wanted to use the name of Jesus Christ—the very name of God—to work their own wonders. However, things didn't work out quite the way they had hoped:

> Then some of the itinerant Jewish exorcists undertook to invoke the name of the Lord Jesus over those who had evil spirits, saying, "I adjure you by the Jesus, whom Paul proclaims." Seven sons of a Jewish high priest named Sceva were doing this. But the evil spirit answered them, "Jesus I know, and Paul I recognize, but who are you?" And the man in whom was the evil spirit

*leaped on them, mastered all of them and overpowered them, so that they fled
out of that house naked and wounded.*—Acts 19:13-16

To understand this story, all we need to know is the third commandment, which says, "You shall not take the name of the LORD your God
in vain, for the LORD will not hold him guiltless who takes his name in
vain" (Exod. 20:7). The seven sons of Sceva misused God's name,
employing it to perform magic tricks for their own personal advantage.
And God did not hold them guiltless, but allowed them to get the beat-
ing they deserved.

Perhaps the most significant part of the story is what happened
next: "And this became known to all the residents of Ephesus, both
Jews and Greeks. And fear fell upon them all, and the name of the
Lord Jesus was extolled" (Acts 19:17). God preserved the honor of his
name. By refusing to allow anyone to manipulate him, God demonstrated his supreme and sovereign authority. He showed that he was
nothing like the pagan gods, who could be controlled. He alone
would decide when to perform a miracle, and he would only do it
through his chosen servants.

What happened to the seven sons of Sceva only served to enhance
God's reputation. The Ephesians understood what it meant: Jesus
Christ was Lord over every other god; his was the Name above all
names. They also saw how dangerous it was to dabble in the occult:
"Many of those who were now believers came, confessing and
divulging their practices. And a number those who had practiced magic
arts brought their books together and burned them in the sight of all.
And they counted the value of them and found it came to fifty thousand pieces of silver" (Acts 19:18-19). The story ends with this thrilling
conclusion: "So the word of the Lord continued to increase and prevail
mightily" (Acts 19:20). When God's name is honored, his kingdom
grows.

## FOR THE HONOR OF HIS NAME

As the story shows, there is a clear connection between honoring God's
name and spreading the gospel. When the name of Jesus Christ is lifted

up and exalted, people come to him for their salvation. Therefore, keeping the third commandment is doubly important. Not only is it the lawful thing to do, but when we do it, sinners believe and are saved. The application is obvious: As servants of the Lord Jesus Christ, we should do everything we can to honor God's name.

Since we are Christians, we bear the very name of Christ. It was by calling on his name that we were saved in the first place (Acts 4:12; Rom. 10:13; 1 John 5:13). We received his name upon entering the church, when we were baptized "in the name of the Father and of the Son and of the Holy Spirit" (Matt. 28:19). Since we always carry the name of Christ, God has a personal stake in our ongoing spiritual progress. The Bible says, "you were washed, you were sanctified, you were justified in the name of the Lord Jesus Christ" (1 Cor. 6:11). Now the very name of Christ is associated with everything we do. Our reputation is a reflection on his reputation; so we should always make it our aim to honor his name.

We must confess that we are sometimes tempted to dishonor God's name. The most obvious temptation is to use it as a swear word. This is what people usually think the third commandment is mainly about. Today many people call down divine damnation on whatever (or whoever) happens to be a source of frustration. Or they use the name Jesus Christ as a kind of exclamation point. All of the bad language on television and at the movies reveals how godless our culture has become. But it also shows that we can never get away from God. People can't seem to swear without using God's name. Why is that? What does it tell us about the human condition? I think it proves the existence of God. Like everything else people say, cursing comes from the heart. When non-Christians use God's name—even in vain—it shows that deep down they know there really is a God. Their rage is direct rebellion against his honor.

As Christians, we need to watch our language. Most Christians try not to curse—at least not out loud (or at least not when anyone else is listening); but it is not uncommon for churchgoing people to use mild oaths: "Gosh darn it!" "Oh, my God!" "What the heck?" "Good Lord!" "I swear to God." Some people think that these are manners of expression, but they are really just a more polite way to swear. They may also be a better indication of our true spiritual condition than what we say in church.

We also have a responsibility to remind others to watch their language. There are good and gracious ways to do this. In his book on the Ten Commandments, Rob Schenck tells how he confronted two men for breaking the third commandment:

> Some years ago, after a long speaking itinerary in the midwest, I boarded a late-night flight to return home. I was tired and looking forward to a rest. Sitting behind me in the airplane were two salesmen whose conversation was peppered with profanity. I had finally had it when they began running the Lord's name into the gutter. I raised myself up from my seat and turned around so that I was looking down on them from my perch. Then I asked, "Are either of you in the ministry?"
>
> The one in the aisle seat raised his eyebrows incredulously and said, "What the . . . would ever make you think that?"
>
> "Well, I am in the ministry," I said with a smile. "And I am amazed at your communication skills. You just said God, damn, hell, and Jesus Christ in one sentence. I can't get all of that into a whole sermon!" They both blushed, and I didn't hear another word from them for the remainder of the flight![8]

God's Spirit can use that kind of godly response to convict someone who swears of how sinful it is to take God's name in vain.

A more serious way to break the third commandment is by using God's name to advance our own agenda. Some Christians say, "the Lord told me to do this." Or worse, they say, "the Lord told me to tell *you* to do this." That is false prophecy! God has already said whatever he needs to say to us in his Word. Of course, there is also an inward leading of the Holy Spirit. But that is only an inward leading, and it should not be misrepresented as an authoritative word from God.

Most Christians don't actually claim to hear God's voice. What we are often tempted to do, however, is to misinterpret Scripture for our own purposes. How easy it is to take one idea from Scripture—or even one verse—lift it out of context, and then use it to support our own personal opinions. We become so certain that God is on our side that we refuse to listen to other believers or to submit to spiritual authority in the church.

Sometimes we use God to endorse our political views, so that he becomes a sort of party mascot. Sometimes we use him to prop up our position so that other people will have to do what we say. Sometimes we fix his stamp of approval to our ministry or to our plans for the church. But whenever we confuse what we want with what God wants, we take his name in vain. Stephen Carter makes this point in a book on the role of religion in public life, a book suitably called *Taking God's Name in Vain*:

> In truth, there is probably no country in the Western world where people use God's name quite as much, or quite as publicly, or for quite as many purposes, as we Americans do—the Third Commandment notwithstanding. Few candidates for office are able to end their speeches without asking God to bless their audience, or the nation, or the great work we are undertaking, but everybody is sure that the other side is insincere. . . . Athletes thank God, often on television, after scoring the winning touchdown, because, like politicians, they like to think God is on their side. Churches erect huge billboards and take out ads in the paper. . . . God's will is cited as a reason to be against gay rights. And a reason to be for them. God is said not to tolerate poverty. Or abortion. Or nuclear weapons. . . . Everybody who wants to change America, and everybody who wants not to, understands the nation's love affair with God's name, which is why everybody invokes it.[9]

There are many other ways to take God's name in vain. We do it when we say "Praise the Lord!" or use some other Christian cliché without really meaning it. We do it when we slap God's name on a T-shirt or bumper sticker and use it as a slogan to boost sales. We do it when we use his Word to make jokes or when we write Christian songs with trite lyrics.

These are all serious violations of the third commandment, but the most subtle and perhaps the most common way we break it is by being careless in our worship. As we look at the church today, it is tempting to wonder whatever happened to God. There seems to be so little reverence and awe, so little trembling before his majesty. Instead, we take God lightly. David Wells calls this "the weightlessness of God."[10] Others have described it as "the trivialization of God."[11] Such a trivial view of God comes from trivial talk about him. We do not recognize his true glory when we come into his presence for worship. Our thoughts wander when we pray. Our eyes pass over the pages of Scripture, but our minds are not open to God's Word. And when we sing, our hearts are not in tune with our voices. We are like Shakespeare's Hamlet, who said, "My words fly up, my thoughts remain below; words without thoughts never to heaven go!"[12] Our worship is casual, careless, and insincere, and in this way we dishonor God's name.

## AT THE NAME OF JESUS

God has said that if we confess these sins, he will forgive them (1 John 1:9). He will do this because Christ was crucified for all our sins, including our violations of the third commandment. We need to confess our misuse of God's name because God has said that he will not hold us guiltless. We will discover this for ourselves at the final judgment, when what we do with God's name will determine what God does with us.

Some people will keep using God's name in vain right up until the day of judgment. Jesus said, "Not everyone who says to me, 'Lord, Lord,' will enter the kingdom of heaven, but the one who does the will of my Father who is in heaven. On that day many will say to me, 'Lord, Lord, did we not prophesy in your name, and drive out demons in your name, and do many mighty works in your name?' And then I will declare to them, 'I never knew you; depart from me, you workers of lawlessness!'" (Matt. 7:21-23). What a shock! At the final judgment there will be people who think they know Jesus but will be lost forever. There will be professing Christians—even people involved in Christian ministry—who will be condemned to hell. The reason is because they were taking God's name in vain all along. Although it was often on their lips, it was never in their hearts.

Something else will also happen at the final judgment: The name of Jesus Christ will be truly praised. The Bible says that Jesus obeyed God to his very death on the cross, where he paid for all our violations of God's law. Then it says that "God has highly exalted him and bestowed on him the name that is above every name" (Phil. 2:9). What name is that? What name is above every name? The Bible continues, "so that at the name of Jesus every knee should bow, in heaven and on earth and under the earth, and every tongue confess that Jesus Christ is Lord" (Phil. 2:10-11). The name that is above every name is not "Jesus," but "Lord." The Son of God was given the name "Jesus" at the time of his incarnation. But his exalted name—the name that demonstrates his deity by identifying him as the sovereign God—is "Lord." "Lord" was God's sacred divine name in the Old Testament, and even then God promised that one day all nations would bow before him as the only Savior and Lord (see Isa. 45:21b-25). That promise was about Jesus Christ, who will soon be revealed as the God of Moses, and then everyone will give him the glory that his special divine name deserves.

If that is the honor that Jesus will receive at the end of history, it is also the honor that he deserves right now, and we should give it to him. Don't take the name of the Lord Jesus Christ in vain!

## STUDY QUESTIONS

1. Why did your parents choose your name (special meaning, named for someone, etc.)?
2. What does God's name—YHWH—tell us about his character?
3. How do you see God's name misused in the world today? How do Christians misuse it?
4. What are some ways to hallow God's name?
5. Read Acts 19:11-17. What did the sons of Sceva do wrong? How did this event end up spreading the gospel?
6. What lessons can we learn from this story about hallowing God's name?
7. Colossians 3:17 tells us, "And whatever you do, in word or deed, do everything in the name of the Lord Jesus, giving thanks to God the Father through him." What does it mean to do something "in the name of the Lord Jesus"? What does it accomplish when we, like Paul, do things in Jesus' name?

8. When you are reminded that it is by God's name you are saved, that you bear his name as a Christian, and that dishonoring God's name is not only unlawful but also dishonoring to his reputation among nonbelievers, how should studying this commandment affect your life? How can you more fully obey it this week?

9. How can you tactfully and appropriately hold others—both Christians and non-Christians—to some level of obedience to this commandment? Have you ever been in a situation where this was handled well? (If so, share your experience.)

# THE FOURTH COMMANDMENT:
# WORK AND LEISURE

*Remember the Sabbath day, to keep it holy. Six days you shall labor, and do all your work, but the seventh day is a Sabbath to the LORD your God. On it you shall not do any work, you, or your son, or your daughter, your male servant, or your female servant, or your livestock, or the sojourner who is within your gates. For in six days the LORD made heaven and earth, the sea, and all that is in them, and rested the seventh day. Therefore the LORD blessed the Sabbath day and made it holy.*

EXODUS 20:8-11

A few years ago a friend telephoned with an urgent request. "Phil," he said, "I'm calling to ask a favor. I need the most precious thing you have."

Can you guess what he needed? He was asking for my time, of course. As the pastor of a large church—not to mention the father of a growing family—few things are more precious to me than my time. I need time to work, worship, rest, and play. I need time to spend with the Lord. I need time to prepare sermons and give people spiritual counsel. I also need time to love my family. It all takes a great deal of time, and there never seems to be quite enough.

Many people have the same frustration. We often feel rushed. We never seem to have time for work and leisure, for family and ministry. So we complain, "If only I had one extra day this week, then I could get all my work done." Or we say, "You know, I could really use some time off." Or "If only I had more time to study the Bible and serve the Lord." In these and many other ways we grumble about being overtired and overworked. It is all part of the frustration of living as finite creatures in a fallen world.

Out of his great mercy, God has provided a remedy: one whole day out of seven to rest in his grace. He has given us a rhythm of work and rest, with six days for labor and one day for leisure. And he grants us our leisure specifically for the purpose of his praise. The Sabbath is a day for worship, a day for mercy, and a day for rest.

### Remembering the Sabbath

Keeping the Sabbath holy may not seem very productive. In fact, sometimes it even keeps people away from Christ. They would rather do something else—anything else—than go to church on Sunday. When billionaire Bill Gates was asked why he didn't believe in God, he said, "Just in terms of allocation of time resources, religion is not very efficient. There's a lot more I could be doing on a Sunday morning."[1]

Even if devoting a whole day to God may not seem very efficient, it must be important, because God has commanded it:

> Remember the Sabbath day, to keep it holy. Six days you shall labor, and do all your work, but the seventh day is a Sabbath to the LORD your God. On it you shall not do any work, you, or your son, or your daughter, your male servant, or your female servant, or your livestock, or the sojourner who is within your gates. For in six days the LORD made heaven and earth, the sea, and all that is in them, and rested the seventh day. Therefore the LORD blessed the Sabbath day and made it holy.—Exod. 20:8-11

This is the longest commandment, and it comes in three parts. Verse 8 tells us *what* to do, verses 9-10 specify *how* we are to do it, and verse 11 explains *why*.

*What* God wants us to do is to "remember the Sabbath day, to keep it holy" (Exod. 20:8). The word "remember" has a double meaning. For the Israelites, it was a reminder that they had heard about the Sabbath before. On their journey to Mount Sinai, God provided manna six days out of seven. The seventh day was meant to be "a day of solemn rest, a holy Sabbath to the LORD" (Exod. 16:23a). So when they reached Mount Sinai, God commanded them to "remember" the Sabbath.

This was something they needed to remember not just once, but every week. It is something we need to remember, too; so the fourth commandment calls us to a weekly remembrance of the Sabbath. We are prone to forget the great work of God in creation and redemption. And when we forget, we fail to praise him for making us and saving us. But the fourth commandment is a reminder. It is God's memorandum to his people, reminding us to give him glory for his grace.

Remembering involves more than just our memories; it demands the total engagement of our whole person in the service of God. Remembering the Sabbath is like remembering one's anniversary. It is not enough to say, "Oh, yes, I remember: It's our anniversary!" It takes dinner and flowers—maybe even jewelry—and a romantic evening for two. In much the same way, remembering the Sabbath means using the day to show our love for God in a special way. It means "keep[ing] it holy." Literally, we are to *sanctify* it, setting it apart for sacred use.

## KEEPING THE SABBATH WHOLLY

*How* are we to do this? The fourth commandment gives explicit instructions for keeping the Sabbath holy. God begins by telling us what he wants us to do with the rest of our week: "Six days you shall labor, and do all your work" (Exod. 20:9). Although this part of the fourth commandment is often overlooked, it is our duty to work. This does not mean that we have to work all day, every day. But it does mean that God governs our work as well as our rest. He has given us six whole days to fulfill our earthly calling.

People generally have a negative attitude about work. At best, work is treated as a necessary evil, and in fact sometimes it is thought that work is the result of sin. In a column for *Time* magazine, Lance Morrow claimed that "When God foreclosed on Eden, he condemned Adam and Eve to go to work. From the beginning, the Lord's word said that work was something bad: a punishment, the great stone of mortality and toil laid upon a human spirit that might otherwise soar in the infinite, weightless playfulness of grace."[2] This is completely false. Work is a divine gift that goes back before the Fall, when "The LORD God took the man and put him in the Garden of Eden to work it and keep it" (Gen. 2:15). We were made to work. The trouble is that our work has been cursed by our sin. It was only after Adam had sinned that God said, "cursed is the ground because of you; in pain you shall eat of it all the days of your life" (Gen. 3:17b). But it was not that way from the beginning. The fourth commandment reminds us to honor God by doing an honest week's worth of work. We find God's blessing in doing what he has called us to do.

According to the Puritan Thomas Watson, having six days to work is a divine concession, and thus a sign of God's favor. God would have been well within his rights to make *every* day a Sabbath. Instead, he has given us six days to do all our work. Watson thus imagined God saying, "I am not a hard master, I do not grudge thee time to look after thy calling, and to get an estate. I have given thee six days, to do all thy work in, and have taken but one day for myself. I might have reserved six days for myself, and allowed thee but one; but I have given thee six days for the works of thy calling, and have taken but one day for my own service. It is just and rational, therefore, that thou shouldest set this day in a special manner apart for my worship."[3]

Watson was right: Six days are for work, but the seventh day is for worship. How do we keep the fourth commandment? By worshiping the Lord on his day. To keep something holy in the biblical sense is to dedicate it exclusively for worship. Whereas the other six days of the week are for us and our work, the Sabbath is for God and his worship. This is the positive aspect of the fourth commandment: "the seventh day is a Sabbath *to* the LORD your God" (Exod. 20:10a). Elsewhere God refers to the seventh day as *his* Sabbath—the day that belongs to him: "you shall keep my Sabbaths: I am the LORD your God" (Lev. 19:3b). The commandment was worded this way to remind the Israelites that their relationship with God was special. No other nation could claim that the Lord was their God; so no other nation kept the Sabbath. There were some other ancient civilizations that divided their time into periods of seven days. However, they generally associated the seventh day with misfortune.[4] Only the Israelites kept the Sabbath as a day for worshiping the one true God as their Savior and Lord.

To keep a Sabbath "to the LORD" is to give the day over to God, setting it apart for him and his glory. The book of Leviticus calls the Sabbath "a holy convocation" (Lev. 23:3), meaning a time to gather for corporate worship. Jesus endorsed this practice by attending weekly Sabbath services at the synagogue (Luke 4:16). This focus on worship led the Puritans to refer to the Sabbath as "the market-day of the soul."[5] Whereas the other six days of the week are for ordinary commerce, this is the day we devote to transacting our spiritual business, trading in the currency of heaven. "This day a Christian is in the altitudes," wrote Thomas Watson. "He walks with God, and takes as it were a turn with him in heaven."[6] We meet with God by prayer and the ministry of the Word, by singing his praises and presenting him our offerings, by celebrating the sacraments and sharing Christian fellowship. The result, according to Watson, is that "The heart, which all the week was frozen, on the Sabbath melts with the word."[7]

The Sabbath is not only a day for worship, but also a day of rest. It is a day for ceasing from work, and especially from common labor. Here we need to notice that the fourth commandment is stated both positively and negatively. It is the only commandment to do so explicitly. The positive requirement comes first: "Remember the Sabbath day, to keep it holy" (Exod. 20:8). Then there is the absolute prohibition: "On it you shall not do any work" (Exod. 20:10).

The word "Sabbath" comes from the Hebrew word meaning "to cease or to rest." It is not a day for "business as usual." Rather, it is a day for relaxation and recuperation, a day to step back from life's ordinary routines in order to rediscover God's goodness and grace. To quote again from Thomas Watson, "To do servile work on the Sabbath shows an irreligious heart, and greatly offends God. To do secular work on this day is to follow the devil's plough; it is to debase the soul. God made this day on purpose to raise the heart to heaven, to converse with him, to do angels' work; and to be employed in earthly work is to degrade the soul of its honour."[8]

To see how strict this command was under the law of Moses,

consider the man who gathered wood on the Sabbath (Num. 15:32-36):
He was stoned to death. Or to take a positive example, consider the
women who wanted to prepare the body of Christ for burial: "Then
they returned and prepared spices and ointments. On the Sabbath they
rested according to the commandment" (Luke 23:56b). Gathering
wood was such a small thing to do; what was the harm in doing it on
the Sabbath? Taking spices to the tomb of Christ was a noble act of
piety; so why not go ahead and do it? The answer was, God had commanded a day of rest.

This rest was for everyone to enjoy: "On it you shall not do any
work, you, or your son, or your daughter, your male servant, or your
female servant, or your livestock, or the sojourner who is within your
gates" (Exod. 20:10b). Here we see that the fourth commandment has
profound implications for the wider community. When it comes to
work and leisure, parents are to set the agenda by teaching their children how to worship and rest. The Sabbath really is a day to spend with
the family.

By including servants, the commandment also teaches that
employers have a responsibility to care for their workers. Some commentators have thus described the fourth commandment as the world's
first workers' bill of rights. In the ancient world there was a sharp divi-
sion between masters and slaves. But here is a new social order, in which
work and leisure are not divided along class lines. Everyone should
work, and everyone should rest, because everyone should be free to
worship God. The law extended this right to the gates of the city,
including everyone in the whole community. It even applied to beasts
of burden. God wanted all his creatures to get some relief from their
labor. Now imagine what the world would be like if everyone kept this
commandment in the biblical way. Imagine the whole creation at rest.
Once a week people all over the world would stop striving and turn
back to God.

What are we commanded to do? To keep the Sabbath holy. How do
we do this? By working six days and then dedicating a day to the Lord
for worship and rest. This is all summarized in Leviticus: "Six days work
shall be done, but on the seventh day is a Sabbath of solemn rest, a holy

convocation. You shall do no work. It is a Sabbath to the LORD in all your dwelling places" (Lev. 23:3).

## GOD'S WORK, GOD'S REST

The reason for this commandment is very simple. We are called to work and rest because we serve a working, resting God. *Why* should we remember the Sabbath? Because "in six days the LORD made heaven and earth, the sea, and all that is in them, and rested the seventh day. Therefore the LORD blessed the Sabbath day and made it holy" (Exod. 20:11). Keeping the Sabbath may be the oldest of the Ten Commandments, because it goes all the way back to the creation of the world.

There are many additional reasons for keeping the Lord's Day holy. It promotes the worship of God. It restores us, both spiritually and physically; so it is for our benefit. As Jesus said, "The Sabbath was made for man" (Mark 2:27). It is good for children and workers; it can even be good for animals. But our fundamental reason for obeying the fourth commandment is not practical but theological: God made the world in six days, and then he rested. His activity in creation thus sets the pattern for our own work and leisure.

We serve a working God, who has been at work from the beginning. The Scripture says that "on the seventh day God finished his work that he had done" (Gen. 2:2a). Part of the dignity of our work comes from the fact that God is a worker. We work because we are made in the image of a working God.

We also serve a resting God. Once his creative work was done, God took his divine leisure. The Scripture says that "he rested on the seventh day from all his work" (Gen. 2:2b). To mark the occasion, "God blessed the seventh day and made it holy, because on it God rested from all his work that he had done in creation" (Gen. 2:3). The first time that God blessed anything, he blessed a day for us to share in his rest. We keep the Sabbath because God made it holy. Like work, leisure is "something that God put into the very fabric of human well being in this world."[9]

There is one further reason for keeping a day of rest. Although it is not mentioned here in Exodus, it is mentioned in Deuteronomy, where

the Ten Commandments are repeated. There the first part of the commandment is virtually identical (Deut. 5:12-14), but the reason is different: "Remember that you were a slave in the land of Egypt, and the
LORD your God brought you out from there with a mighty hand and
an outstretched arm. Therefore the LORD your God commanded you
to keep the Sabbath day" (Deut. 5:15). There is no contradiction here.
The Sabbath looked back not only to creation, but also to redemption.
It reminded God's people that they had been delivered from slavery in
Egypt. One of the benefits of their rescue was that now they didn't have
to work all the time. Back in Egypt they had to work seven days a week,
fifty-two weeks a year, without ever getting a vacation. But now they
were set free. The Sabbath was not a form of bondage to them, but a
day of freedom. It was a day to celebrate their liberation by giving glory
to God.

## BUSINESS AS USUAL

Sadly, the Israelites often forgot to remember the Sabbath. And when
they did, they inevitably fell back into spiritual bondage. There is a story
about this in the book of Nehemiah—the story of the governor and the
salesmen.

God's people had returned from their captivity in Babylon to
rebuild the city of Jerusalem. Under Nehemiah's leadership, the whole
community was restored. They rebuilt the city walls, reestablished their
homes, and started gathering again for public worship. They read the
law and kept the feasts; they repented of their sins and promised to keep
covenant with God. They also reestablished the priesthood. The Levites
were serving, the choirs were singing, and God was blessing the holy
city.

Then the governor went back to Babylon for a short time. Sadly, on
his return to Jerusalem, Nehemiah found that the Israelites were failing to keep God's covenant. In particular, they were breaking the
Sabbath by using it as a day to conduct commerce. They had promised,
"If the peoples of the land bring in goods or any grain on the Sabbath
day to sell, we will not buy from them on the Sabbath or on a holy day"
(Neh. 10:31a). Yet here is what Nehemiah said was happening:

*In those days I saw in Judah people treading winepresses on the Sabbath, and bringing in heaps of grain and loading them on donkeys, and also wine, grapes, figs, and all kinds of loads, which they brought into Jerusalem on the Sabbath day. And I warned them on the day they sold food. Tyrians also, who lived in the city, brought in fish and all kinds of goods and sold them on the Sabbath to the people of Judah, in Jerusalem itself!—*Neh. 13:15-16

These businessmen were not residents of Jerusalem, but traveling salesmen. To them, one day was no different from the next; so they assumed that the Sabbath was a day for business as usual. This proved to be a source of temptation for the people of God. Many of the people in Jerusalem were genuine believers. They attended public worship and supported God's work with their tithes and offerings. They knew God's law, including all ten of the commandments (see Neh. 9:14-15). Yet they were breaking the Sabbath. Frankly, they were like many Christians today. Although basically they were committed to following God, under pressure from the surrounding culture they treated the Sabbath pretty much like the rest of the week.

Nehemiah needed to take strong action. First he spoke out against Israel's sin: "Then I confronted the nobles of Judah and said to them, 'What is this evil thing that you are doing, desecrating the Sabbath day? Didn't your forefathers do the same things, so that our God brought all this calamity upon us and upon this city? Now you are stirring up more wrath against Israel by profaning the Sabbath'" (Neh. 13:17-18). Nehemiah had a good point. When God explained why he sent his people into captivity, he often mentioned their failure to keep the Sabbath holy (see Jer. 17:19-27; Ezek. 20:12-13). As the city's governor, Nehemiah knew that keeping the fourth commandment was a matter of public safety.

Nehemiah did more than preach, however. The governor also enforced public laws for keeping the Sabbath special: "As soon as it began to grow dark at the gates of Jerusalem before the Sabbath, I commanded that the doors should be shut and gave orders that they should not be opened until after the Sabbath. And I stationed some of my servants at the gates, that no load might be brought in on the Sabbath day" (Neh. 13:19). It didn't take long for the salesmen to take the hint: "Then the merchants and sellers of all kinds of wares lodged outside Jerusalem once or twice. But I warned them and said to them, 'Why do you lodge outside the wall? If you do so again, I will lay hands on you.' From that time on they did not come on the Sabbath. Then I commanded the Levites that they should purify themselves and come and guard the gates, to keep the Sabbath day holy" (Neh. 13:20-22).

We need to be careful how we follow Nehemiah's example. God is not calling us to establish the Sabbath by force. However, there is a principle here that we can apply. In order to preserve a day of worship and rest, we need to bar the gates against the clamor of our culture. Otherwise, we will end up mixing the business of this world with the pleasure of spending time with God.

## THE LORD'S DAY

What does the fourth commandment mean for the Christian? Like the Israelites, we are made in the image of a working, resting God. We still need to work, we still need our rest, and we can still receive the creation blessing of God's holy day. The main thing that has changed is that we have received a new and greater deliverance. We no longer look back to the old exodus for our salvation; we look to Jesus Christ, who accomplished a greater exodus by dying for our sins and rising again. Jesus is the fulfillment of the fourth commandment, as he is of all the others. The Old Testament Sabbath pointed to the full and final rest that can only be found in him.

Jesus gives a whole new meaning to work, and a whole new meaning to rest. He came into the world to finish the work of his Father (John 4:34), and on the basis of that work, he is able to give rest to our souls (Matt. 11:29). There is no need to strive for our salvation. All we need to do is repose in the finished work of Jesus Christ. David said, "My soul finds rest in God alone; my salvation comes from him" (Ps. 62:1, NIV). The way for us to find that rest is by trusting in Christ alone for our salvation, depending on his work rather than our own. The Scripture assures us that in Christ, "There remains a Sabbath rest for the people of God, for whoever has entered God's rest has also rested from his works as God did from his" (Heb. 4:9-10). This is the primary fulfillment of the fourth commandment.

Christ's saving work has transformed the weekly Sabbath. It is no longer the seventh day of the week, but the first, and it is no longer called the Sabbath, but the Lord's Day. This is because the apostles observed their day of worship and rest on the day that Jesus rose from the dead (John 20:19; Acts 20:7; 1 Cor. 16:2). Already by the end of the first century, Ignatius was able to write that Christians "no longer observe the Sabbath, but direct their lives toward the Lord's day, on which our life is refreshed by Him and by His death."[10] B. B. Warfield explained it like this: "Christ took the Sabbath into the grave with him and brought the Lord's Day out of the grave with him on the resurrection morn."[11]

Keeping the Lord's Day holy preserves the Sabbath principle of resting one whole day out of seven. Although the specific day was provisional—a sign of Israel's coming salvation—the commandment is perpetual. Like the rest of the Ten Commandments, it was written in stone. Back in Chapter 1 we drew a distinction between three types of law: the moral, the civil, and the ceremonial. The Old Testament teaching on the Sabbath included aspects of all three. As a nation Israel executed strict civil penalties for Sabbath-breaking. Since these are no longer in effect, to a certain extent the fourth commandment has been made less severe. There was also a ceremonial aspect to the Sabbath. The rest it provided was a sign pointing to salvation, and its observance on the seventh day was part of the whole Old Testament system that found its fulfillment in Christ (see Col. 2:17). But even if the fourth commandment has found its primary fulfillment in Christ, there remains an obligation—based on the eternal standard of God's law—to rest one whole day in seven. To summarize, the civil aspect of the command has expired, the ceremonial aspect has been fulfilled, but the moral aspect remains. In the words of the Westminster Confession of Faith, keeping the Sabbath holy is "a positive, moral, and perpetual commandment" (XXI.7).

## REST ASSURED

God is honored when Christians celebrate the Lord's Day. However, we need to be on our guard against legalism in all its forms. We do not base our standing before God on what we do on Sunday. We do not judge others for the way they keep—or fail to keep—the Lord's Day holy (see Rom. 14:5-6a; Col. 2:16). And we do not have a set of man-made regulations for keeping the Sabbath. This is what the Pharisees did, and Jesus condemned them. When they heard that they couldn't work on the Sabbath, the Pharisees wanted to know exactly what counted as work and what didn't; so they developed their own guidelines. Eventually these became so elaborate that the true purpose of the Sabbath was lost entirely.

The way to avoid all this legalism is to remember that the Lord's Day is for celebrating the freedom that we have in Christ. Jesus said, "The Sabbath was made for man, not man for the Sabbath" (Mark 2:27). This does not mean that anything goes. A call to freedom, like the one we are given in the fourth commandment, is never an excuse for seeking our own pleasure (see Isa. 58:13). However, the freedom we have in Christ does mean that for the Christian, the Sabbath is not a straitjacket.

Keeping the Lord's Day holy begins with working hard the rest of the week. In America we usually work at our play and play at our work, but God has given us six days for the ordinary business of life, and we are called to use them for his glory. Christians ought to be the most faithful and diligent workers. Our industry is an important part of our piety, while sloth is a very great sin. To waste our time is to squander one of the most precious resources that God has given us.

The duty to work is for everyone, not just for people who get paid. It is for housewives, for retired people, for the disabled and the unemployed—all of us are called to do something useful with our time. Even if we don't need to earn an income, we need to glorify God in whatever work we do. Today many Americans assume that they will work for the first sixty years of their lives and then take the rest of their lives off. That is not the biblical view of work and leisure, because the Bible calls all of us to maintain the rhythm of work and rest that is essential to our humanity.

The week begins with the Lord's Day. This is not a day for inactivity, but a day for worship, mercy, and rest. One of the best summaries of how to keep the day holy comes from the Westminster Confession of Faith: "This Sabbath is then kept holy unto the Lord, when men, after a due preparing of their hearts, and ordering of their common affairs before-hand, do not only observe an holy rest, all the day, from their own works, words, and thoughts about their worldly employments and recreations, but also are taken up, the whole time, in the public and private exercises of His worship, and in the duties of necessity and mercy" (XXI.8). The choice of the word "recreations" is unfortunate, because one purpose of the Lord's Day is to refresh us in the joy of our Creator—as it were, to "re-create" us. It is a day to "catch our breath," which can include God-centered recreation. But the Confession is right that this is not a day for worldly recreations.

The Lord's Day is for worship. It is a day for attending corporate worship, for enjoying fellowship with the people of God, for catching up on our spiritual reading, and for spending the whole day in ways that really make it the *Lord's* Day. In order to worship well, we need to be prepared. Thus keeping the Lord's Day holy also means getting ready the night before. Thomas Watson wrote, "When Saturday evening approaches, sound a retreat; call your minds off from the world and summon your thoughts together, to think of the great work of the approaching day. . . . Evening preparation will be like the tuning of an instrument, it will fit the heart better for the duties of the ensuing Sabbath."[12]

The Lord's Day is for mercy. This was one of the things the Pharisees failed to understand. Some rabbis maintained "that if a wall fell on top of someone on the Sabbath, only enough rubble could be removed to find out how badly the person was injured. If he was not injured too badly, then he must be left until the Sabbath ended, when the rescue could be completed."[13] But Jesus said it was a day for mercy, which is why he performed so many miracles on the Sabbath. He was not violating the fourth commandment—as the Pharisees thought—but was fulfilling its true purpose. We follow his example whenever we use the Lord's Day to welcome the stranger, feed the poor, or visit the sick.

Finally, the Lord's Day is for rest, for ceasing from our labor. The fourth commandment teaches us to have a leisure ethic as well as a work ethic.[14] The businessman should rest from his business, the housewife from her housework, the student from his studies. Of course, Christians have always recognized that some work is necessary. Workers who provide medical care or preserve public safety need to do their jobs, as do ministers and various workers in the church. People who do such work are wise to set aside another day of the week for rest, if not for public worship. There are also some basic daily chores that need to be done. But this is a day to close the calendar, go off the clock, and put away the "to do" list. It is a day to step out of the frenzy, stop buying and selling, and quit worrying about the profit margin. In a culture that increasingly treats Sunday like any other day of the week, thereby turning what is sacred into something secular, we need to resist the tendency to let our work enslave us. Keeping the Lord's Day holy is the biblical answer to workaholism.

At this point many Christians still want to know what they can and cannot do on the Sabbath. Can I watch TV? Can I play Frisbee? Can I go to a restaurant? Can I catch a flight back home? Can I play Monopoly, or do I have to stick to Bible trivia games? The danger in making universal applications is that we are prone to Pharisaism; it is easy for us to slip back into legalism. In keeping the fourth commandment there is room for Christian freedom, the wise exercise of godly judgment. For example, even the Puritans recognized that there were times when it might be appropriate or even necessary to dine at a public inn.[15] However, when we start asking these kinds of questions, it is usually because we want to know what we can get away with. We want to know how far we can go without actually breaking the fourth commandment. But if we are looking for a loophole in the Lord's Day, then we are missing the whole point of the fourth commandment. God is calling us away from our own business to transact the most important business of all, which is to glorify him in our worship. And when we try to make as much room as we can for our own pleasures, then we miss the greatest pleasure of all, which is fellowship with the living God.

Our problem is that we find it so hard to take genuine delight in the sanctified pleasures of God. Dare I say it? God bores us. We are willing to spend some of our time worshiping him, but then we feel like we need a break, and so we go right back to the world's lesser pleasures. But the more we learn to delight in God, the more willing we are to keep his day holy. And then we discover that we are able to answer the questions that once seemed so vexing: Can I take a job that will require me to work on Sundays? Is it okay to catch up on my work? Should we let our kids play Little League baseball on Sunday? Is it a good day for watching television? Most of the practical applications are easy when we want to honor the Lord on his day. The strain and struggle come when we want to use it to do our own thing.

Dr. Robert Rayburn once told the story of a man who was approached by a beggar on the street.[16] The man reached into his pocket to see what he had. Finding seven dollars and feeling somewhat sorry for the beggar, he held out six bills and said, "Here you go." Not only did the beggar take the six dollars, but with his other hand he struck his benefactor across the face and grabbed the seventh dollar, too.

What do you think of the beggar? Don't you think he was a scoundrel? Then what do you think of a sinner, saved by the grace of Jesus Christ, who insists on taking seven days a week—or even six and a half—for himself? The way to avoid this scandal is to remember the Lord's Day by keeping it holy.

## STUDY QUESTIONS

1. What's your favorite way to spend a Sunday?
2. Why does God command us to keep the Sabbath?
3. What are the benefits of obeying this commandment?
4. What are the essential elements of a God-honoring Sabbath?
5. What activities are inappropriate for Sundays? Why?
6. What are some forms of work that you genuinely enjoy and find fulfilling? (You may not even think of them as work!)
7. How would you answer someone who says, "I know I shouldn't work on Sunday, but I really need to catch up on my work," or "What's the harm in working on Sunday?"
8. In what ways are you tempted to "forget" the Sabbath? What factors contribute to your spending a Sunday in ways that do not honor God?

9. Read Nehemiah 10:31; 13:15-22. Why were the people of Nehemiah's day no longer keeping the Sabbath?

10. Why was it so important for Nehemiah to make sure that God's people honored the Sabbath?

11. We can't—and shouldn't—force others to honor the Sabbath like Nehemiah did. But what principles can we learn and apply from this story as we think about the way Sunday is treated in our own lives, in the church, and in society at large?

12. What are some practical ways you can honor the Lord's Day without becoming legalistic about it? Are there attitudes, focuses, or activities that you need to work on changing in order to better honor the Lord's Day?

# 8

# THE FIFTH COMMANDMENT:
# RESPECT AUTHORITY

*Honor your father and your mother, that your days may be long in the land that the LORD your God is giving you.*
EXODUS 20:12

Many historians believe that a significant shift in American attitudes toward authority took place during the 1960s. It was the decade of the anti-establishment. Young people were anti-business, anti-government, anti-military, and anti-school. But of all the institutions that came under attack, perhaps the most significant was the family.

Annie Gottlieb is one of many participants who identify "the Sixties" as "the generation that destroyed the American family." She writes, "We might not have been able to tear down the state, but the family was closer. We could get our hands on it. And . . . we believed that the family was the foundation of the state, as well as the collective state of mind. . . . We truly believed that the family had to be torn apart to free love, which alone could heal the damage done when the atom was split to release energy. And the first step was to tear ourselves free from our parents."[1]

What makes Gottlieb's analysis so chilling is the connection she draws between the family and the state. She's right: The way to destroy a nation is to destroy the family, and the way children can destroy the family is by disobeying their parents.

## CHARITY BEGINS AT HOME

God's plan for preserving the family calls for keeping the fifth commandment: "Honor your father and your mother, that your days may
be long in the land that the LORD your God is giving you" (Exod.
20:12). The placement of this commandment shows the special importance of the family. When God gave his law, he wrote it down on two
tablets (Exod. 31:18). Most likely this means that he provided Moses
with two copies. This was customary in ancient times whenever two
parties established a covenant. Or perhaps the law was divided into two
parts. Traditionally, the first four commandments are distinguished
from the last six. The first table of the law consists of the four commandments that govern our response to God. The second table consists
of the six commandments that govern the way we treat one another.
Obviously, our human relationships cannot be separated from our relationship to God, but there is a distinction: The first four commandments teach us to love God, while the last six teach us to love our
neighbor.

Love for God must come first. We cannot truly love one another
unless we love God. If we do not respect God, we will not respect one
another. So we can hardly begin to keep the last six commandments
until we learn how to keep the first four. According to John Calvin,
"The first foundation of righteousness is the worship of God. When this
is overthrown, all the remaining parts of righteousness, like the pieces
of a shattered and fallen building, are mangled and scattered.... [A]part
from the fear of God men do not preserve equity and love among themselves. Therefore we call the worship of God the beginning and foundation of righteousness."[2]

If we analyze the Ten Commandments this way, then the second
table of the law would begin with the fifth commandment. This is significant. In telling us how to treat one another, God starts with our families. Loving our neighbor starts at home: "Just as the relationship with
Yahweh is the beginning of the covenant, so this relationship [i.e.,
between parents and children] is the beginning of society, the inevitable
point of departure for every human relationship. The first relationship
beyond the relationship with Yahweh, who according to the OT is the

giver of life, is the relationship to father and to mother, who together are channels of Yahweh's gift of life. No other human relationship is so fundamental, and none is more important."[3]

Augustine emphasized the importance of the fifth commandment by posing a rhetorical question. He asked, "If anyone fails to honor his parents, is there anyone he will spare?"[4] Presumably not, because the relationship between parent and child is the first and primary relationship, the beginning of all human society. Under ordinary circumstances, the first people a child knows are his parents. God intends the family to be our first hospital, first school, first government, first church.[5] If we do not respect authority at home, we will not respect it anywhere. Charity really does begin at home!

## HONOR YOUR FATHER AND YOUR MOTHER

Like the rest of God's law, the fifth commandment needs to be studied carefully. The first word is "honor." This is a heavy word—literally. The word is *kaved*, which is Hebrew for "heavy" or "weighty." It is the word the Old Testament uses for the glory of God, for the weightiness of his divine majesty. To honor one's parents, therefore, is to give due weight to their position. It is to give them the recognition they deserve for their God-given authority. To honor is to respect, esteem, value, and prize fathers and mothers as gifts from God.

The opposite of honor is dishonor. Just as the fifth commandment requires respect for parents, so it forbids showing them any disrespect. If parents are weighty, then they should not be treated lightly, as if the fifth commandment didn't even matter. Sadly, rebelling against parents has become a common sin. The cover of one magazine for teen-aged girls asked, "Do you really hate your parents? Like, who doesn't?" The magazine proceeded to offer advice on "how to deal with your detestables."

The Bible has a deep revulsion to this kind of disrespect, treating it almost with a kind of horror. When I was a youth pastor, I once took my high school students through the biblical passages that deal with disobedience to parents. We discovered that some of the most frightening curses in the Old Testament are reserved for children who rebel against their parents. Here are two examples:

*For anyone who curses his father or his mother shall surely be put to death; he has cursed his father or his mother; his blood is upon him.*—Lev. 20:9

*If a man has a stubborn and rebellious son who will not obey the voice of his father or the voice of his mother and, though they discipline him, will not listen to them, then his father and his mother shall take hold of him and bring him out to the elders of his city at the gate. . . . Then all the men of the city shall stone him to death with stones. So you must purge the evil from your midst, and all Israel shall hear and fear.*—Deut. 21:18-19, 21

Not surprisingly, by the time I finished reading these and many similar passages, the kids in my youth group were very quiet. Like most young people, they had always assumed that breaking the fifth commandment was part of their job, an ordinary part of growing up. God obviously considers dishonoring one's parents to be one of the worst sins that anyone can possibly commit. This is true even if the Old Testament penalties for breaking this commandment are no longer in effect. In the New Testament, disobedience to parents is listed as one of the signs that we are living in the "terrible times" (NIV) of "the last days" (2 Tim. 3:1-2).

Notice that the commandment includes both fathers and mothers: "Honor your father *and* your mother." Elsewhere the Bible makes it clear that fathers have a unique responsibility for the spiritual leadership of their families. However, this does not mean that mothers deserve any less honor. The Scripture says, "My son, keep your father's commandment, and forsake not your mother's teaching" (Prov. 6:20). In fact, Leviticus 19:3 mentions mothers first: "Every one shall revere his mother and his father." God commands children not to try to take advantage of their mothers, but to give them equal respect.

This commandment was without parallel in the ancient world. Although today the Bible is often considered patriarchal—especially in the Old Testament—it always strikes the proper balance, confronting every culture's structures of sin. Here the Bible insists that mothers should receive as much as honor as fathers (this part of the fifth commandment obviously rules out same-sex parents). Unless a parent is removed by death, every child is expected to honor both a father and a mother. This is God's pattern for all people in all places. Where there are exceptions—as in the case of orphans, for example, or when one parent dies—they are exceptions to the biblical rule.

## LIVE LONG AND PROSPER

Why should children respect their parents? For many reasons. Parents deserve to be honored for the many sacrifices they make on behalf of their children. They deserve to be listened to because of their wealth of life experience. There is also the simple fact that keeping the fifth commandment glorifies God, which is reason enough. The Bible says, "Children, obey your parents in everything, for this pleases the Lord" (Col. 3:20). It also says that honoring one's parents is the right thing to do: "Children, obey your parents in the Lord, for this is right" (Eph. 6:1).

These are all good reasons to keep the fifth commandment, but the reason given in the commandment itself is that honoring our parents serves our own best interest: "Honor your father and your mother, that your days may be long in the land that the LORD your God is giving you" (Exod. 20:12). The apostle Paul said this was "the first commandment with a promise" (Eph. 6:2), and the promise is intended to give special encouragement to children. God knows how hard it is to obey our parents. He also knows that children find it easier to obey when they are promised a reward; so the fifth commandment comes with the promise of long life in God's land.

This promise had special meaning for the Israelites. They had just been brought out of the land of slavery, and God had promised to lead them to a new and better country. One way they could ensure that they would keep living in the promised land was to honor their fathers and mothers in the faith.

This general promise should not be taken as an automatic guarantee that children who obey their parents will live to be ninety. Nor does it necessarily mean that someone who dies young is guilty of breaking the fifth commandment. For reasons concerning his greater glory, God sometimes allows people to meet what we consider an untimely end, even if they almost always obeyed their parents. There are many providences that determine the length of a person's life. But the promise still stands: Children who honor their parents receive the gift of life.

Here it helps to know that when the Bible talks about living long in the land, it is not simply talking about how old people are when they die. The expression "live long in the land" is a Hebrew phrase for the fullness of God's blessing. It means to have an abundant life. This is confirmed by the New Testament, which says, "Honor your father and mother . . . that it may go well with you and that you may live long in the land" (Eph. 6:2-3). Anyone who wants to live long and prosper should honor his mother and father.

There is one more reason to keep the fifth commandment, and it may be the most important reason of all: Parents have a God-given responsibility to teach their children how to know and serve God. But children will not learn those lessons if they do not respect their parents; so keeping the fifth commandment is essential to God's plan for passing down the faith. Of all the ways children honor their parents, the most important is listening to what they say about God and the way of salvation.

Spiritual instruction is a responsibility for both fathers and mothers. Solomon said, "Hear, my son, your father's instruction, and forsake not your mother's teaching" (Prov. 1:8), and "My son, do not forget my teaching, but let your heart keep my commandments, for length of days and years of life and peace they will add to you" (Prov. 3:1-2). These words are a commentary on the fifth commandment. Solomon repeats the promise of long life and prosperity and ties it specifically to biblical teaching in the home. This is the heart of the fifth commandment: receiving the gift of life by respecting our parents in the faith. Today God commands us to honor our fathers and mothers because this is how many people first come to know Jesus Christ.

Learning God's plan for the family sometimes brings sadness and disappointment to people who never had a good family background. Is a person who was not raised in a Christian home at a spiritual disadvantage? In a way, yes. We are always damaged by the sins of others, including the sin of parents in not raising their children "in the discipline and instruction of the Lord" (Eph 6:4). But God is gracious, and by the saving work of his Spirit he adopts orphan sinners into the best and most important family of all—the family of God. The Bible gives every child of God this precious promise: "For my father and mother have forsaken me, but the LORD will take me in" (Ps. 27:10).

## HONOR TO WHOM HONOR IS DUE

In order to make the fullest and best use of the fifth commandment, we need to understand that it is not just for children, but it really applies to everyone. According to the Westminster Shorter Catechism, "The fifth commandment requireth preserving the honour, and performing the duties, belonging to everyone in their several places and relations, as superiors, inferiors, or equals" (A. 64). In other words, respecting authority applies to every person in every relationship.

Here we need to remember one of our rules for interpreting the Ten Commandments. According to "the rule of categories" (see Chapter 3), every commandment stands for a whole category of sins and duties. By implication, when God tells us to respect our parents, he is telling us to respect anyone who has legitimate authority over us. This is something the Israelites would have readily understood because they often used the term *father* in relationships outside the home. For example, the Israelites referred to the king as their father (e.g., 1 Sam. 24:11). On occasion they used the same title for the prophets. Elisha called out to Elijah, "My father, my father!" (2 Kings 2:12). Similarly, Israel's elders were honored as the fathers of their people (see Acts 7:2). So the Israelites naturally would have applied the fifth commandment to other relationships that involved authority.

We should do the same. The fifth commandment rules our relationship to the government. The Bible says, "Be subject for the Lord's sake to every human institution. . . . Honor everyone. . . . Fear God. Honor the emperor" (1 Pet. 2:13, 17). Today honoring the king means respecting officers of the law and representatives of the state. It means praying for politicians. It means obeying the laws of government and paying our taxes. In all these ways we are called to "be subject to the governing authorities. For there is no authority except from God . . . instituted by God" (Rom. 13:1).

The fifth commandment also regulates our work. We are to respect our bosses and show honor to our employers. After telling children to obey their parents, Paul proceeded to tell slaves to serve their masters. It was all part of respecting authority. He wrote: "Slaves, obey your earthly masters with fear and trembling, with a sincere heart . . . knowing that whatever good anyone does, this he will receive back from the Lord" (Eph. 6:5, 8). Keeping the fifth commandment on the job means working hard and speaking well of the management.

The fifth commandment also requires respect for our leaders in the church. Specifically, it requires submission to our pastors, elders, and deacons—the leaders who serve as our spiritual fathers in the household of God. The Scripture says, "Let the elders who rule well be considered worthy of double honor, especially those who labor in preaching and teaching" (1 Tim. 5:17). To honor our leaders is to pray for them, encourage them, and assist them in their efforts for our spiritual progress. It is to accept their counsel and discipline with humility, for the Scripture says, "Obey your leaders and submit to them" (Heb. 13:17a).

In all of these relationships, "we should look up to those whom God has placed over us, and should treat them with honor, obedience, and gratefulness."[6] We should do this even when those in authority don't seem to deserve our respect. The Heidelberg Catechism is right when it says that the fifth commandment requires "that I show honor, love, and faithfulness to my father and mother and to all who are set in authority over me; that I submit myself with respectful obedience to all their careful instruction and discipline; *and that I also bear patiently their failures, since it is God's will to govern us by their hand*" (A. 104, italics added). Respect for those who are in authority is respect for God, because all authority comes from him. Our respect is not based on their personal qualities or professional qualifications, but on the position God has given them.

There is another side to all this, which is that people in authority have a responsibility to exercise it in ways that are pleasing to God. We may not abuse our authority by using it harshly or by overstepping our bounds. Nor may we fail to do our duty. Leaders in government are called to protect their citizens. Spiritual leaders are called to serve God's people in the church, not to abuse them. And people in management are called to care for the people who work for them.

The fifth commandment has special relevance for fathers and mothers. Our family duties are reciprocal. If children are supposed to obey their parents, then obviously parents are supposed to give them proper discipline. The New Testament makes this explicit when it attaches these words to the fifth commandment: "Fathers, do not provoke your children to anger, but bring them up in the discipline and instruction of the Lord" (Eph. 6:4; cf. Col. 3:21). When parents place unreasonable demands on their children, when they correct them in anger rather than in love, or when they stunt their growth by stifling their freedom, they abuse their authority.

Parents are called to give their children many other things besides proper discipline. We are called to pray for them, encourage them, counsel them, protect them, and provide for their daily needs. We are called to set a godly example, for although children don't always listen to their parents, they never fail to imitate them. We are called to educate our children, preparing them for their life's work, including marriage and parenthood, according to the providence of God. Most important of all, if children are commanded to listen to their parents, then we are commanded to teach them the Scriptures and lead them in the worship of God.

## GOD SAVE THE KING

It is not always easy to respect authority, and there is a story about this in the Bible—the story of two best friends, David and Jonathan. These brave young men were spiritual brothers, bound by a covenant of friendship. Both were mighty warriors, both had a courageous faith in the God of Israel, and both had proven themselves in battle. David is well-known for killing Goliath, but Jonathan was just as brave. On one occasion the Israelites faced the Philistines without any weapons. Only Jonathan had a sword. Yet he said, "It may be that the LORD will work for us, for nothing can hinder the LORD from saving by many or by few" (1 Sam. 14:6b). With those words, he launched a one-man attack, killing twenty Philistines and sending the rest of their army into a panic.

The only person who gave David and Jonathan more trouble than the Philistines was Jonathan's father, King Saul. God had anointed Saul king over Israel; yet he was an angry, impetuous, ill-tempered man who often made rash threats against his own people. During one battle Saul swore an oath cursing any soldier who had anything to eat before he could avenge his enemies. Unfortunately, Jonathan didn't hear his father's oath; so when he saw honey oozing on the ground, he went ahead and dipped his staff into the honeycomb and tasted it. When Saul eventually learned what had happened, he said to his son, "God do so to me and more also; you shall surely die, Jonathan" (1 Sam. 14:44). The other soldiers intervened to spare Jonathan's life, but that episode showed what kind of man Saul was. He was the kind of man who would do violence to his own son over a mouthful of food.

Saul treated David even worse. At first he was pleased with David because he loved to hear him play the harp. Then after David killed Goliath, Saul welcomed him into his own house and gave him a high rank in the army. David excelled in everything the king asked him to do. However, he soon became more famous than Saul, which aroused the king's jealousy. One day, in a fit of anger, the king hurled his spear, trying to pin David to the wall. David escaped, but this only added to Saul's anger. Next Saul tried to get rid of David by having him killed in battle. He promised David his daughter's hand in marriage if he would kill a hundred Philistines. Saul's secret hope was that the young warrior would die at the hands of his enemies. But David killed two hundred Philistines without getting a scratch.

Saul could see from all this that David had God's blessing, which of course made him angrier than ever. Swearing eternal enmity, the king ordered his soldiers—including his son Jonathan—to kill David. This put Jonathan in a bad position. He knew he was supposed to honor his father, but he also knew that murder was wrong. So Jonathan did the right thing: He honored God by disobeying his father. First he warned David what his father was planning to do so that he had a chance to escape. Then he interceded with his father, saying, "Why then will you sin against innocent blood by killing David without cause?" (1 Sam. 19:5). By doing this, Jonathan was not dishonoring his father, but was preserving his honor. On this occasion Saul listened to his son. He repented of his anger and welcomed David back into his home. Their truce didn't last for long, however. David had more success in battle, Saul became more jealous, and once again he hurled his spear in anger.

The point of telling this unhappy story is that if ever there was a father who failed to deserve the respect of his son, or a king who failed to deserve the respect of his subjects, it was Saul. And yet David and Jonathan both honored the king. They respected his God-given authority, honoring him because they honored God.

The way David honored Saul was by refusing to take his life. After the king had his last blowup, David left for good. Saul chased him into the hills, where on two separate occasions David had an easy opportunity to take the king's life. Once Saul came alone into the very cave where David was hiding. David's men told him to seize his chance: "Here is the day of which the LORD said to you, 'Behold, I will give your enemy into your hand, and you shall do to him as it shall seem good to you'" (1 Sam. 24:4a). But David decided not to kill Saul. Instead he sneaked up and cut off the corner of the king's robe. Yet afterwards David was sorry for what he had done. Even after everything Saul had done to him, David's conscience told him that it was dishonorable for him to show disrespect to Israel's king. David said, "The LORD forbid that I should do this thing to my lord, the LORD's anointed, to put out my hand against him, seeing he is the LORD's anointed" (1 Sam. 24:6). Notice David's reasoning. His repentance was not based on how Saul had treated him. He said nothing about what kind of king Saul was. The only thing that mattered was that his kingship came from God and therefore demanded David's respect. So after Saul left, David stepped out of the cave and cried, "My lord the king!" Then he said, "See, my father, see the corner of your robe in my hand! For . . . I cut off the corner of your robe and did not kill you" (1 Sam. 24:8, 11a). David called Saul "father" as a sign of respect for his kingly authority.

Jonathan honored Saul too, and he did so by trying to stop him from sinning against David. This put a tremendous strain on their relationship. On one occasion Saul was so angry with Jonathan for siding with David that he hurled a spear at him and said, "You son of a perverse, rebellious woman" (1 Sam. 20:30-33). Naturally this made Jonathan angry. It also grieved him because he loved his friend David. But even after all the violent outbursts, Jonathan remained loyal to his father. Although he was not blind to the man's faults, he still loved him as his father. The last we see of Jonathan he is at his father's side, desperately trying to defend him from the Philistines. Jonathan was an honorable son who died fighting to save his father (1 Sam. 31:1-6).

Obviously Saul is not a very good model of the proper exercise of authority. There were times when David and Jonathan had to disobey him. In doing so they did not break the fifth commandment, but kept it by honoring their higher commitment to obey their Father in heaven. There were also times when David and Jonathan had to protect themselves. Submitting to authority never means subjecting ourselves to violence, domestic or otherwise. Perhaps this point needs to be emphasized: When there is physical abuse, the duty to preserve life takes precedence over the duty to obey one's parents. But the difficulties these friends faced make their example all the more remarkable. David and Jonathan understood that there is something sacred about authority. Because it comes from God, it demands our highest respect.

## A LIFETIME OF RESPECT

There are many ways to honor God by honoring our parents. The fifth commandment is for young children. God wants boys and girls to speak respectfully to their parents, using good manners. He wants them to obey their parents all the time, doing everything they ask with a good attitude. The Puritans said, "A child should be the parents' echo; when the father speaks, the child should echo back obedience."[7]

The fifth commandment is for teenagers. Many high school students are amazed at how out of touch their parents are—how little they seem to know about life. Most parents deserve more credit than that, of course, but even the ones who don't still need to be obeyed. Honoring father and mother means speaking well of them to friends. It means listening to what they say, including their warnings about spending time with the wrong friends or experimenting with things that can cause permanent physical and spiritual damage. It also means talking to parents, letting them know what's happening. I once heard a mother say that her son went through his entire senior year of high school doing nothing more than grunting at her. He dishonored his parents, although apparently he did know how to use words, because within several years he could once again carry on intelligent conversations with his parents in English!

The fifth commandment is for young adults. Often around age twenty children finally recognize that their parents are gifts from God. One recent college graduate told me that he was pleased (and a little surprised) that he was starting to have a better relationship with his parents. With apologies to Mark Twain, who said something along similar lines, I said, "You know, it's amazing how much your parents have matured in the last couple of years!" Young adults have major decisions to make about education, career, and sometimes marriage. Children honor their fathers and mothers by seeking their counsel. The decisions are theirs to make, especially once they leave the home, but it is wise to get whatever help and blessing their parents have to offer.

Here we need to consider what children should do when their parents fail to give them godly advice. Remember, the Israelites were told to honor their parents so they could learn to know God. But what if someone's parents don't know God? What if they aren't Christians? And what if they try to stop their children from doing what God is calling them to do? What does it mean to honor your father and mother then?

This situation is not uncommon. Some parents find it very hard to accept their children's putting Christ first in decisions about education, career, family, and ministry. Where there is faith, Jesus brings families together; but where there is unbelief, he drives them apart. Christians can never let honoring their parents get in the way of following Christ. This is what Jesus meant when he said, "Whoever loves father or mother more than me is not worthy of me, and whoever loves son or daughter more than me is not worthy of me" (Matt. 10:37). If it comes down to a choice, the Christian's true Father is in heaven, and it is his will that we must follow. This is one of the reasons the Bible tells us to obey our parents "in the Lord" (Eph. 6:1; Col. 3:20). This is an important qualification. The honor we owe our parents can never come at the expense of the honor we owe to God.

When Christians who need guidance cannot rely on their parents for godly counsel, they should turn to the church, which after all is our fundamental and eternal family. But even when we cannot accept our parents' advice, we still need to show them honor and respect. This means listening to what they say, caring for their needs, and strengthening the family ties in any way we can.

The fifth commandment remains in force even after children grow up and move out on their own. Honoring father and mother means giving them a certain precedence in life, making them a priority. It means loving them and appreciating them. It means caring for them to the very end of their lives. The Scripture says, "Listen to your father who gave you life, and do not despise your mother when she is old" (Prov. 23:22). One ancient writer expanded on this by saying, "My child, support your father in his old age, do not grieve him during his life. Even if his mind should fail, show him sympathy, do not despise him in your health and strength."[8] Yet this is precisely what many people do: They despise their parents. Barely half of Americans think that children have a responsibility to care for elderly parents.[9] Many children abandon their parents or, worse, try to help them die. This shows flagrant contempt for God's law.

When Jesus saw some of the Pharisees refusing to provide for their parents in old age, he accused them of violating the fifth commandment: "For God commanded, 'Honor your father and your mother,' and, 'Whoever reviles his father or mother must shall surely die.' But you say, 'If anyone tells his father or his mother, What you would have gained from me is given to God, he need not honor his father.' So for the sake of your tradition you have made void the word of God" (Matt. 15:4-5). Instead of taking care of their parents, the Pharisees were keeping their money for themselves and then claiming that they had dedicated it to God. But children have a responsibility to make sure that their parents get all the physical, medical, spiritual, and emotional care they need. To honor one's father and mother in these ways is to honor God. For the Scripture says, "You shall stand before the gray head and honor the face of an old man, and you shall fear your God: I am the LORD" (Lev. 19:32).

## THE PERFECT CHILD

It is good to ask ourselves whether we are keeping the fifth commandment. Does our relationship with our father or mother bring glory to God? The truth is that it is hard for children to honor their parents. One man complained: "Youth today love luxury. They have bad manners, contempt for authority, no respect for older people, and talk nonsense when they should work. Young people do not stand up any longer when adults enter the room. They contradict their parents, talk too much in company, guzzle their food, lay their legs on the table, and tyrannize their elders."[10] Who was this man? It was Socrates, the philosopher who lived four hundred years before Christ! His words describe what young people are still like today because they describe what young people are always like.

Like the rest of God's law, the fifth commandment is impossible for us to keep. Here are some questions for self-examination: Do you ever talk back to your parents? Do you ever hide anything from them? Do you ever silently curse them? Do you speak well of your parents? Are you taking the time to strengthen your relationship with them? Are you giving them the care they need and the honor they deserve for their position in your life? We all fail somewhere. The fifth commandment is part of God's law, and like the rest of God's law, we have broken it. No one is the perfect child.

Except Jesus. When Jesus died on the cross, he paid the penalty for our breaking the fifth commandment as much as for any other sin. But Jesus has done more than that: He has also kept the fifth commandment in our behalf. It was not enough for Jesus to pay the price for our sin; he also had to offer God the obedience that his law demands. And Jesus did that. He honored his parents. The Bible says explicitly that Jesus "went down with them and came to Nazareth and was submissive to them" (Luke 2:51a). The only times their relationship was strained were when Jesus stayed behind at the temple in Jerusalem (Luke 2:41-50) and when he kept preaching instead of stopping to visit with his family (Luke 8:19-21), but even then he kept the fifth commandment by honoring his higher commitment to his Father in heaven. And Jesus honored his earthly parents right to the very end of his life. He was not able personally to care for his mother in her old age, but he provided for her in his dying moments by asking his friend John to be like a son to her (John 19:26-27).

From the manger to the cross, Jesus was an obedient son who brought honor to his earthly parents and his heavenly Father. In respecting his parents' authority he is more than our example: He is the perfect child God demands that we should be. Everyone who trusts in Jesus has offered perfect obedience to the fifth commandment, because when Jesus obeyed his parents, he was keeping God's law on our behalf.

To illustrate this, consider the way I once chastised my son for failing to clean his room. "You didn't clean your room," I said. "I told you to clean your room, and you didn't do it." After hearing my son's excuse—which although carefully developed nevertheless was thoroughly unpersuasive—I said, "I don't care what happened. I told you to clean your room, and you didn't do it." Then, trying to help him understand the gospel, I said, "You know, you like to think you're a pretty good boy. But the truth is that you're not a good boy. Actually, you're a bad boy. God wants you to obey me all the time, but sometimes you don't. How can God accept you if you keep disobeying your parents?"

My son wasn't sure, but his father was a pastor, so of course he knew that the answer was probably Jesus. And he was right: Jesus *is* the answer. God does not accept us on the basis of what we have done, but on the basis of what Jesus has done. And one of the things Jesus has done is to keep the fifth commandment. So instead of looking at what we have done—all the times we dishonored and disobeyed our parents—God looks at what Jesus did when he obeyed his parents perfectly. It is almost as if Jesus cleaned our room for us and then did everything else a child is supposed to do. One of the reasons he is the perfect Savior is because he was the perfect child.

## STUDY QUESTIONS

1. Share a childhood memory of a time when you disobeyed your parents. What were the consequences?
2. "We cannot truly love one another unless we love God." How does God's love help us love others better? What aspects of human love are we unable to experience if we don't love God?
3. How does a child's relationship with his or her parents affect the way he

or she relates to others throughout life? How does this affect society as a whole?

4. In what ways do society and the media encourage disrespect for parents among children? Among adults?

5. What scriptural reasons do we have for obeying the fifth commandment?

6. What responsibilities do parents have in helping their children obey this commandment?

7. Are there people in authority over you who are not receiving the respect they are due? How can you improve in this area? Read 1 Samuel 14:24-30, 43-45; 18:10-11; 19:1-7; 24:2-12.

8. What did Saul do that made it hard to honor him?

9. How did David and Jonathan show respect even to this bad authority figure? What were the results of their actions?

10. What principles can we learn from their examples about how to obey this commandment?

11. What are some specific responsibilities incumbent on children as they follow this commandment in their relationship with their parents?

12. How does our responsibility to honor our parents change when we become adults? Are there some specific things God is calling you to do to show greater honor to your parents?

# 9

# THE SIXTH COMMANDMENT:
# LIVE AND LET LIVE

*You shall not murder.*

EXODUS 20:13

Apparently some Americans consider the Ten Commandments dangerous. Put them up—at work, in the classroom, or at the courthouse—and someone will try to make you take them down. Hence the recent cartoon depicting two public school administrators watching a line of students pass through a metal detector. "It's the latest in school safety devices," one of them explains. "That light and horn go off if a student tries to smuggle in a gun, knife, bomb or a copy of the ten commandments!"[1]

Which commandments cause the controversy? Almost all of them. People strongly object to the first commandment, which rules out other gods. They don't really see the point of the fourth commandment, which requires a weekly day of rest. They enjoy indulging in a little sexual sin every now and then; so they don't care for the seventh commandment.

Just about the only commandment everyone still seems to accept is number six. No one approves of murder. It is so contrary to the law of nature that every culture has some sort of prohibition against it. Even in America, homicide is still a criminal act. However, when we study the sixth commandment carefully and come to understand its full implications, we find that no commandment is more blatantly or brutally violated.

## Lawful and Unlawful Killing

The sixth commandment is one of the shortest. It is just two words in the original: *lo ratzach*, or "Don't kill." But what kind of killing does the Bible have in mind? The Hebrew language has at least eight different words for killing, and the one used here has been chosen carefully. The word *ratzach* is never used in the legal system or in the military. There are other Hebrew words for the execution of a death sentence or for the kind of killing a soldier does in mortal combat. Nor is the word *ratzach* ever used for hunting and killing animals. So the King James Version, which says "Thou shalt not kill" (Exod. 20:13), is somewhat imprecise. What the commandment forbids is not killing, but the unlawful killing of a human being.

The English Standard Version (among other translations) comes closer to the truth when it says, "You shall not murder" (Exod. 20:13). Murder is what the sixth commandment mainly has in mind: the premeditated taking of an innocent life, the deliberate killing of a personal enemy. However, even "murder" is somewhat imprecise because *ratzach* can be used for any form of wrongful death. It is used for voluntary manslaughter, a crime of passion. It is also used for involuntary manslaughter. Some accidental deaths, although unintentional, are nevertheless culpable, which is why God's law includes legal sanctions for "anyone who kills his neighbor unintentionally, without being at enmity with him in time past" (Deut. 4:42).

To summarize, what the sixth commandment forbids is the unjust taking of a legally innocent life. It applies to "murder in cold blood, manslaughter with passionate rage, [and] negligent homicide resulting from recklessness or carelessness."[2] Perhaps the best translation is, "You shall not kill unlawfully."

God's people have always recognized that there are some situations where taking a life is not only permitted, but actually warranted. One such situation is self-defense, the protection of one's self and one's family from violent attack. To extend the principle, we may also kill in the defense of our nation. As Stephen Carter explains, "War is horrible and should be fought rarely, and only to avoid greater horrors."[3] But this view has increasingly come under attack. After the horrific attack on the World

Trade Center in New York City, some people said, "If we kill as a response to this great tragedy, we are no better than the terrorists who launched this awful offensive. Killing is killing, and killing is wrong."[4] This is not the biblical position. The Bible teaches that it is not unlawful to kill enemies in wartime, provided that the war is just. Of course, the justice of a war needs to be considered carefully, especially by nations as heavily armed as the United States. Christians have long believed that a war is just only if it is waged by a legitimate government; for a worthy cause; with force proportional to the attack; against men who are soldiers, not civilians; when all other means of resolution have failed.

Another situation where killing is lawful is the execution of a death sentence. It is always wrong for us to take the law into our own hands. If justice is to be done, the plaintiff may not serve as the jury, the judge, and the executioner. However, the Bible makes a distinction between private individuals and the state. Capital punishment—when it is justly administered by the governing authorities—is one lawful form of killing. For a public official "to kill an offender is not murder, but justice."[5] This is taught not only in the Old Testament, but also in the New. Paul told the Romans, who were then under imperial authority, that the government "does not bear the sword in vain," because the one who governs "is the servant of God, an avenger who carries out God's wrath on the wrongdoer" (Rom. 13:4b). Although it is always wrong to avenge ourselves (see Rom. 12:19), the government has a God-given responsibility of vengeance.

These examples show that not all killing is morally wrong. But why does God permit some forms of killing? What makes them lawful? The answer is that their goal is not the destruction of life, but its preservation. This is obviously true in the case of self-defense. Sometimes it is necessary to take a life in order to save a life. In the case of a just war, the same principle applies on a larger scale. The purpose of having an army is not to kill people, but to keep a country's citizens safe.

The same life-preserving principle even holds true for capital punishment. The execution of a murderer stops him from killing again and deters other would-be criminals from doing the same. His execution is also a matter of justice. The Bible says, "Whoever sheds the blood of man, by man shall his blood be shed, for God made man in his own image" (Gen. 9:6). This is the biblical logic behind capital punishment. It is precisely *because* life is precious that someone who takes it unlawfully must be put to death. What makes life so precious is that every human being is made in God's image. God has put his stamp on every one of us the way a great artist signs his name to a work of art. Therefore, to damage a life is to deface one of God's masterpieces. Calvin wrote, "Our neighbor bears the image of God: to use him, abuse, or misuse him is to do violence to the person of God who images himself in every human soul."[6]

The sixth commandment preserves the sanctity of human life. It also preserves God's sovereignty over life and death. Jesus Christ is the Lord of life. He is its author and inventor, its ruler and sustainer. Since he is the giver of life, it is also his prerogative to take it, and to do so at his own time, in his own way. The sovereignty of God is always at stake in matters of life and death. Now God has delegated his authority, so that in some situations it is lawful for one person to take another person's life. But this can only be done according to God's will. To take a life unlawfully is to violate God's sovereignty over life and death.

It is also to rob God of his glory. God has given us life and breath so that we might live for his praise. The psalmist wrote, "I shall not die, but I shall live, and recount the deeds of the LORD" (Ps. 118:17). Life is not given for its own sake, but for God's glory, and for this reason it may not be taken unlawfully. One theologian has observed that "A person may not be killed for this reason, that he is, either actually or potentially, someone who declares God's praise, and therefore anybody who kills another person thereby robs God."[7]

## THE UNSANCTITY OF LIFE

The sixth commandment has important implications for contemporary society. We like to think of America as a civilized country, but we are living in angry, violent times, and murder in all its forms is very common. There is such a callous disregard for human life that many people say we are now living in what Pope John Paul II has rightly called a "culture of death." Death is everywhere. There is death in the city. In places like Philadelphia there is a shooting almost every day of the year; hundreds of people die. There is death at school. There has been a rash of shootings from Kentucky to Columbine, and teachers have to watch out for students who carry weapons. Little League parents want to kill the ump, and sometimes they do. There is death on the highway, where motorists get into a rage or drive under the influence of alcohol. There is even violence at home, where parents violate their sacred trust by striking in anger.

Where does all this violence come from? From evil hearts that have turned away from God. But the rapid spread of brutality in America has been accelerated by violence in the media, where an entire industry promotes the breaking of the sixth commandment. According to the American Psychological Association, by the time the average child finishes elementary school, he or she will have watched eight thousand televised murders and a hundred thousand acts of on-screen violence. And things are getting worse. The *New York Times* comments, "If you have the impression that movies today are bloodier and more brutal than ever in the past, and that their body counts are skyrocketing, you are absolutely right. Inflation has hit the action-adventure movie with a big slimy splat."[8]

Something else is happening too. Movies are not just getting more violent; they are also treating violence as a form of humorous entertainment. Movie critic Michael Medved writes:

> The current tendency is to make mayhem a subject of mirth. As the on-screen mutilation and dismemberment become progressively more grotesque and horrible, film makers make light of their characters' pain by introducing sadistic humor as an indispensable element of entertainment. . . . [I]t's the violence itself that's supposed to be hilarious, and that leaves audiences howling with laughter. . . . The nightmarish mix of comedy and carnage demonstrates more clearly than anything else that the brutality in today's films is different in kind, not just extent, from the screen violence of the past.[9]

What is so disturbing about all of this is that it affects the way people live. In 1998 the American College of Forensic Psychiatry conducted a comprehensive review of scientific studies on the relationship between violence on the screen and violence in real life. Out of a thousand studies, more than 980 established a definite link between violence on the screen and violence in real life.[10] According to the best estimates, media violence has doubled America's homicide rate. David Grossman is not surprised. A retired military psychologist, Lt. Col. Grossman is an expert on teaching people to overcome their natural reluctance to kill. He was shocked to realize that children who watch TV and play violent video games are subjected to the same methods—the conditioning and the desensitization—that the army uses to train soldiers. We are teaching our children how to kill, and we should not be surprised when they do.[11]

Not all forms of murder are violent. Sometimes death carries a clipboard and wears a lab coat. In a recent book called *Culture of Death*, Wesley J. Smith argues that "a small but influential group of philosophers and health-care policy makers" actively seek to persuade our culture that "killing is beneficent, suicide is rational, natural death is undignified, and caring properly and compassionately for people who are elderly, prematurely born, disabled, despairing, or dying is a burden that wastes emotional and financial resources."[12] This kind of thinking is a direct assault on the biblical view of personhood. Often the assault is intentional. In the words of one medical professor:

> We can no longer base our ethics on the idea that human beings are a special form of creation made in the image of God, singled out from all other animals and alone possessing an immortal soul. Once this religious mumbo-jumbo has been stripped away, we may continue to see normal members of our species as possessing greater capacities of rationality, self-consciousness, communication, etc. than members of other species, but we will not regard as sacrosanct the life of each and every member of our species.[13]

This kind of rhetoric has convinced many Americans that some lives are less worth living than others, that in fact some lives are not worth living it all. The result is that abortion, infanticide, euthanasia, and assisted suicide are exceedingly common. In some cases they are protected by law, but they are all forms of murder—violations of the sixth commandment.

Christians have always believed that an unborn child is a person made in the very likeness of God. To cite just one example, Calvin insisted that "the *foetus*, though enclosed in the womb of its mother, is already a human being, and it is almost a monstrous crime to rob it of the life which it has not yet begun to enjoy."[14] This is what Christians have always believed because it is what the Bible teaches. "You formed my inward parts," wrote the psalmist; "you knitted me together in my mother's womb. . . . My frame was not hidden from you, when I was being made in secret, intricately woven in the depths of the earth. Your eyes saw my unformed substance" (Ps. 139:13, 15-16a). A child in the womb is a living human being who has a relationship with God and with its mother. To kill such a child is a violation of the law of God.

What is true of the unborn is true of all God's children. The young and the helpless, the elderly and the infirm, the diseased and the disabled—we are all made in the image and likeness of God. Every life is precious in his sight. None can be discarded; all must be preserved.

This means that as Christians we have a duty to oppose euthanasia. God alone is the Lord of life, and he alone has the right to determine when it is time for someone to die. The difficulty is that we now have the medical capacity to keep a body functioning long after that time has come. This raises many more ethical questions than we can address here. But briefly, although we always have a duty to provide basic nourishment, we do not always have a duty to provide extraordinary measures such as artificial respiration. There is a legitimate moral distinction between killing and allowing someone who is terminally ill to die. In other words, there is a difference between terminating life—which is never permissible—and terminating treatment—which can be a way of turning life (and thus also death) back over to God. But this calls for constant vigilance, because many people (including many health professionals) don't know the difference, and thus they often cross the line that should never be crossed.

We also have a duty to oppose suicide. God has not given us the right to kill ourselves. To commit suicide is to claim lordship over our own

lives. Physician-assisted suicide, in which a doctor becomes an accessory
to his patient's self-murder, is especially dangerous. Such voluntary
euthanasia is wrong in itself, but there is another danger: Voluntary
euthanasia almost always becomes involuntary. This has been the experience in the Netherlands, where thousands of medical patients are killed
every year. What is especially frightening is that most of the requests for
these so-called mercy killings do not come from the patients themselves,
but from their families, who frankly are trying to get rid of them.

These are only some of the many signs that we are living in a culture of death. And we are not the only ones. Such is the hatred of the
human heart that people are killing one another all over the world.
There is ethnic violence in Europe, attempted genocide in Africa, religious warfare in the Middle East. Communists persecute Christians in
China, and there is a threat of terror wherever militant Islam confronts
the West. Even if we do not face these terrors ourselves, the sixth commandment demands a global perspective. John Calvin rightly said,
"The purpose of this commandment is: the Lord has bound mankind
together by a certain unity; hence each man ought to concern himself
with the safety of all."[15]

## THE PRO-LIFE SAMARITAN

Many Bible stories illustrate the sixth commandment. Perhaps the
most obvious is the story of Cain and Abel: the first murderer and his
victim. There is also the story of Lamech, who performed the original
gangsta rap:

> *Adah and Zillah, hear my voice;*
> *you wives of Lamech, listen to what I say:*
> *I have killed a man for wounding me,*
> *a young man for striking me.*
> *If Cain's revenge is sevenfold,*
> *then Lamech's is seventy-sevenfold.*—Gen. 4:23

And these examples come from only the first few chapters of
Genesis. The rest of the Bible contains so many acts of violence that it
is hard to know which to choose.

There is one story, however, that hits closer to home than almost any other. It is a story Jesus told about a man who got mugged and what happened to him afterwards. It began like this: "A man was going down from Jerusalem to Jericho, and he fell among robbers, who stripped him and beat him and departed, leaving him half dead" (Luke 10:30). It was a terrible crime, and if there were any justice in the world, the men who committed it would be punished for violating the sixth commandment. Although they did not actually kill the man, they almost did, and God forbids any form of lawless violence.

But the robbers were not the only men who broke the sixth commandment that day. There were two fine, upstanding citizens who also broke the law—not by killing, but by leaving a man to die when they could have helped him live. Jesus continued: "Now by chance a priest was going down the same road, and when he saw him he passed by on the other side. So likewise a Levite, when he came to the place and saw him, passed by on the other side" (Luke 10:31-32).

Like many of the stories Jesus told, this one was intended to shock and offend. The priest and the Levite were respected religious leaders. Think of them as pastors, elders, or deacons. They both saw that the man was in need, but neither of them did anything to help. It's not hard to imagine reasons why. Maybe they were late for worship. Maybe they told themselves he was already dead. Maybe they just didn't want to get involved. Whatever the reason, they both made a deliberate choice not to save the dying man. The priest and the Levite saw that he was in need; yet they made a conscious decision to avoid him. They looked the other way, pretending not to notice, and they went to the other side of the road. It was a shocking thing for men in their position to do. In a way, the worst thing that happened to the victim that day was not getting mugged, but getting rejected by his spiritual leaders, who were too busy to save his life.

What this story shows is that sometimes all it takes to break the sixth commandment is to do nothing at all. Martin Luther said:

> This commandment is violated not only when a person actually does evil, but also when he fails to do good to his neighbor, or, though he has the opportunity, fails to prevent, protect, and save

him from suffering bodily harm or injury. If you send a person away naked when you could clothe him, you have let him freeze to death. If you see anyone suffer hunger and do not feed him, you have let him starve. Likewise, if you see anyone condemned to death or in similar peril and do not save him although you know ways and means to do so, you have killed him. It will do you no good to plead that you did not contribute to his death by word and deed, for you have withheld your love from him and robbed him of the service by which his life might have been saved.[16]

These are sobering words for Christians who live in a culture of death. Media violence, homicide, rape, abortion, euthanasia, assisted suicide, warfare, terrorism—the evils are so overwhelming that it is tempting to do nothing at all. But we must at least do what we can. We can teach our children how to resolve conflict without resorting to violence. We can pray for peace in the troubled parts of the world. We can intercede on behalf of the unborn, the disabled, and the elderly. We can help save children through adoption and foster care. We can care for the sick and the dying. We can send relief to those who are oppressed. We can work to make laws that bring justice and promote life.

This is the positive side to keeping the sixth commandment. At the same time that God forbids us to take life unjustly, he commands us to guard it carefully. We are called to protect life, one life at a time. In other words, we are called to be like the hero of Jesus' story, the Good Samaritan. Here is how the story ends: "But a Samaritan, as he journeyed, came where he was, and when he saw him, he had compassion. He went to him and bound up his wounds, pouring on oil and wine. Then he set him on his own animal and brought him to an inn and took care of him. And the next day he took out two denarii and gave them to the innkeeper, saying, 'Take care of him, and whatever more you spend, I will repay you when I come back'" (Luke 10:33-35).

There is more to keeping the sixth commandment than not mugging people. The Samaritan took the time to see what the man needed, and when he saw the need, he was filled with compassion. Rather than closing off his emotions, he opened his heart to be touched by someone else's suffering. He got involved, even when things were messy. He invested his own valuable time and money to provide what was needed. And he followed through, making sure that the victim was fully restored. But what is most remarkable of all is that he did all this for someone outside his own people group. In those days Jews did not associate with Samaritans, but rather than giving in to that kind of ethnic hatred, the Good Samaritan treated his enemy the same way he would treat a friend.

Jesus told the story of the pro-life Samaritan to a man who wanted to know who counted as his neighbor. The man knew that he was supposed to love his neighbor, but that seemed awfully open-ended. It might include anyone! Hoping to find some way to limit his obligations, he asked Jesus, "And who is my neighbor?" (Luke 10:29). In response, Jesus told his story about the man who got mugged on the Jericho road. When he had finished, Jesus asked, "Which of these three, do you think, proved to be a neighbor to the man who fell among the robbers?" (Luke 10:36). The answer was obvious. The man questioning Jesus replied, "The one who showed him mercy." Then seizing the opportunity to drive his point home, Jesus said, "You go, and do likewise" (Luke 10:37).

That is what Jesus says to us too. Keeping the sixth commandment means more than not murdering anyone. It means loving our neighbor. It means showing kindness to strangers and mercy to our enemies. The Heidelberg Catechism says it well: "Is it enough then, if we do not kill our neighbor in any such way?" The answer is, "No; for when God condemns envy, hatred, and anger, he requires us to love our neighbor as ourselves, to show patience, gentleness, mercy, and friendliness toward him, to prevent injury to him as much as we can, and also to do good to our enemies" (A. 107).

## MURDER OF THE HEART

Like the rest of God's law, the sixth commandment is a lot harder to keep than it seems at first. Most people don't think of themselves as murderers. Sometimes even murderers don't think of themselves that way. Back in 1931 one of "America's most wanted" was Two-Gun Crowley. Two-Gun was charged with a string of brutal homicides, including a cop-killing. That spring he was finally captured after a fierce gun battle in his girlfriend's apartment. When the police searched him, they found a blood-spattered note that read, "Under my coat is a weary heart, but a kind one, one that would do nobody any harm."[17]

Two-Gun was wrong. His heart *was* unkind; he *did* want to do somebody harm. But we are all guilty of the same kind of self-deception. We like to think of the sixth commandment as one of the few we actually keep. At least we haven't murdered anyone! But Jesus said, "You have heard that it was said to those of old, 'You shall not murder, and whoever murders is liable to judgment.' But I say to you that anyone who is angry with his brother will be liable to judgment" (Matt. 5:21-22).

Here we need to remember one of our rules for interpreting the Ten Commandments. According to the "inside/outside" rule (see Chapter 3), each commandment covers inward attitudes as well as outward actions. The Heidelberg Catechism explains it like this: "I am not to dishonor, hate, injure, or kill my neighbor by thoughts, words, or gestures, and much less by deeds" (A. 105). So instead of being one of the easiest commandments to keep, "You shall not murder" actually is one of the hardest, because even if we do not kill one another with our deeds, we often dishonor one another with our words and in our thoughts.

How easy it is to commit what Calvin called "murder of the heart"![18] By this standard, it is as wrong to hate those who carry out abortions as it is for them to perform them in the first place. To quote again from the Heidelberg Catechism, "By forbidding murder God teaches us that He hates the root of murder, such as envy, hatred, anger, and desire of revenge, and that He regards all these as murder" (A. 106). But these are the kinds of homicide we have all committed. Envy in the biblical sense is not simply the desire to have what someone else has, but to take it away from them so that they are harmed in the process. Hatred is a settled resentment, a permanent and vindictive grudge, the desire to get back at someone. It is really a way of wishing someone were dead, for as the Bible says, "Everyone who hates his brother is a murderer" (1 John 3:15; cf. Lev. 19:17). Anger is an even more sudden and more violent passion. Sometimes we say, "If looks could kill . . ." The point Jesus was trying to make was that sometimes they can. There is almost always something murderous about our anger. There is a place for righteous anger, of course, but we are not very righteous, and our unrighteousness usually shows up in our anger.

We also break the sixth commandment with our words. Jesus said, "out of the abundance of the heart the mouth speaks" (Matt. 12:34b). This means that when we use angry words—when we put people down, when we whisper about their reputations, when we make racist or sexist remarks—we reveal that there is murder in our hearts. According to Proverbs, "rash words are like sword thrusts" (Prov. 12:18), which is another way of saying that our words can be used as murder weapons. What we say can be deadly at home, on the job, and in the church.

Are you a murderer? Do you ever say anything to hurt someone? Do you ever take secret satisfaction in their misfortune? Do you have an enemy—someone you are out to get? Do you want to make somebody pay for what they've done? Do you ever get so angry that you're out of control? There are many ways to break the sixth commandment, and we are all guilty of some of them, if not all of them. This is a real problem because the Bible explicitly excludes murderers from the kingdom of God. When the book of Revelation lists the kinds of sinners who will be sent into "the lake that burns with fire and sulfur" (Rev. 21:8), murderers are mentioned. Elsewhere the Bible says that anyone who is guilty of "hatred, discord . . . fits of rage . . . and envy . . . will not inherit the kingdom of God" (Gal. 5:20-21, NIV). So if we commit murder—even if only in our hearts—then we deserve to go to hell. If there is no way for murderers to be saved, there is no way for anyone to be saved. We all need a Savior.

It's a good thing Jesus kept God's law, including the law that said, "You shall not kill unlawfully." The Bible says that Jesus was "oppressed, and . . . afflicted . . . although he had done no violence" (Isa. 53:7a, 9). It says further that he was "like a lamb . . . led to the slaughter . . . he opened not his mouth" (Isa. 53:7b). In other words, Jesus was peaceable even when he was provoked, and in this way he offered perfect obedience to the sixth commandment.

It's a good thing, too, that when Jesus died on the cross, he died for murderers as much as for anyone else. We know this because he offered forgiveness to the very people who murdered him (Luke 23:34). Afterwards, when Jesus had ascended into heaven, the apostle Peter preached in Jerusalem to the same people who had called for Christ to be crucified. He basically accused them of murder, of killing the one who came to be their Savior. When they realized what they had done, they desperately wanted to know what they could do about it. Peter said, "Repent and be baptized every one of you in the name of Jesus Christ for the forgiveness of your sins" (Acts 2:38a). There was a way for their murderous sin to be forgiven. The very death that they were guilty of demanding—Christ's death on the cross—was the death that atoned for their sin.

If you're the kind of person who breaks the sixth commandment, then there is hope for you in the cross of Christ. If you are prone to get angry, if there is someone you secretly resent, if there is murder in your heart—or if you have ever committed any other kind of murder in thought, word, or deed (including abortion, infanticide, or euthanasia)—then repent and believe in Jesus Christ for the forgiveness of your sins. Save a life (your own life!) by trusting in him.

## STUDY QUESTIONS

1. Under what circumstances—if any—do you think you would be capable of killing someone (war, threat to family, etc.)?
2. What are the biblical and theological reasons for why murder is wrong?
3. What current movies or TV shows take the breaking of the sixth commandment too lightly?
4. How does violence in the media affect our attitude toward death? How has it changed social mores? Read Luke 10:29-37.
5. Discuss how this story would play on the evening news with a homeless person, a local pastor, a prominent politician, and a social outcast as the principal characters. Can you think of any recent stories in the news that remind you of this story from the Bible?
6. What are some ways to break the sixth commandment by not doing something you ought to do?
7. How can you stand up for the sanctity of life in your daily life?

8. What are some specific ways to follow the Good Samaritan's example and obey the positive side of the sixth commandment?
9. If there is someone in your life who is hard to love, what are some specific ways you can obey the inward demand of the sixth commandment in the way you treat him or her?
10. Is it fair for God to consider envy and hatred to be as wrong as murder? Why or why not?

# 10

# THE SEVENTH COMMANDMENT:
# THE JOY OF SEX

*You shall not commit adultery.*
EXODUS 20:14

In one of the more embarrassing experiences of my adolescence, my father's name appeared on the cover of *Christianity Today*. Why was this an embarrassment? Because the title of his cover article—which was printed in bold white letters against a black background—was "The Puritans and Sex."

Although it offended my teenage sensibilities, the article's title had the kind of frankness that many Puritans might have appreciated. Prior to the Reformation the church generally regarded sex—even within marriage—as a necessary evil. Tertullian regarded the extinction of the human race as preferable to procreation. Ambrose said that married couples ought to be ashamed of their sexuality. Augustine was willing to admit that intercourse might be lawful but taught that sexual passion was always a sin. Many priests counseled couples to abstain from sex altogether. The Catholic church gradually began to prohibit sex on certain holy days, so that by the time of Martin Luther, the list had grown to 183 days a year![1]

Thank God for the Reformation, which began to restore sexual sanity by celebrating the physical act of lovemaking within marriage. According to my father, "The Puritan doctrine of sex was a watershed in the cultural history of the West. The Puritans devalued celibacy, glorified companionate marriage, affirmed married sex as both necessary and pure, established the ideal of wedded romantic love, and exalted the role of the wife."[2] In other words, they promoted a more biblical view of human sexuality.

## THE GIFT OF SEX

The biblical view of sex begins with acknowledging our sexuality as a gift from God. After all, the physical union between a husband and wife was God's idea in the first place. It was part of the goodness of his creation. God told Adam to cleave to his wife so that they could be fruitful and multiply (Gen. 1:28a). And it is by the inspiration of God's Spirit that the Bible includes the following duet between the lover and his beloved:

> *Let him kiss me with the kisses of his mouth!*
> *For your love is better than wine. . . .*
> *Draw me after you; let us run!*
>     *The king has brought me into his chambers;*—Song 1:2, 4a

> *Behold, you are beautiful, my love;*
>     *Behold, you are beautiful;*
>     *your eyes are doves.*
> *How beautiful you are, my darling!*
>     *Oh, how charming!*
>     *And our bed is verdant.*—Song 1:15-16, NIV

> *How delightful is your love, my sister, my bride!*
>     *How much better is your love than wine,*
>     *and the fragrance of your oils than any spice!*
> *Your lips drip nectar, my bride;*
>     *honey and milk are under your tongue.*—Song 4:10-11a

> *I slept, but my heart was awake.*
>     *A sound! My lover is knocking.*
> *"Open to me, my sister, my love,*
>     *my dove, my perfect one,*
> *for my head is wet with dew,*
>     *my locks with the drops of the night."*

*I had put off my garment;*
  *how could I put it on?*
*I had bathed my feet;*
  *how could I soil them?*
*My beloved put his hand to the latch,*
  *and my heart was thrilled within me.*
*I arose to open to my beloved,*
  *and my hands dripped with myrrh,*
*my fingers with liquid myrrh,*
  *on the handles of the bolt.*—Song 5:2-5

It doesn't take much imagination to understand what kind of sexual intimacy the Holy Spirit has in mind. Although God's Word is never pornographic, it is unashamedly erotic. If this comes as an embarrassment to some Christians, it is only because we are more prudish than God is. The Bible celebrates the sexual act of love—exclusively within marriage (see Prov. 5:15-19)—as a gift from God.

The traditional Roman Catholic view of sex was utilitarian. Intercourse was only for procreation, the propagation of the human race. The biblical view is that sex is not merely procreational, but also relational, and even recreational. Sex is for love, for pleasure, and for joy. And it is in order to protect this joy that God has given us the seventh commandment: "You shall not commit adultery" (Exod. 20:14).

## EROS DEFILED

What does it mean to commit adultery? The simplest answer is that adultery is marital infidelity. It is sexual intercourse that breaks the bonds of a marriage covenant. So the primary purpose of this commandment is to protect marriage. Adultery is the greatest sexual sin because it violates the trust between a husband and wife. It breaks the marriage covenant, a promise made before God. For this reason, adultery does more damage than other forms of sexual sin, such as having sex before marriage. The Bible confirms this by making the penalty for adultery so severe: "If a man commits adultery with the wife of his neighbor, both the adulterer and the adulteress shall surely be put to death" (Lev. 20:10). Was this punishment just? Douglas Wilson comments: "Certainly an adulterer is worthy of death; a man who will betray his wife will betray anyone and anything. Adultery is treason against the family, and God hates it."[3]

Having sex is not the only way to commit adultery, however. As we have seen, the Ten Commandments generally rule out the most extreme form of every kind of sin, but by implication they also rule out all the lesser sins that lead up to it. In the case of the seventh commandment, what is forbidden is everything that causes adultery. Most adulterous relationships don't start with sex; they start with inappropriate intimacy. The seventh commandment thus forbids a married man to flirt with another woman, or a single man to get close to someone else's wife. In order to forestall temptation, a certain social distance needs to be maintained. The commandment also forbids a married woman to seek primary emotional support from some other man, whether at work, at church, or in an Internet chat room. To put things more positively, the seventh commandment requires husbands and wives to nurture their love for one another, emotionally and spiritually as well as sexually.

Furthermore, committing adultery is not the only way to break the seventh commandment. According to "the rule of categories" (see Chapter 3), each commandment applies to every sin of the same kind. So the seventh commandment rules out any form of sexual immorality, or what the Greek New Testament calls *porneia*. "You shall not commit adultery" also means, to use the proper terminology, "you shall not fornicate." Fornication is sexual intercourse in a relationship outside the covenant commitment of marriage. It refers most specifically to premarital sex, which is a violation of the seventh commandment.

Couples that are dating often wonder how far they can go. The Bible doesn't say where the line is. Certainly any form of genital stimulation is ruled out. Until a man and a woman are actually married, they do not have the right to enjoy the sexual parts of one another's bodies. But the real problem is the question itself. Instead of wondering what they can get away with, couples ought to be asking questions like "How can I protect my sexual purity?" and "How can I preserve the joy of the person I love?" As Christians we are called to purity, not because we are sexually repressed, but because we are unwilling to settle for illicit pleasures that rob people of the joy of marital intercourse.

What else is ruled out? Prostitution is forbidden on the same grounds as adultery and fornication. Homosexual intercourse is ruled out because the biblical pattern calls for sex to be shared only between a husband and wife. Also forbidden is sexual violence, including rape, pedophilia, incest, or any form of sexual abuse within a marriage. In short, the seventh commandment forbids any sexual activity that violates the covenant of marriage. Period. There are no exceptions and no loopholes.

Why is adultery, in all its forms, forbidden? Not because sex is bad, but because it is designed to be such a powerful force for good. Sex is like superglue. When used properly, intercourse seals the bond of matrimony. It is the glue—the "covenant cement," as New York City's Tim Keller calls it—that helps to hold a marriage secure. This is why husbands and wives are required to have sexual relations. The Bible says, "The husband should give to his wife her conjugal rights, and likewise the wife to her husband. . . . Do not deprive each other" (1 Cor. 7:3, 5a; cf. Heb. 13:4). God has made us sexual beings to seal the love between a husband and wife. Their sexual union cements their total spiritual communion.

Sex only has God's blessing within the security of a total life commitment, and whenever intercourse is divorced from such a commitment, it loses its true purpose and its highest joy. According to C. S. Lewis:

> The Christian idea of marriage is based on Christ's words that a man and wife are to be regarded as a single organism. . . . [T]he male and the female were made to be combined together in pairs, not simply on a sexual level, but totally combined. The monstrosity of sexual intercourse outside marriage is that those who indulge in it are trying to isolate one kind of union (the sexual) from all the other kinds of union which were intended to go along with it and make up the total union. The Christian attitude does not mean that there is anything wrong about sexual pleasure, any more than about the pleasure of eating. It means that you must not isolate that pleasure and

try to get it by itself, any more than you ought to try to get the pleasures of taste without swallowing and digesting, by chewing things
and spitting them out again.[4]

Whenever people try to isolate the pleasures of sex, they always end
up harming themselves and others. Since sex is like superglue, squeez-
ing it out at the wrong time or in the wrong place always creates an
awful mess. The wrong things get joined together, and getting them
unstuck again tears at the soul. This is why adultery is forbidden. It is
because sex is a great force for good, but only when it is used to join one
man and one woman for life.

Another reason God forbids adultery is because there is a close connection between our sexuality and our spirituality. The union between
a husband and wife is intended to exemplify the exclusive relationship
between God and his people. There is something transcendent about
our sexuality. In the same way that husbands and wives give themselves
to one another—holding nothing back—God gives himself to us and
wants us to give ourselves to him. In the Old Testament God often
compared his relationship with his people to the romance between a
husband and wife. When his people were unfaithful—when they broke
their love covenant with him—they were guilty of committing spiritual
adultery (see, e.g., Jer. 3:1-10; 5:7-11; Hos. 2; Mal. 2:10-16).

The New Testament deepens the mystery by defining marriage in
terms of our relationship to Jesus Christ. Paul quotes from Genesis: "A
man shall leave his father and mother and hold fast to his wife, and the
two shall become one flesh" (Eph. 5:31). Then he adds this comment:
"This mystery is profound, and I am saying that it refers to Christ and
the church" (Eph. 5:32). In other words, the union between husband
and wife exemplifies the union between Christ and his church.

This has major implications for our sexuality. For the Christian,
every act of sexual immorality is a kind of spiritual desecration. It is an
offense against God the Son. "The body is not meant for sexual
immorality," Paul told the Corinthians, "but for the Lord, and the Lord
for the body. . . . Do you not know that your bodies are members of
Christ?" (1 Cor. 6:13b, 15a). If that is true—if our bodies are in Christ
and for Christ—then sexual immorality is a sin against God the Son.

Paul continues, "Shall I then take the members of Christ and make them members of a prostitute? Never! Or do you not know that he who is joined to a prostitute becomes one body with her? For, as it is written, 'The two will become one flesh.' But he who is joined to the Lord becomes one spirit with him" (1 Cor. 6:15b-17). For Christians to have sex with someone who is not a spouse is to violate the holiness of their union with Christ. We show our covenant loyalty to God by maintaining our sexual fidelity to our spouse (or our future spouse).

Sexual sin also dishonors the Holy Spirit. Paul goes on to say this: "Flee from sexual immorality. Every other sin a person commits is outside the body, but the sexually immoral person sins against his own body. Do you not know that your body is a temple of the Holy Spirit within you, whom you have from God? You are not your own, for you were bought with a price. So glorify God in your body" (1 Cor. 6:18-20). Our bodies were purchased for God when Christ died on the cross. Now they are inhabited by God's Spirit. This means that whatever we do with our bodies is directly related to our fellowship with the triune God. In addition to damaging ourselves and others, committing adultery dishonors the Father, the Son, and the Holy Spirit.

## THE DEADLY SIN OF LUST

Sexual immorality is common in our culture. People are looking for love, but they are settling for sex. Consider the casual sex on the college campus, the aggressive promotion of homosexuality as a lifestyle, and all the sexual material on television. With all the encounters and innuendoes, the average American views sexual material more than ten thousand times a year.[5] And by a ratio of more than ten to one, the couplings on television involve sex outside of marriage. This is because, as one TV producer explained, "married or celibate characters aren't as much fun."[6] Consider as well the vast pornography industry: the video stores, the strip clubs, the phone lines, and the cable channels. And consider the way that sex is used to sell—the soft pornography of the advertising industry. Then consider the personal consequences of all this sexual immorality: divorce, disease, and the sexual abuse of children.

It is tempting to think that our hypersexed culture is the problem, but of course sexual immorality is nearly as common in the church. Christians, including pastors and other spiritual leaders, get caught up in all the same kinds of sexual sin. On any given Sunday, there are people sitting in church who only the night before watched a pornographic video or had sex outside of marriage. This shows that the problem is not our culture, even for all its temptations; the problem is our own sinful hearts.

Jesus said, "You have heard that it was said, 'You shall not commit adultery.' But I say to you that everyone who looks at a woman with lustful intent has already committed adultery with her in his heart" (Matt. 5:27-28; cf. 15:19). When Jesus spoke these famous words, he was using the "inside/outside rule" (see Chapter 3) for interpreting the Ten Commandments: The law governs our inward thoughts as well as our outward actions. It covers both the desires of the heart and the deeds of the body. For the seventh commandment, this means that we are forbidden to lust.

To lust is to look at a woman—or a man, for that matter—and to imagine the sexual possibilities. Jesus told his disciples not to look at anyone *lustfully*. Looking is not the problem. The problem is looking at someone in a way that leads to sexual arousal. Whenever we look at someone that way, viewing a person as an object to satisfy our desire, we are lusting after sin. That sin is compounded when our lust leads to sexual self-gratification (i.e., masturbation), which is an act of self-worship.

There are many other ways to commit inward adultery. Martin Luther said, "[T]his commandment applies to every form of unchastity, however it is called. Not only is the external act forbidden, but also every kind of cause, motive, and means. Your heart, your lips, and your whole body are to be chaste and to afford no occasion, aid, or encouragement to unchastity."[7] The Westminster Shorter Catechism states the matter more simply: "The Seventh Commandment requireth the preservation of our own and our neighbor's chastity, in heart, speech, and behavior" (A. 71). To apply these principles, we break the seventh commandment by reading sexual literature, such as most romance novels. We break it by fantasizing about relationships that include sexual intimacy. We also break it by what we say, by making suggestive comments or telling dirty jokes. The Bible says, "But sexual immorality and all impurity or covetousness must not even be named among you, as is proper among saints. Let there be no filthiness or foolish talk nor crude joking, which are out of place" (Eph. 5:3-4). These are all ways of breaking the seventh commandment in the heart.

Most people have a higher tolerance for their inward sins than they do for their outward sins. We're less concerned about the sins of our hearts because no one else knows about them (or so we think). But our inward flaws are just as fatal. This is true of lust, which the medieval church rightly listed as one of the seven deadly sins. No doubt there are more than seven, but however many there are, lust certainly belongs on the list!

Lust has many unhappy consequences. It's expensive. It will cost a man his money, and maybe even his life: "Do not desire her beauty in your heart, and do not let her capture you with her eyelashes; for the price of a prostitute is only a loaf of bread, but [the adulteress] hunts down a precious life" (Prov. 6:25-26). Giving in to lust is like playing with fire. Solomon asked, "Can a man carry fire next to his chest and his clothes not be burned?" (Prov. 6:27). Lust leads men and women into shame and disgrace (Prov. 6:32-33). But worst of all, sexual sin brings us under the wrath of God: "Do you not know that the unrighteous will not inherit the kingdom of God? Do not be deceived: neither the sexually immoral, nor idolaters, nor adulterers, nor men who practice homosexuality . . . will inherit the kingdom of God" (1 Cor. 6:9-10). "Let marriage be held in honor by all, and let the marriage bed be undefiled, for God will judge the sexually immoral and adulterous" (Heb. 13:4).

Thankfully, God gives grace to sinners who repent of their lust and come to faith in Jesus Christ. Having listed the various kinds of people who are excluded from eternal life, Paul goes on to say, "And such were some of you. But you were washed, you were sanctified, you were justified in the name of the Lord Jesus Christ and by the Spirit of our God" (1 Cor. 6:11). Through the death and resurrection of Jesus Christ, God offers forgiveness to lusty sinners.

But God offers something more than forgiveness. By his Spirit he gives grace in the time of temptation. He has also provided a practical way to preserve our chastity. It's called marriage. Admittedly, there are some Christians who have the gift of continence, or celibacy. For some physical or spiritual reason, they have a special capacity for refraining from sexual sin. However, most Christians do not have that gift, and obviously it would be good for them to get married. The apostle Paul said, "Each has his own gift from God, one of one kind and one of another. To the unmarried and the widows I say that it is good for them to remain single, as I am. But if they cannot exercise self-control, they should marry. For it is better to marry than to be aflame with passion" (1 Cor. 7:7b-9).

Every unmarried Christian is called to sexual purity. As we shall see, there are practical ways to live out that calling. God gives grace to those who seek to honor him by preserving their chastity. However, anyone who struggles with sexual self-control should make spiritual preparations for marriage. For men, this means learning to live for others, practicing the self-sacrificing love of Christ. For women, this means learning to serve others, living in submission to Christ. Unfortunately, many Christian men are too self-centered to get outside themselves and love others. Often they get caught up in secret sexual sin, including pornography and masturbation. Relationally broken, they settle for the false intimacy and false acceptance of self-fulfillment without ever learning how to love a woman. The sad result is that many good Christian women suffer for the want of a good Christian man. It would be better for all concerned if these men (and also these women) made spiritual preparations for marriage, and the best way to do this is to grow in submission and sacrifice.

Submission and sacrifice are the virtues that marriage demands, and not surprisingly, they also prove to be the virtues that bring joy to sex. Our culture places far too much emphasis on technique, trying to turn lovemaking into some kind of scientific skill. But husbands and wives are called to do more than "have sex"; they are called to find joy in the sexual love that they share. When couples are not finding satisfaction, usually the problem is not sexual but relational, and therefore spiritual. Often there is a lot of blame-shifting, with husbands and wives criticizing one another for their shortcomings. What is the answer?

At the risk of oversimplifying, the answer is for husbands to love their wives in sacrificial ways. The husband's spiritual leadership is fundamental for everything that happens in a marriage, including what happens in bed. Of course wives have an obligation to their husbands, including a sexual obligation. As mentioned earlier, "The husband should give to his wife her conjugal rights, and likewise the wife to her husband" (1 Cor. 7:3). Interestingly, here is one place where the Bible teaches mutual submission: "For the wife does not have authority over her body, but the husband does. Likewise the husband does not have authority over his own body, but the wife does" (1 Cor. 7:4). So husbands and wives must offer themselves to one another in what the Puritans called "the mutual communication of bodies." This is their marital duty. But it will always be a chore if a wife is not cherished by her husband. The key to a happy marriage, sexually and otherwise, is, "Husbands, love your wives, as Christ loved the church and gave himself up for her" (Eph. 5:25).

## DAVID'S FOLLY

The poet Wendell Berry once defined sexual love as "the power that joins a couple together" and marriage as "the way we protect the possibility that sexual love can become a story."[8] Berry is right: When a man and a woman are joined together in marriage, their love becomes a story. However, when their love is betrayed, that story turns into a tragedy, as in the story of David and Bathsheba.

David was the king of Israel, and the Bible tells how one night "he arose from his couch and was walking on the roof of the king's house" (2 Sam. 11:2a). That warm spring evening David had everything a man could ever want. He had conquered his enemies and established his kingdom. He was living in royal luxury. He was famous and handsome. More than that, he was righteous, a man after God's own heart. He wrote beautiful hymns of praise to the God who had promised him an eternal kingdom. As he strolled around the roof, David was the master of all that he surveyed. There was nothing more for him to gain . . . but he still had everything to lose.

Tragically, David had exposed himself to temptation. Walking around the roof seems innocent enough, but David had no business being there at all. He should have been out defending his people in battle. Instead, he was walking back and forth, going nowhere, killing time. The story of his tragic downfall began with these ominous words: "In the spring of the year, the time when kings go out to battle, David sent Joab, and his servants with him, and all Israel. And they ravaged the Ammonites and besieged Rabbah. But David remained at Jerusalem" (2 Sam. 11:1).

This verse does more than simply tell us where David was; it tells us where he should have been and what he should have been doing. His nation was still at war, and as the king, it was his duty to lead his armies into battle. Instead, David decided to take it easy. When the Bible tells us that he "remained at Jerusalem," this is meant as a reproach. The king had stopped serving, sacrificing, and giving his life away for others. It is not at all surprising that it was at this time that he indulged in sexual sin.

Committing adultery is sometimes considered a masculine thing to do. "That's just the way men are," people say. But David's example shows that the real truth is just the opposite: Sexual sin is a failure of godly manliness. Elsewhere the Bible says that to break the seventh commandment is to "give your honor to others and your years to the merciless" (Prov. 5:9). The man of God does not live for himself, but for others, and this enables him to keep his sexual desire under the power of love. But when a man turns inward, he is vulnerable to all kinds of sexual temptation.

This is a key insight for anyone who struggles with sins against the seventh commandment. Sexual sin is never just about sex; it is always connected to the rest of life. David never would have committed adultery if he had been doing what God had called him to do. Instead, he abdicated his royal responsibility and retreated to his palace. There, in his idleness and isolation, he gave in to temptation. This shows how vulnerable we are to sexual sin when we are living for ourselves and not for others. What we do with our bodies is not just physical, but also spiritual. It comes from the deepest desires of the heart. One way to gain victory over sexual sin is to live self-sacrificially rather than self-indulgently, and to do so in every area of life. Godliness in one area promotes godliness in others.

David made a strategic blunder when he stopped giving himself away in love. Then he made a serious tactical mistake: "He saw from the roof a woman bathing" (2 Sam. 11:2). If David had simply caught a glimpse of the woman, he would not have been guilty, but he did more than that. His glance became a gaze. He ogled the woman, looking her up and down, thinking about what he'd like to do with her.

This gives us a further insight into sexual temptation and how to avoid it. The eye is a window to sinful desire. One way to gain victory over sexual sin, therefore, is to turn away our lusty gaze. Godly women have always understood that this requires modesty in the way they dress. And godly men have always understood that preserving sexual purity means being careful about what we keep looking at. The apostle Peter wisely warned against having "eyes full of adultery" (2 Pet. 2:14; cf. 1 John 2:16). Job's remedy was this: "I made a covenant with my eyes not to look lustfully at a girl" (Job 31:1, NIV).

Being careful what we see has never been more important than it is today, when there are sexual images almost everywhere we look. Porn has become the norm, and the greatest danger of all is the Internet, which is the most powerful purveyor of pornography in the history of the world. What makes the Internet so dangerous is that it is anonymous, accessible, and affordable.[9] Anyone with a computer can download pornography in complete privacy. And the stream of sexual material is endless. Other forms of pornography eventually lose their appeal because the images have all been seen before, but on the Internet there is always something new. According to one popular men's magazine:

> What makes sex online far more compelling than any shrink-wrapped smut [is] instant gratification in endless variety—you never get to the end of the magazine and have to start looking at the same pictures again. With old porn, once you view it, you've consumed it. You've chewed the flavor out of the gum. This can't be

done on the Net. The gum never runs out of flavor. A new piece of flesh waits behind every old one, and expectation bids you to go further. Much further. Because as long as there's more to come, you'll keep looking. This is all so new. No stimulus like this ever existed before.[10]

As long as there is more to see, some people will keep looking, including some Christians. One Internet expert wrote the following letter to his pastor:

> I'm deeply concerned about the avenues for decadent content that have been opened into the home.
>
> I'm fortunate to have many good Christian male friends that I can confide in and talk openly with about their faith and areas in their life where they are struggling. What has been alarming to me is that out of a dozen or so close friends that I have talked to, all but one has admitted that they struggle in this area and frequently fail. All of these friends are very committed followers of Christ, many involved in full time Christian service. What I see is that Christians who would have never even considered going into an adult store, renting an R/X rated movie, or dialing a 900 number, are now continually failing in this area because of the anonymity and free and easy access to this type of content on the Internet. What is worse, is seeing the grip and pull it has on people once they start down this path.
>
> Based on my experience, the Internet has become Satan's number one tool in the 21st century and it seems to be a more silent infection into the body of believers because it typically only involves the user and their computer.[11]

The silent infection of pornography in the church is deadly. It denigrates women, damages relationships, and destroys a man's spiritual ability to lead. The Puritan Thomas Watson rightly said that pornographic pictures "secretly convey poison to the heart."[12]

To see how deadly lust is, look what happened to David. The more he looked at the woman, the more he wanted her. Sin was starting to take control, and as David began to fantasize, he found himself unable to turn away. Rather than fleeing from temptation (see Gen. 39:12; Prov.

5:8; 2 Tim. 2:22), he began to "make . . . provision for the flesh, to grat-
ify its desires" (Rom. 13:14). He toyed with the possibilities: "The
woman was very beautiful. And David sent and inquired out about
the woman. And one said, 'Is not this Bathsheba, the daughter of
Eliam, the wife of Uriah the Hittite?'" (2 Sam. 11:3).

The whole matter should have ended right there. Bathsheba was a
married woman. Giving her any further thought was out of the question for a man of God, but David felt like he had to have her. Bathsheba
had become an obsession. This is the way lust works. It takes on a power
of its own, pulling us in deeper and deeper until we feel powerless to
resist. And since David was the king, he could do what most men can
only dream of doing. If he wanted a woman, he could take her, and so
he did: "So David sent messengers and took her, and she came to him,
and he lay with her" (2 Sam. 11:4a).

It seemed like such a small thing—only a moment of weakness,
that's all. But soon Bathsheba discovered that she was pregnant, and the
cover-up started. By the time David was finished, Bathsheba's husband
was dead, and the king was guilty not only of adultery, but also of lying,
stealing, and murder. And for a while, it seemed like he would get away
with it all, too. Sure, he had to scramble a little bit to make it happen,
but everything went according to plan. Except for this: "The thing
David had done displeased the LORD" (2 Sam. 11:27b).

Like David, Christians often seem to think that they can sin with
impunity. We engage in a little sexual fantasy. Why not? Then we look
at some pornography. Who doesn't? At first it doesn't seem all that
harmful. We can still carry out our ministry as effectively as ever. No
one will ever know. But God always knows. Solomon said, "Why
should you be intoxicated, my son, with a forbidden woman and
embrace the bosom of an adulteress? For a man's ways are before the
eyes of the LORD, and he ponders all his paths" (Prov. 5:20-21). God
sees everything we do with our bodies. He knows what we look at,
think about, desire, and touch, and he will hold us accountable.

God certainly held David accountable! From the moment the king
decided to act on his lust, his life became a tragic series of disappoint-
ments. He lost almost everything he had worked so hard to obtain.

Bathsheba's son died. David's family was torn apart by rape, incest, and fratricide. His kingdom was divided. His beloved son rebelled against him, even having sex with David's wives on top of the palace, bringing shame to his father's house. And all for the sake of a few minutes in bed.

Do you think it was worth it? If not, then what about your own sexual sins? What do you really gain, and what are you willing to lose?

## EROS REDEEMED

In this whole sordid affair there was only one thing that David did right: He confessed his sin. God loved David, and out of his marvelous mercy and amazing grace, he sent his prophet Nathan to confront him. Once his sin was exposed, David knew that he was guilty. More than that, he knew that what he had done was worthy of death. So he did the only thing a guilty sinner can do, and that is to cry out to God for mercy. He said, "I have sinned against the LORD" (2 Sam. 12:13a).

There are many lessons to learn from David's interview with Nathan. We learn that we cannot hide our sin from God. We learn that sin always has consequences. We learn that because sexual immorality thrives on secrecy, we need the open assistance of other believers—especially pastors—to help us turn away from sin. But we also learn this: When we sin, we should go straight back to God and confess it.

David's full confession is recorded in Psalm 51. He began by crying out for God to forgive him:

> Have mercy on me, O God,
>    according to your steadfast love;
> according to your abundant mercy
>    blot out my transgressions.
> Wash me thoroughly from my iniquity,
>    and cleanse me from my sin.—Ps. 51:1-2

David made his appeal for forgiveness on the basis of an atoning sacrifice, the blood of a lamb applied to the guilt of his sin:

> Purge me with hyssop, and I shall be clean;
> wash me, and I shall be whiter than snow.—Ps. 51:7

Then he prayed for God's ongoing work of sanctification in his life:

*Create in me a pure heart, O God,*
  *and renew a right spirit within me.*
*Cast me not away from your presence,*
  *and take not your Holy Spirit from me.*
*Restore to me the joy of your salvation,*
  *and uphold me with a willing spirit.*—Ps. 51:10-12

David got it right at last. He made a full and open confession, and God had mercy on him, as he does on every sinner who truly repents. Nathan said to David, "The LORD also has put away your sin; you shall not die" (2 Sam. 12:13b). To be sure, David still had to face the consequences of his sin. But his sin was forgiven; his guilt was taken away.

So often when we break the seventh commandment, we feel so guilty that it is all we can do to drag ourselves back to the cross, when what we ought to do is to run back to the cross and confess our sin. At the cross we can find a sacrifice for our sin, with cleansing for our guilt and the power to start living again for Christ.

When God confronts us with the guilt of sexual sin, we have a choice. If we keep hiding our sin, we may be sure that it will destroy us in the end. But if we repent of our sin, God will have mercy. In a sermon on adultery, Martyn Lloyd-Jones said, "Even adultery is not the unforgivable sin. It is a terrible sin, but God forbid that there should be anyone who feels that he or she has sinned himself or herself outside the love of God or outside His kingdom because of adultery. No; if you truly repent and realize the enormity of your sin and cast yourself upon the boundless love and mercy and grace of God, you can be forgiven and I assure you of pardon."

Lloyd-Jones could have stopped there, except he added this comment: "But hear the words of our blessed Lord: 'Go, and sin no more.'"[13] These were Jesus' words to the woman caught in adultery, and they are also his words to us, for the Bible says:

*This is the will of God, your sanctification: that you should avoid sexual immorality; that each one of you should know how to control his own body in holiness and honor, not in the passion of lust like the Gentiles who do not know God; that no one transgress and wrong his brother in this matter, because the Lord is an avenger in all these things, as we told you beforehand and solemnly warned you. For God has not called us for impurity, but in holiness. Therefore whoever disregards this, disregards not man but God, who gives his Holy Spirit to you.*—1 Thess. 4:3-8

## STUDY QUESTIONS

1. What is your reaction to the passages quoted from Song of Songs (1:2, 4a; 1:15-16; 4:10-11a; 5:2-5) when you consider that they are in the Bible?
2. What does the seventh commandment teach us about how God views sex?
3. Why is adultery treated as such a serious sin? What far-reaching effects does it have?
4. What immediate and potential consequences of premarital sex make it such a dangerous sin?
5. In what ways does the relationship between a husband and wife mirror the relationship between God and his people?
6. How does adultery dishonor the Father, the Son, and the Holy Spirit?
7. What lesser or inward forms of adultery are people tempted to excuse as being "not that serious"?
8. Read 2 Samuel 11:1-17; 12:1-15. What poor decisions led up to David's temptation?
9. What principles can we learn from David's fall about how to keep the seventh commandment?
10. Read Psalm 51. What are the main components of David's confession? (It might be helpful to write a brief outline of this psalm.)
11. How can you apply this study of the seventh commandment to your own life? Are you doing anything that could lead to inward or outward adultery? How can you avoid these temptations?

# THE EIGHTH COMMANDMENT:
# WHAT'S MINE IS GOD'S

*You shall not steal.*

EXODUS 20:15

In his book on the Ten Commandments, Cecil Myers describes a picture by Norman Rockwell. The well-known painting, which first appeared on the cover of *The Saturday Evening Post*, shows a woman buying a turkey for Thanksgiving dinner. The turkey is being weighed on the scale. Behind the counter is the jolly butcher, with his apron stretched tightly over his ample belly and his pencil tucked neatly behind one ear. His customer is a respectable looking woman of perhaps sixty. Like the butcher, she looks pleased. The two of them exchange a knowing smile, almost as if they are sharing a joke, but the joke is really on them because the painting shows what they are secretly doing. The butcher is pressing the scale down with his big fat thumb, to raise the price. At the same time, the woman is trying to get a better deal by pushing the scale up with her forefinger. The reason both of them look pleased is that neither is aware of what the other is doing!

In typical Rockwell style, the painting is a charming scene from American life that makes us laugh at our own foibles. But really what the butcher and his customer were doing was violating the eighth commandment. Myers comments: "Both the butcher and the lovely lady would resent being called thieves. The lovely lady would never rob a bank or steal a car. The butcher would be indignant if anyone accused

him of stealing; and if a customer gave him a bad check, he would call
the police, but neither saw anything wrong with a little deception that
would make a few cents for one or save a few cents for the other."[1] In
a word, they were stealing.

## On the Take

Everyone knows that stealing is wrong. Even people who don't read the
Bible know the eighth commandment, which says, "You shall not steal"
(Exod. 20:15). To steal is to take something that doesn't belong to you.
The Hebrew word for stealing (*ganaf*) literally means to carry something
away, as if by stealth. To give a more technical definition, to steal is to
appropriate someone else's property unlawfully.

What the eighth commandment forbids seems very simple.
However, most people fail to understand its full meaning. Like the rest
of God's law, the prohibition on stealing is comprehensive:

> *Ganaf*—stealing—covers all conventional types of theft: burglary
> (breaking into a home or building to commit theft); robbery (tak-
> ing property directly from another using violence or intimidation);
> larceny (taking something without permission and not returning
> it); hijacking (using force to take goods in transit or seizing control
> of a bus, truck, plane, etc.); shoplifting (taking items from a store
> during business hours without paying for them); and pickpocketing
> and purse-snatching. The term *ganaf* also covers a wide range of
> exotic and complex thefts . . . [such as] embezzlement (the fraud-
> ulent taking of money or other goods entrusted to one's care).
> There is extortion (getting money from someone by means of
> threats or misuses of authority), and racketeering (obtaining money
> by any illegal means).[2]

This is only a partial list of the countless ways people violate the
eighth commandment. They pilfer public property, stealing supplies
from hospitals, building sites, and churches. In fact, one hotel reported
in its first year of business having to replace thirty-eight thousand
spoons, eighteen thousand tiles, three hundred and fifty-five coffee pots
. . . and one hundred Bibles![3]

Citizens steal from the government by underpaying their taxes or making false claims for disability and Social Security. The government steals too. With its huge bureaucracy, the federal government commits theft on a national scale by wasting public money and by accumulating debt without fully planning to repay. Deficit spending is really a way of stealing from future citizens.

There is theft at work. Employees fill in false time cards and call in sick when they want a day off. They help themselves to office supplies, make personal long-distance phone calls, and pad their expense accounts. Sometimes they go so far as to embezzle, but a more common workplace theft is simply failing to put in a full day's work. Instead workers idle away their time, sitting in their offices and surfing the Internet, sending e-mail to friends—even playing computer games. Whenever we give anything less than our best effort, we are robbing our employer of the productivity we owe.

These are not victimless crimes. Employee theft of time and property costs American businesses and their investors more than two hundred billion dollars a year. This affects all of us. According to some estimates, as much as one-third of a product's cost goes to cover the various forms of stealing that occur on its way to the marketplace. This "theft surcharge," as analysts call it, is a drag on our whole economy.

For their part, employers often steal from their workers. They demand longer hours than contracts allow. They reorganize their workforce to improve their profits, and then the workers who still have jobs end up doing all the work that used to be done by the people who got laid off (plus their own of course)! This is just a sophisticated way for companies to steal from their best employees.

Large corporations steal from the general public. They keep some of their transactions off the books. They hide their losses in offshore accounts. They manipulate securities by providing false information. One of the worst offenders in recent history was Enron, the vast energy company whose spectacular collapse in 2001 injured the whole U.S. economy and cost some people their life savings. Enron's fall was quickly followed by a series of others as Arthur Andersen, WorldCom, Adelphia, Rite-Aid, and other well-known corporations were caught cheating the public. The nefarious executives from these companies knew all the tricks, but this is hardly a recent phenomenon. Martin Luther identified certain men of his day as "gentlemen swindlers or big operators. Far from being picklocks and sneak-thieves who loot a cash box, they sit in office chairs and are called great lords and honorable, good citizens, and yet with a great show of legality they rob and steal."[4] And John Calvin said, "It follows, therefore, that not only are those thieves who secretly steal the property of others, but those also who seek gain from the loss of others, accumulate wealth by unlawful practices and are more devoted to their private advantage than to equity."[5]

Many common business practices are immoral, even if technically they are not illegal. This is especially true in marketing. What many business people consider good salesmanship actually violates the eighth commandment. There is price gouging, in which the laws of supply and demand are used to take advantage of helpless consumers. There is false advertising and deceptive packaging, which is designed to make a product look bigger and better than it actually is. Salesmen exaggerate the value of their products, trying to sell people things they really don't need. Before the sale, every car is touted as the finest vehicle in automotive history; but once the sale is made, and it's time to talk about a service contract, suddenly the car is going to need all kinds of repairs that ought to be paid for in advance! And so it goes.

These practices are all violations of the eighth commandment. Calvin was right when he said, "Let us remember that all those arts whereby we acquire the possessions and money of our neighbors—when such devices depart from sincere affection to a desire to cheat or in some manner to harm—are to be considered as thefts."[6] Similarly, Luther said that we break the eighth commandment whenever we "tak[e] advantage of our neighbor in any sort of dealing that results in loss to him."[7] How much business fails to measure up to that simple standard?

Then there is all the theft that is tied up with credit. There is usury, the lending of money at exorbitant rates of interest in order to make unjust profits. Today the most blatant offenders are the credit card companies that charge interest at nearly 20 percent. The same sin is committed on a larger scale when international banks hold debtor nations in fiscal bondage. This is only one small aspect of a much wider problem, which is that a small minority uses the vast majority of the world's resources—and does everything they can to protect their advantage. But the Bible teaches that the poor need our help and that they should receive loans free of interest, at least within the community of God's people (Lev. 25:35-38; Deut. 15:7-8). There is another side to this, of course, which is that some people buy on credit without ever intending to repay. No doubt this helps explain why in recent decades credit card debt has risen from five billion to more than five hundred billion dollars.

The list goes on. There is insurance fraud, the filing of false claims. There are the deliberate cost overruns that make up the difference between the estimate and the final price whenever work is contracted. There is the theft of intellectual property, the violation of copyrights, including the unlawful duplication of music and videos. There is plagiarism, the misappropriation of someone else's work. Then there is identity theft, in which personal information is stolen off the Internet and used to run up outrageous charges.

There are countless ways to steal. The Heidelberg Catechism summarizes by saying that in the eighth commandment, "God forbids not only outright theft and robbery, but also such wicked schemes and devices as false weights and measures, deceptive merchandising, counterfeit money, and usury; we must not defraud our neighbor in any way, whether by force or by show of right. In addition God forbids all greed and all abuse or squandering of his gifts" (A. 110). The trouble is that when it comes to stealing, nearly everyone is doing it. Yet nearly 90 percent of evangelical Christians claim that they never break the eighth commandment.[8] This statistic is hardly encouraging. What it shows is that Christians have forgotten what stealing really means. The truth is that theft is pervasive at every level of American society, and like everyone else, we are in on the take. But this is not just an American problem. The whole human race is a band of thieves, and we all suffer the loss. Martin Luther said, "If we look at mankind in all its conditions, it is nothing but a vast, wide stable full of great thieves."[9] He also speculated what would happen if we were all brought to justice. "It is the smallest part of the thieves that are hung," he said. "If we're to hang them all, where shall we get rope enough? We must make all our belts and straps into halters."[10]

## GOD'S PROVIDENCE, OUR STEWARDSHIP

What's wrong with stealing, anyway? Like the rest of God's law, the eighth commandment has deep spiritual significance. Whenever we take something that doesn't belong to us—however we do it—we sin against God as well as our neighbor.

Stealing is a sin against God in at least two ways. First, every theft is a failure to trust in his provision. Whenever we take something that doesn't belong to us, we deny that God has given us or is able to give us everything we truly need. Therefore, keeping the eighth commandment is a practical exercise of our faith in God's providence.

Every theft is also an assault on God's providence for others. This is a second way that stealing is a sin against God: It robs what he has provided for someone else. Here it is important to understand that the eighth commandment assumes a right of ownership. By saying, "You shall not steal," God indicated that people have a right to own their private property. Otherwise, the whole concept of stealing would fail to make any sense. Only something that belongs to someone can be stolen from him or her. But the reason that anything belongs to anyone is because it comes from God, and we do not have the right to take for ourselves what God has given to others.

This brings us to the positive side of the eighth commandment. What the Bible means by ownership is not possessing things to use for our own purposes, but receiving things from God to use for his glory. So at the same time that we are forbidden to take things that don't belong to us, we are required to use what we have in ways that are pleasing to our God. To put it very simply, the eighth commandment isn't just about stealing; it's also about stewardship.

A steward is someone who cares for someone else's property. He is not free to use it however he pleases, but only to manage it in accordance with his master's intentions. This is our situation exactly. Whatever we possess is God's property, and he has given us the sacred trust of looking after it. This is the way it has been since the beginning. Adam did not own any property—he just managed it: "The LORD God took the man and put him in the garden of Eden to work it and keep it" (Gen. 2:15). As Calvin explained:

> [T]he custody of the garden was given in charge to Adam, to show that we possess the things which God has committed to our hands, on the condition, that being content with a frugal and moderate use of them, we should take care of what shall remain. . . . [T]hat this economy, and this diligence, with respect to those good things which God has given us to enjoy, may flourish among us; let every one regard himself as the steward of God in all things which he possesses. Then he will neither conduct himself dissolutely, nor corrupt by abuse those things which God requires to be preserved.[11]

Like Adam, we are called to be good stewards of God's world.

Good stewardship means taking care of what we have been given, not letting things fall into disrepair. It means not being wasteful. Whenever we squander money that could be better spent on something else, we are guilty of a kind of theft. This is one of the problems with gambling, which has become one of the most common ways of breaking the eighth commandment. Each year Americans spend more money on various forms of gambling than they do on food or clothing. "What's wrong with that?" some may ask. The Southern Baptist Convention has provided an excellent answer:

> While the Bible contains no "thou shalt not" in regard to gambling, it does contain many insights and principles which indicate that gambling is wrong. The Bible emphasizes the sovereignty of God in the direction of human events (see Matthew 10:29-30); gambling looks to chance and good luck. The Bible indicates that man is to work creatively and use his possessions for the good of others (see Ephesians 4:28); gambling fosters a something-for-nothing attitude. The Bible calls for careful stewardship; gambling calls for reckless abandon. The Bible condemns covetousness and materialism (see Matthew 6:24-34); gambling has both at its heart. The moral thrust of the

Bible is love for God and neighbor (Matthew 22:37-40); gambling seeks personal gain and pleasure at another person's loss and pain.[12]

Good stewardship also means working hard. The Bible is very specific about this. The book of Proverbs teaches that laziness leads to poverty (Prov. 6:10-11). That's not the only cause of poverty, of course, but it is one of them. Poverty, in turn, brings the temptation to steal (Prov. 30:8-9). One obvious way to avoid this temptation is to work hard for honest gain, with the goal of becoming financially independent (see 1 Thess. 4:11-12). The Bible says, "Let the thief no longer steal, but rather let him labor, doing honest work with his own hands, so that he may have something to share with anyone in need" (Eph. 4:28). In other words, the burglar must become a benefactor, as Zacchaeus did when he made restitution for his many sins against the eighth commandment (Luke 19:8). As soon as we realize what we have stolen, it is our responsibility to pay back what we owe, and then some.

This brings us to the last aspect of good stewardship, which is giving away what God has given to us so that other people will have what they need. Jerry Bridges has observed that there are three basic attitudes we can take toward possessions. The first says, "What's yours is mine; I'll take it." This is the attitude of the thief. The second says, "What's mine is mine; I'll keep it." Since we are selfish by nature, this is the attitude that most people have most of the time. The third attitude—the godly attitude—says, "What's mine is God's; I'll share it."[13]

Christians are called to live generously. We do not work simply to satisfy our own desires, but also to provide for others. This is not to say that we can never enjoy what God has given us. After all, enjoying God's gifts is one aspect of good stewardship. But Christians who are as wealthy as we are should always be thinking about what we can give to someone else. It is only in this way that money loses its power over us. As Kent Hughes has said, "Every time I give, I declare that money does not control me. Perpetual generosity is a perpetual de-deification of money."[14]

Good stewardship starts with meeting the needs of our families. Then it extends to the church and to the global work of the gospel. Finally, it reaches out to the poor in our own community and around the world. The Bible says, "Give . . . freely . . . your heart shall not be grudging . . . because for this the LORD your God will bless you in all your work and in all that you undertake" (Deut. 15:10). The consequences of such generosity will last forever. As A. W. Tozer once explained, "Any temporal possession can be turned into everlasting wealth. Whatever is given to Christ is immediately touched with immortality."[15] To put this another way, the only money we can count on ever seeing again is the money we invest in the kingdom of God. Jesus said, "Do not lay up for yourselves treasures on earth, where moth and rust destroy and where thieves break in and steal, but lay up for yourselves treasures in heaven, where neither moth nor rust destroys and where thieves do not break in and steal. For where your treasure is, there your heart will be also" (Matt. 6:19-21).

If we fail to make this investment, we are guilty of breaking the eighth commandment. The famous fourth-century preacher Chrysostom served a wealthy congregation in the great city of Constantinople. Chrysostom was well-known for challenging his people not to be stingy. On one occasion he said:

> This also is theft, not to share one's possessions. Perhaps this statement seems surprising to you, but do not be surprised. . . . Just as an official in the imperial treasury, if he neglects to distribute where he is ordered, but spends instead for his own indolence, pays the penalty and is put to death, so also the rich man is a kind of steward of the money which is owed for distribution to the poor. He is directed to distribute it to his fellow servants who are in want. So if he spends more on himself than his needs require, he will pay the harshest penalty hereafter. For his own goods are not his own, but belong to his own fellow servants. . . . I beg you remember this without fail, that not to share our own wealth with the poor is theft from the poor and deprivation of their means of life; we do not possess our own wealth but theirs.[16]

## THE TENT OF THIEVES

There are many thieves in the stories of the Bible, but the most audacious was probably Achan. Achan was a soldier in Israel's army. He fought in the battle of Jericho, when the Israelites marched around the city until the walls fell down.

On the morning of that famous victory, General Joshua gave his troops the order of the day. He commanded them, "Shout, for the LORD has given you the city. And the city and all that is within it shall be devoted to the LORD for destruction. . . . But you, keep yourselves from the things devoted to destruction, lest . . . you . . . make the camp of Israel a thing for destruction and bring trouble upon it. But all silver and gold, and every vessel of bronze and iron, are holy to the LORD; they shall go into the treasury of the LORD" (Josh. 6:16b-17a, 18-19). This was holy war. The Israelites were not fighting for their own advantage, but for the glory of God. They were agents of his divine justice, and as such, they were not allowed to claim the spoils of battle. Everything was to be devoted to the Lord, upon the pain of death.

In the battle everything went according to plan. The people cried out, the walls collapsed, and the Israelites conquered the Canaanites: "They devoted the city to the LORD and destroyed with the sword every living thing in it. . . . Then they burned the whole city and everything in it, but they put the silver and gold and the articles of bronze and iron into the treasury of the LORD's house" (Josh. 6:21a, 24, NIV). The soldiers did everything that Joshua commanded.

Except for Achan. In the aftermath of the battle, as he rummaged through the wreckage, Achan's heart was captured by the city's treasure: gold, silver, and fancy clothes with designer labels. "There's so much stuff here," he must have said to himself, "that if I took something, no one would ever notice it was missing." The more treasure he saw, the more he wanted some of it for himself. "After all," Achan reasoned, "I'm a soldier in this army, and I deserve some kind of reward for fighting!"

Achan started thinking about how he could smuggle some of the treasure back to his tent. As his mind worked through the possibilities, he decided to go for it. He "saw among the spoil a beautiful cloak from Shinar, and 200 shekels of silver, and a bar of gold weighing 50 shekels" (Josh. 7:21a). He coveted them, he stole them, and then he hurried back to his tent. When he arrived—breathless—he dug a hole in the ground to hide all his loot. It would be their little family secret.

As robberies go, Achan didn't take much. In today's market it would amount to something like a five hundred dollar suit, a few hundred dollars of silver, and several thousand dollars' worth of gold. Yet that one somewhat modest theft brought death and destruction on Israel. The defeat came quickly. After his great success against Jericho, Joshua was eager to attack the next city. The general sent his scouts to spy out the region, and soon they returned to say that their next target would be easy pickings. Joshua didn't even need to send out his whole army; several thousand soldiers would be more than enough. Yet to their shock and dismay, the Israelites were badly beaten.

To Joshua this seemed like a military crisis. After he had managed to retreat, he threw himself down on the ground and complained to God. But the Lord said to him,

> *Get up! Why have you fallen on your face? Israel has sinned; they have transgressed my covenant that I commanded them; they have taken some of the devoted things; they have stolen and lied and put them among their own belongings. Therefore the Israelites cannot stand before their enemies. They turn their backs before their enemies, because they have become devoted for destruction. I will be with you no more, unless you destroy the devoted things from among you.*—Josh. 7:10-12

The problem was that someone had violated the eighth commandment. So God proceeded to give instructions for identifying and then executing the thief.

The next morning the whole nation was brought before Joshua for judgment. Achan was there, at first wondering what it was all about, and then desperately hoping that his sin would remain undiscovered. He probably said to himself, "Come on—with a million people here, how could the general ever find out?" The tribes were called forward, Judah was taken by lot, and Achan's heart jumped into his throat. Judah! Why, that was *his* tribe. What were the chances of that! Then all the clans of Judah stepped forward, and the descendants of Zerah were taken, and guess whose grandfather that was! Achan's, of course, and the blood

drained from his face. The Zerahites came forward, and the family of
Zimri was taken. Then Achan knew that he was a dead man, because
Zimri was his father. One by one every member of the family went for-
ward, until finally Joshua came to Achan, the thief.

Shortly before he died, Moses had told the Israelites that if they
obeyed God, the Lord would give them the Promised Land. But he also
warned them, "[I]f you will not do so, behold, you have sinned against
the LORD; and be sure your sin will find you out" (Num. 32:23). That's
exactly what happened to Achan: His sin found him out, which is not
surprising, because it was such a stupid sin to commit in the first place.
It's one thing to hide stolen property, but to really gain anything by his
theft, Achan would have to use what he had taken. Think about it:
When would he ever be able to wear his fancy robe or show off his cache
of precious metals?

Achan never got the chance, and in the end he lost everything. Joshua
forced him to confess his crime in front of the whole nation. Then messengers were sent to look for the stolen goods. Sure enough, they were
buried in the thief's tent. The messengers brought everything back where
everyone could see it. "And Joshua and all Israel with him took Achan the
son of Zerah, and the silver and the robe and the bar of gold . . . and all
that he had. And they brought them up to the Valley of Achor. And Joshua
said, 'Why did you bring trouble on us? The LORD brings trouble on you
today.' And all Israel stoned him" (Josh. 7:24-25). Achan lost everything—
including his life—and all for the sake of ill-gotten treasure.

Why did God treat Achan so harshly? It was partly to make an
example of Achan, so everyone would know that God is holy and that
he wants his people to be holy too. What better way to deter other
would-be thieves from even thinking about taking something that
belonged to God? But it was also a matter of justice. Achan was guilty
of breaking the eighth commandment. He had broken it, not just by
stealing from Jericho, but by stealing from God. This is what made his
crime so heinous. All the spoils of battle belonged to God. They were
designated for his house, where they would be dedicated to his praise.
What Achan took belonged to God, and thus he was guilty of the greatest of all thefts: robbing God of his glory.

## BETWEEN TWO THIEVES

Achan's sin and its punishment stand as a warning to anyone who steals anything that belongs to God. There are many ways to do this. One of the most obvious is to use our money for ourselves rather than giving generously back to God. Everything we have belongs to God. While he gives us the freedom to use what we need, he also calls us to give for the work of his gospel, and to neglect this duty is to rob God.

Most Christians would deny that they are stealing from God. They would deny it the way the Israelites denied it in the days of Malachi. When that faithful prophet told them that they were robbing God, they were deeply offended. "How do we rob him?" they asked. God answered by saying, "In your tithes and contributions. You are cursed with a curse, for you are robbing me, the whole nation of you. Bring the full tithes into the storehouse, that there may be food in my house. And thereby put me to the test, says the LORD of hosts, if I will not open the windows of heaven for you and pour down for you a blessing until there is no more need" (Mal. 3:8-9). A tithe is 10 percent, and this is a useful guideline for Christian giving, but God does not operate on a percentage basis. How much we give to the church is a matter of Christian freedom. However, we should always try to give more and more, and to give less than we can is spiritual theft.

Another way to rob God is to fail to give him the best of our time and our talents. All our abilities and opportunities come from God, and they are all to be used for his glory. The Bible says, "Whatever you do, work heartily, as for the Lord and not for men" (Col. 3:23). When we waste our time or fail to develop our gifts to their highest potential, we are robbing God.

Still another way to rob God is to break his law, and thus to deny him our obedience. Every violation of the Ten Commandments involves some form of theft. Bowing down to idols steals God's worship. Desecrating the Sabbath steals his holy day. Murder steals life; adultery steals purity; lying steals the truth. But the real theft is that every sin we commit dishonors God and thus steals the glory that our lives ought to give him.

Are you a thief? One of the benefits of studying the Ten

Commandments is that they confront us with our sin. When we explore their full implications, we discover that there is not a single commandment that we are able to keep in all its integrity. So the law condemns us. It declares, "You are the idolater. You are the foul-mouthed sinner. You are the Sabbath-breaker and the rebel. You are the murderer, the adulterer, and the thief." The law says all this to show that we are guilty sinners who need the gospel.

The gospel is the good news that Jesus died on the cross and rose again to give salvation to everyone who believes in him. Jesus died on the cross in the place of sinners—specifically, in the place of thieves. The Bible says that when Jesus was crucified, "two robbers were crucified with him, one on the right and one on the left" (Matt. 27:38), thus fulfilling the prophecy that the Savior would be "numbered with the transgressors" (Isa. 53:12). In his crucifixion, Jesus was considered a thief. Martin Luther explained the situation like this:

> Christ is innocent so far as His own Person is concerned; therefore He should not have been hanged from the tree. But because, according to the Law, every thief should have been hanged, therefore, according to the Law of Moses, Christ Himself should have been hanged; for He bore the person of a sinner and a thief—and not of one but of all sinners and thieves. For we are sinners and thieves, and therefore we are worthy of death and eternal damnation. But Christ took all our sins upon Himself, and for them He died on the cross. Therefore it was appropriate for Him to become a thief and, as Isaiah says (53:12), to be "numbered among the thieves."[17]

It is a well-known fact that Christ was crucified between two thieves. But as far as God's justice was concerned, there were really *three* thieves on the cross that day: two who died for their own crimes and one who took our sins upon himself. Luther gave this illustration:

> [A] magistrate regards someone as a criminal and punishes him if he catches him among thieves, even though the man has never committed anything evil or worthy of death. Christ was not only found among sinners; but of His own free will and by the will of the Father He wanted to be an associate of sinners, having assumed the flesh

and blood of those who were sinners and thieves and who were immersed in all sorts of sin. Therefore when the Law found Him among thieves, it condemned and executed Him as a thief.[18]

This is a great comfort to everyone who has ever broken the eighth commandment. When Christ died on the cross, he died for thieves, so that every thief who trusts in him will be saved. The first thief to be saved was the one hanging next to him on the cross, the one who said, "Jesus, remember me when you come into your kingdom" (Luke 23:42). Jesus gave him the answer he gives to every lawbreaker who turns to him in repentance and faith: "[Y]ou will be with me in paradise" (Luke 23:43).

## STUDY QUESTIONS

1. What is your most valued possession? If your home were on fire, what would you run back to retrieve?
2. What forms of stealing are considered "okay," even by Christians?
3. Have you ever been a victim of theft—by an employer, salesman, business partner, or friend? Describe the situation and how you responded to it.
4. Why is stealing a sin against God?
5. How does it change the way we treat the things we own to think of them as belonging to God?
6. What attitudes and actions does good stewardship require?
7. What are some specific ways you can be a better steward of what God has given you? (Think of various categories: possessions, time, talents, opportunities, etc.)
8. Share about a time when you gave generously and noticed that money or possessions lost some of their power over you. Read Joshua 6:16-21; 7:1; 7:10-26.
9. What rules were the soldiers given regarding plunder? Why did Joshua make these rules?
10. What actions and thoughts led up to Achan's sin?
11. What were the consequences—for Achan and Israel—of Achan's sin? Does this punishment seem severe? Why or why not?
12. What principles can we take from this story and apply to our own lives?

# 12

# THE NINTH COMMANDMENT:
# TO TELL THE TRUTH

*You shall not bear false witness against your neighbor.*
EXODUS 20:16

In December 2001 George O'Leary was on top of the world. He had just been named head football coach at the University of Notre Dame—the Fighting Irish. It was the dream of a lifetime. O'Leary was in charge of one of the most prestigious sports programs in the world.

Then two days later, at the end of his first day on the job, the call came. A reporter had been trying to contact some of the guys who had played college football with O'Leary back at New Hampshire. The strange thing was that nobody could remember anyone named George O'Leary. So Notre Dame's sports information director telephoned to check it out. O'Leary reluctantly admitted that he hadn't actually *played* football at New Hampshire. Let's see, he had a knee injury one year, then he had mono . . . someone must have made a mistake.

Indeed, someone *had* made a mistake, and the next day the reporter called to say that he had documentation. Years before, when O'Leary applied for a job at Syracuse, he had been asked for information about his athletic background. Some of what he provided was true, like the high school football championships, but somehow it didn't look impressive enough; so the applicant decided to improve his résumé. There it was twenty-one years later, in his own handwriting: "College—Univ. of New Hampshire—3 yr. lettered." It was just a small lie, really, but it was big enough to turn O'Leary's dream into a nightmare, cost-ing him not only his job, but his reputation.

Perhaps the most telling response came from the coach's brother, who said, "Is anyone trying to tell me that résumés are truthful? In the America we live in, the willingness to lie on a résumé is an indication of how much you want the job."[1] Sadly, this attitude is all too typical. According to a survey of nearly three million job applicants, nearly 50 percent of American résumés contain one or more falsehoods.[2]

We all know that lying is wrong; yet we are so used to massaging the truth for personal advantage that we have trouble holding the line against falsehood. A columnist for *Time* magazine wrote: "The injunc-tion against bearing false witness, branded in stone and brought down by Moses from the mountaintop, has always provoked ambivalent, con-flicting emotions. On the one hand, nearly everybody condemns lying. On the other, nearly everyone does it every day." Then he asked this question: "How many of the Ten Commandments can be broken so easily and with so little risk of detection over the telephone?"[3]

## NOTHING BUT THE TRUTH

Long before anyone ever lied over the phone, God gave his people the ninth commandment: "You shall not bear false witness against your neighbor" (Exod. 20:16; NIV: "give false testimony"). The immediate context for this commandment is a court of law; it governs the legal testimony a witness gives in a public trial before a jury. The word "neighbor" suggests a trial that takes place within the covenant com-munity (see Lev. 19:8), but it is not limited to that. After all, Jesus taught that everyone is our neighbor (see Luke 10:25-37). Therefore, what God most specifically condemns in the ninth commandment is a lying witness, someone who testifies falsely against anyone accused of a crime.

To understand this commandment it helps to know more about the justice system in the ancient world. In those days, people who were charged with a crime had little protection. They were not presumed innocent until proven guilty, but presumed guilty until proven inno-cent. There were few standards for the presentation of evidence, and sometimes the accused didn't even get the chance to mount a defense. Furthermore, most ancient courts were willing to convict someone on the strength of a single witness.

Obviously, this whole legal system was subject to abuse, which explains why God stated the ninth commandment the way that he did: "You shall not bear false witness against your neighbor" (Exod. 20:16). In the days before forensic evidence, almost everything depended on the witness. Usually it came down to one person's word against another's, and since many crimes were treated as capital offenses, often the defendant's life was at stake. The words of a false witness could be fatal.

In the wisdom and providence of God, the situation was different in Israel. When a member of the covenant community was put on trial, he appeared before a jury of elders. There had to be more than one witness, for as God said in his law, "A single witness shall not suffice against a person for any crime or for any wrong in connection with any offense that he has committed. Only on the evidence of two witnesses or three witnesses shall a charge be established" (Deut. 19:15). This was especially important in a trial for a capital offense: No one could be put to death by a single witness (Num. 35:30; Deut. 17:6).

Another protection concerned the execution of judgment. When someone was sentenced to die, his accuser had to throw the first stone (Deut. 17:7; cf. John 8:7). This was a significant safeguard because it is one thing to accuse someone, but quite another to put him to death. Furthermore, if the allegations proved to be false, the accuser was punished: "The judges shall inquire diligently, and if the witness is a false witness and has accused his brother falsely, then you shall do to him as he had meant to do to his brother" (Deut. 19:18-19). These legal safeguards were designed to protect the innocent from injustice. God's people were not allowed to bear false witness against one another. As the prophet Zechariah later said: "Speak the truth to one other, render in your gates judgments that are true and make for peace" (Zech. 8:16b).

These principles are still relevant for trials today, whether civil or ecclesiastical. Many people have lost confidence in public justice, and it can only be restored by the rejection of every form of falsehood. Where there is no truth, there can be no justice. Jochem Douma states that when we consider the ninth commandment,

> we must always include reference to the significance of the system of justice. Past interpreters of the ninth commandment never hesitated to mention various persons who have a role in administering justice. These interpreters would demand of a *judge* that he be incorruptible and not judge rashly. . . . They required of the *accuser* that he never accuse somebody unnecessarily, out of antipathy or revenge. They expected the *witness* to tell the truth and nothing but the truth. The *lawyer* was forbidden to call black white and white black, even when he had the valuable function of coming to the aid of the accused and demanding that proof of guilt—if there was any—be airtight. These interpreters required the *accused* to confess his guilt where such guilt was proved.[4]

In other words, everyone involved in the entire legal process has an obligation to maintain the truth, the whole truth, and nothing but the truth.

## LIAR, LIAR!

A courtroom is not the only place where someone can give false testimony. Remember how the Ten Commandments work. What they forbid is the most extreme form of any particular sin. Murder is the worst kind of hatred, adultery is the most destructive sexual sin, and so on. Similarly, the ninth commandment forbids the deadliest lie: one that condemns an innocent man for a crime he did not commit.

According to "the rule of categories" (see Chapter 3), each commandment also applies to lesser sins of the same kind. In the case of the ninth commandment, the underlying principle is that God forbids every form of falsehood. This is confirmed by the prophet Hosea, who accused the Israelites of "swearing, lying, murder, stealing, and committing adultery" (Hos. 4:2a). Hosea was clearly referring to the Ten Commandments, but rather than using the Hebrew term for false testimony (*shaqar*), he used a more general word that refers to any kind of lying (*kachash*). The ninth commandment means "You shall not lie." It is not just about the false testimony that people give in court, but also about the lies they tell their neighbors over the backyard fence and the rumors they whisper between the pews at church.

There are many different ways to lie. *Roget's Thesaurus* offers an impressive list of synonyms. A falsehood can be described as an invention, an equivocation, a falsification, a fabrication, or a prevarication. Dishonesty also comes in all different sizes. There are the big lies—the whoppers and the grand deceptions. Then there are all the little lies we tell—the half-truths, the flatteries, and the fibs. What we say may be true, as far as it goes, but we leave out the details that might put us at a disadvantage. Or we say something that is technically true, yet nevertheless intended to deceive. We overstate our accomplishments, putting ourselves in the best possible light. At the same time we exaggerate other people's failings, thinking and saying the worst about others. We mislead, misquote, and misinterpret. We twist people's words, taking things out of context. In these and many other ways, we exchange the truth for a lie.

The most blatant violation of the ninth commandment is any lie that harms someone else. What is especially forbidden is falsehood *against* our neighbor. God has given us the capacity to speak so that we can use our words to praise him and to bless others. However, our speech is corrupted by our sin; so it has the power to do great damage. The apostle James said that the tongue "stain[s] the whole body, setting on fire the entire course of life, [being] set on fire by hell" (James 3:6). Like a massive forest fire set by a single careless individual, a lying tongue consumes everything in its path. James also said, "no human being can tame the tongue. It is a restless evil, full of deadly poison" (James 3:8). Truly the tongue is the most dangerous part of the body!

Given how dangerous words can be, it is not surprising that when the New Testament lists the sins we need to avoid, it often tells us to watch what we say. The apostle Paul warned the Corinthians about quarreling, slander, and gossip (2 Cor. 12:20). He told the Galatians that discord and dissensions were acts of the sinful nature (Gal. 5:19-20). He told the Ephesians to get rid of slander and malice (Eph. 4:31). These sins of speech all violate the ninth commandment, because rather than being used to build people up, words are used to tear them down.

When the Bible condemns gossip, it means something more than just casual talk about other people's business. Gossip is talking about people in a way that damages their reputation with others. Reputations are important. The Bible says, "A good name is to be chosen rather than great riches, and favor is better than silver or gold" (Prov. 22:1). One problem with gossip is that it tries to steal this treasure. When this is done in speech, it is called slander; when it appears in print, it is called libel. Either way, the victims of gossip never get to defend themselves. They never have a chance to explain their circumstances, clarify their motives, or correct the misconceptions people have about them. Instead, they are charged, tried, and convicted in the court of public opinion.

Most gossip contains a fair amount of misinformation. People who gossip trade in hearsay, rumor, innuendo, and other notoriously unreliable forms of communication. However, even true words can violate the ninth commandment. Sometimes what a gossip reports is true, but it is said to the wrong person or for the wrong reason, to the injury of others. The words may contain some version of the truth, but the testimony is false because it is malicious. Jochem Douma comments:

> Perhaps the one spreading gossip is not lying, but he or she is being untruthful: saying things that are true, but in the context of slander, is deceitful. The neighbor's mistakes, faults, and shortcomings are discussed in minute detail. People realize this kind of chatter gets them an attentive audience. For it is a universal phenomenon that we would rather hear something bad about our neighbor than something good. And something dirty always sticks long after the conversation has died. As Martin Luther put it in his Large Catechism, reputation is something quickly stolen, but not quickly returned.[5]

Gossip is such a common sin that we forget how ungodly it is, but before we open our mouths and start talking about someone else, we need to ask ourselves some hard questions: *Is what I am about to say true? If so, does it really need to be said to this person in this conversation? Would I put it this way if the person I'm talking about were here to listen?* If our words fail these simple tests, then it would be better for us not to speak at all.

There is another side to this too. As wrong as it is to gossip, it is just as wrong to listen to gossip. This too is injurious to the truth. According to an old rabbinic saying, slander "kills three: the one who speaks it, the one who listens to it, and the one about whom it is spoken."[6] The Puritan Thomas Watson made a similar point when he said, "He that raises a slander, carries the devil in his tongue; and he that receives it, carries the devil in his ear."[7] Watson was right: Whenever we listen to gossip, we become implicated in its sin. We get drawn into making judgments about others when it is not our place to judge. The problem is that most of us like to hear a little gossip. We have an appetite for it, especially if it's juicy. According to Proverbs, "The words of a whisperer are like delicious morsels; they go down into the inner parts of the body" (Prov. 18:8). But no matter how tasty it is, gossip is still poison.

What should we do when someone tries to tell us something we know we shouldn't hear? Interrupt! We should say, "You know, this is starting to sound like gossip; we need to talk about something else." Or we should say, "Wait, before you say anything more, why don't we stop and pray about this?" Then, after bringing the matter before the Lord, we can say, "Now, what was it you wanted to talk about?" Or we should say, "I'm sorry, I'm not sure I can listen to any more of this. Tell me, have you gone and spoken about it to the people involved? Because if you haven't, it wouldn't be right for us to talk about it."

All too often, people who like to complain about others are unwilling to do the hard spiritual work of helping them grow in godliness. But the Bible is very clear about the right way to deal with the sins of others. First, before talking with anyone else, we need to go directly to them and discuss it (Matt. 18:15). If they are not willing to confess their sin, there are appropriate ways to involve other people from the church in addressing the issue. But the only time we can talk about someone else's sin is when it is our God-given responsibility to give them spiritual help. Otherwise, it is none of our business. If only everyone would follow these simple guidelines, there would be no one left for gossips to talk to!

## THE BEST POLICY

According to "the two-sided rule" (see Chapter 3), there is something that each commandment forbids and also something that it requires. For the ninth commandment this rule is easy to apply. If lying is forbidden, then what is required is telling the truth.

It is not easy to stand up for the truth. George Orwell said, "In a time of universal deceit, telling the truth is a revolutionary act."[8] If that is true, then Christians are called to be revolutionaries, because we are certainly living in a time of universal deceit, when everyone seems to be lying. As we saw in the previous chapter, there are the lies that business people tell—all the ways they put their own spin on the truth. There are the lies that academics tell. These days the biggest lie on campus is that there is no universal truth, only different versions of reality. This is part of what some scholars call postmodernism. It is the big lie that makes it possible for academics to tell all sorts of other lies. Then there are all the lies that politicians tell, especially during campaign season. After all the attack ads and broken promises, voters are more cynical than ever. We often find ourselves asking the question *Time* magazine posed before a recent presidential election: "Is anyone telling the truth in this campaign?"[9] There are also the lies that journalists tell. When the story is more important than the truth, the line between fact and fiction gets blurry. With all the lies going around, it is hardly surprising to learn that fewer than half of Christian young people believe there is an objective standard of truth.[10]

In a culture of lies—what Charles Colson has termed a "Post-Truth Society"[11]—we are called to be people of the truth. If we are scholars, we are called to be careful with our quotations and fair with our criticisms. If we are politicians, we are called to be honest about our record, as well as that of our opponents. If we are in business, we are called to deal honestly with people. If we are journalists, we are called to get the story straight. These are only examples, of course. Every discipline has its own deceptions, but whatever lies people tell in our line of work, *we* are called to tell the truth.

The reason we are called to be people of the truth is because we serve a truth-telling God. God the Father is true. The Bible says, "Let

God be true though every one were a liar" (Rom. 3:4). God the Son is true. The Bible says that he came "from the Father, full of grace and truth" (John 1:14), and "there was no deceit in his mouth" (Isa. 53:9), for he is truth personified. Jesus said, "I am . . . the truth" (John 14:6), and "Everyone who is of the truth listens to my voice" (John 18:37). God the Holy Spirit is also true. In fact, the Bible calls him "the Spirit of truth" (1 John 4:6). If God is true—Father, Son, and Holy Spirit— then he must be true to his word. And he is. Everything that God has ever said—including every word on every page of the Bible—is absolutely, unmistakably, and entirely true. Therefore, we can always take God at his word: "your word is truth" (John 17:17b).

If God is true to us, then we must be true to him, and also to one another. The Scripture says, "You shall not deal falsely; you shall not lie to one another. You shall not swear by my name falsely, and so profane the name of your God: I am the LORD" (Lev. 19:11-12). It also says, "having put away falsehood, let each of you speak the truth with his neighbor, for we are all members one of another" (Eph. 4:25). John Calvin summarized the biblical teaching as follows: "The purpose of this commandment is: since God (who is truth) abhors a lie, we must practice truth without deceit toward one another."[12] Honesty really is the best policy, not simply because it helps us get along with other people, but because our interpersonal communication ought to be grounded in the character of God.

Telling the truth means thinking and saying the best about people. Rather than being suspicious of their motives, we should put the best construction on what they have said or done. Telling the truth also means defending people when they are unfairly attacked. All too often, people stand by in silence. But as William Barclay writes, "It is an important principle that a cowardly or careless and irresponsible silence can be as senseless a crime as false and lying speech. The sin of silence is as real as the sin of speech."[13]

Sometimes sin needs to be confronted, and in those cases keeping the ninth commandment means "speaking the truth *in love*" (Eph. 4:15, emphasis added). Unfortunately, the love is usually what's missing. Some Christians are more than willing to "tell it like it is," but there is something brutal about their honesty. Understand that keeping the ninth commandment does *not* mean saying whatever comes to mind. There are many situations in life when it is better to say nothing at all. What the ninth commandment means is saying the honest thing—when it is our duty to say it—in a loving way.

People sometimes wonder whether there is ever a time when it is permissible to lie. What about telling a tall tale for comic effect or pulling someone's leg? Provided they are told with affection, these kinds of jokes really do not violate the ninth commandment because ultimately there is no intention to deceive. However, it is always wrong to use humor to damage someone else's dignity.

What about times of warfare or persecution? Is it okay to lie then? Going back to Augustine, many theologians have said no. However, there were a number of incidents in the Bible when deception was not condemned. Consider, for example, the Hebrew midwives Shiphrah and Puah, who deceived Pharaoh to avert genocide. There was Rahab, who deceived the Canaanites to save Joshua's spies. There was Gideon, who used concealment as a stratagem of war. The Bible does not condemn these falsehoods. However, each of them was told to prevent evil men from committing even greater sins, such as murder. But we should not use these extreme cases to justify falsehood when we are in a tight spot or when we think the end justifies our means. Even in those rare cases when a lie seems necessary to protect others, it is still wrong in itself.

## THE DROP-DEAD LIE

There are lots of liars in the Bible. There was the serpent who lied to Eve in the Garden of Eden. There was Jacob who tricked his brother into selling his birthright. There were the men Jezebel bribed to testify against Naboth. There were the lying prophets who criticized Jeremiah. And of course there were all the people who told lies about Jesus Christ. But the most terrifying story of deception comes from the early church. It's the story of a husband and wife and their drop-dead lie.

Ananias and Sapphira were members of the first church in Jerusalem. It was an exciting time to be a Christian. Jesus had returned to heaven and had poured out his Spirit on the church. The apostles were preaching the gospel and performing miraculous signs and wonders. People were coming to faith in Christ every day!

Almost as remarkable was the way the first Christians cared for one another's practical needs. The Bible says: "Now the full number of those who believed were of one heart and soul, and no one said that any of the things that belonged to him was his own, but they had everything in common. . . . There was not a needy person among them, for as many as were owners of lands or houses sold them and brought the proceeds of what was sold and laid it at the apostles' feet, and it was distributed to each as any had need" (Acts 4:32, 34-35; cf. 2:45). When the first Christians did this, they were saying something significant. They were testifying that since they had found their treasure in Jesus Christ, they were willing to give everything they had for the work of his kingdom. When they sold their property and gave it all back to God, it was a public gesture of total commitment to Christ.

One of the people who did this was a man from Cyprus named Joseph. The Bible says that he "sold a field that belonged to him and brought the money and laid it at the apostles' feet" (Acts 4:36-37). Joseph wasn't even from Jerusalem; yet he gave to God's work in that great city. It was such a generous offering that the apostles gave him a new nickname. They called him Barnabas, which means "Son of Encouragement."

Ananias and Sapphira saw what Barnabas did. They also noticed how his offering enhanced his reputation in the church. The couple realized that if they wanted to get the kind of attention they thought they deserved, they needed to make a major donation to the apostles, and so they did: "A man named Ananias, with his wife Sapphira, sold a piece of property, and with his wife's knowledge he kept back for himself some of the proceeds and brought only a part of it and laid it at the apostles' feet" (Acts 5:1-2). *No one will ever know*, they must have thought to themselves.

Understand that Ananias and Sapphira had the right to use their property any way they wanted. They were not required—by God or by anyone else—to sell their field. And once they sold it, they were not obligated to give all their money to God. It was a matter of stewardship, and they had the freedom to use what they had however they chose. God would have accepted them if they had given only some of it to the church, or even none at all, as long as ultimately they did it for his glory.

The problem was not what Ananias and Sapphira did, but what they said. They said they were paying God full price when in fact they were taking a discount. It's not entirely clear how Ananias said this. Maybe he said it out loud, or maybe it was simply implied by the act of putting money at the apostles' feet. But however he did it, Ananias lied. He acted like he had done something totally for God when in fact he had done it partly for God and partly for himself.

Somehow Peter knew what Ananias had done, because no sooner had he received the offering than he gave this stinging rebuke: "Ananias, why has Satan filled your heart to lie to the Holy Spirit and to keep back for yourself part of the proceeds for the land? While it remained unsold, did it not remain your own? And after it was sold, was it not at your disposal? Why is it that you have contrived this deed in your heart? You have not lied to men but to God" (Acts 5:3-4).

Peter said three important things to Ananias. First, he told Ananias what his sin was. It was not primarily a sin of theft, or even of covetousness, but of deception. What he broke was the ninth commandment, not just the eighth and the tenth commandments.

Second, Peter told Ananias where his sin came from. His sin came from a heart infected by the poison of demonic deception. Satan is the one who filled Ananias's heart with lies, which is not surprising because Satan was a liar from the very beginning. Jesus called him "a liar and the father of lies" (John 8:44). Ultimately every lie comes from Satan. This helps us understand why lying is so despicable and why God hates it so much (see Prov. 6:16-19; Zech. 8:17). Whereas every truth comes from our Father in heaven, every lie comes from the devil himself.

The third thing Peter did was to tell Ananias whom he had sinned against. He had not sinned primarily against Peter and his apostolic authority, or even against the church, but against God first and foremost. Peter said that Ananias "lie[d] to the Holy Spirit" (Acts 5:3). Then he said, "You have not lied to men but to God" (Acts 5:4). This is what lying really is: a sin against the God of all truth.

Here again—as with so many other commandments—we are confronted with the absolute folly of sin. How can anyone lie to God and expect to get away with it? And of course he didn't get away with it: "When Ananias heard these words, he fell down and breathed his last. And great fear came upon all who heard of it. The young men rose and wrapped him up and carried him out and buried him" (Acts 5:5-6). End of story, except that for some reason Sapphira didn't hear about it: "After an interval of about three hours his wife came in, not knowing what had happened" (Acts 5:7). Peter gave her a chance to repent of her sin. He said, "Tell me whether you sold the land for so much" (Acts 5:8a). The price Peter mentioned was not the full price of the sale; it was only the amount of the offering, as Sapphira well knew. But she said, "Yes, for so much" (Acts 5:8b).

Whenever we lie, there is always the danger that we will get trapped in the web of our own deception. But in this case Sapphira never saw it coming. First Peter accused her of deception. "How is it that you have agreed together to test the Spirit of the Lord?" he asked (Acts 5:9a). Then with the impeccable timing of God's justice, he said, "Behold, the feet of those who have buried your husband are at the door, and they will carry you out" (Acts 5:9b). No sooner had the men stepped across the threshold than they had to turn around and go back to the burial ground because "immediately she fell down at his feet and breathed her last. When the young men came in they found her dead, and they carried her out and buried her beside her husband" (Acts 5:10).

## THE TRUTH ABOUT US

Are you shocked by what God did to Ananias and Sapphira? Imagine what it would be like if this happened at your church. Imagine a well-respected couple dropping dead at the pastor's feet for what most people would consider a trivial deception—a little white lie about how much they put in the offering plate. Everyone would be amazed . . . and afraid, which is exactly how people responded in Jerusalem. The Bible says, "Great fear came upon the whole church and upon all who heard of these events" (Acts 5:11). No kidding! The whole episode sent a chill down their collective spine. The punishment was so severe and so sudden. One day Ananias and Sapphira were in church, singing hymns and going to Bible study. The next day they were dead! Within a matter of hours they were both dragged off and buried. Was it really fair for God to do that?

Of course it was fair! It was fair because lying is a deadly sin. King David said, "You destroy those who speak lies" (Ps. 5:6a), and when Ananias and Sapphira dropped dead, his words came true. David also asked this question: "O LORD, who shall sojourn in your tent? Who shall dwell on your holy hill?" (Ps. 15:1). The king answered, "He . . . who speaks truth in his heart; who does not slander with his tongue" (Ps. 15:2-3). The implication is that the only people who are worthy to enter the kingdom of God are people who keep the ninth commandment. But what about people who break it? Jesus said that the place where liars belong is "in the lake that burns with fire and sulfur" (Rev. 21:8), and that "everyone who loves and practices falsehood" will be shut out from his eternal city forever (Rev. 22:15). Every liar deserves to die, and after that, to suffer God's eternal wrath against sin.

No wonder everyone was scared: What happened to Ananias and Sapphira was a preview of the judgment to come. They were scared because they knew that they were liars too. They realized that what Ananias and Sapphira had done was no worse than many of the lies that they had told. It was just an exaggeration, that's all—an error in mathematics. If God killed people for something like that, then they deserved to die too, and pretty soon there wouldn't be any church left! No doubt for weeks afterwards they were very careful not to claim that they had done anything more for God than they actually had!

If there is one thing God hates, it is the lies that Christians tell to make themselves look more righteous than they really are. Our testimony is that we are unrighteous, that there is no way we could ever be saved apart from the grace of God in Jesus Christ. The real truth about us is that we are so guilty that the very Son of God had to be crucified to pay for our sins. If that is true, then why would we ever pretend to be anything more than sinners saved by grace? To act like we have it spiritually together is a lie. But more than that, it is a denial of the grace of God, which alone has the power to save us.

At a local church meeting another pastor confronted me. He rebuked me for being a legalist, for not demonstrating God's grace. Frankly, he was a little forward, and I'm not sure his rebuke was fair. But what could I say? He was right, of course. I am a Pharisee at heart. And that's not the worst of it either. I am a lawbreaker who likes to follow other gods. Even though I have a sacred ministry, I profane God's name. I am guilty of murderous intentions, lustful thoughts, covetous desires. And yet I am able to cover most of that up most of the time (or at least I think I can). But that's the real truth about me, the truth that people would be able to see if it weren't covered up with so many lies.

What's the truth about you? What lies have you been telling? What are the lies you tell yourself? What are the lies you try to sell to others? The biggest lie is the one we live with every day, the lie we work so hard to maintain. It is the lie that we are on the inside what we pretend to be on the outside. But Jesus said, "Woe to you . . . hypocrites! . . . you . . . outwardly appear righteous to others, but within you are full of hypocrisy and lawlessness" (Matt. 23:27-28).

Something wonderful happens when we're willing to confess the real truth about ourselves and all our sin. What happens is that we are able to see the real truth about Jesus and what he has done for our salvation. It is only when we tell the truth about our sin that we are able to see how much we need a Savior—the Savior who said, "you will know the truth, and the truth will set you free" (John 8:32).

## STUDY QUESTIONS

1. What is the biggest lie you have ever been told? (It could be by someone you know or someone in the media.) How did you react when you learned the truth?
2. What safeguards against injustice did God provide in his law?
3. What forms of lying are easiest for Christians to justify, and why?
4. What are some of the results and consequences of these "little" lies?
5. What makes gossip such a damaging form of lying (even if parts of what is said are true)?
6. What are some practical ways to avoid spreading or listening to gossip or other types of false testimony?
7. In what everyday life situations are you called to stand up for the truth?

8.  What is your response to someone who says there is no universal truth—how would you defend the idea of absolute truth?
9.  Read Acts 4:32—5:11. What made Ananias and Sapphira's sin so severe?
10. How do you think this situation affected the church? How would a similar situation affect your church?
11. What lies are you tempted to tell yourself or others?
12. Tell about a time you told the truth when it would have been easier to lie. What were the results of standing up for the truth?

# 13

## THE TENTH COMMANDMENT:
## BEING CONTENT

*You shall not covet your neighbor's house; you shall not covet your neighbor's wife, or his male servant, or his female servant, or his ox, or his donkey, or anything that is your neighbor's.*

EXODUS 20:17

Jesus said many things that stand directly at odds with the way most people live. He said, "Blessed are the meek, for they shall inherit the earth" (Matt. 5:5), and "Love your enemies, do good to those who hate you" (Luke 6:27). But of all the things that Jesus said, none contradicts the values of our consumer culture more directly than this: "Take care, and be on your guard against all covetousness, for one's life does not consist in the abundance of his possessions" (Luke 12:15).

But of course today most Americans seem to believe that life *does* consist in the abundance of our possessions. We are always trying to get more for less, always spending but never satisfied. One pastor confessed:

> I belong to the Cult of the Next Thing. It's dangerously easy to get enlisted. It happens by default—not by choosing the cult, but by failing to resist it. The Cult of the Next Thing is consumerism cast in religious terms. It has its own litany of sacred words: *more, you deserve it, new, faster, cleaner, brighter*. It has its own deep-rooted liturgy: *charge it, instant credit, no down-payment, deferred payment, no interest for three months*. It has its own preachers, evangelists, prophets, and

apostles: ad men, pitchmen, and celebrity sponsors. It has, of course, its own shrines, chapels, temples, meccas: malls, superstores, club warehouses. It has its own sacraments: credit and debit cards. It has its own ecstatic experience: the spending spree. The Cult of the Next Thing's central message proclaims, "Crave and spend, for the Kingdom of Stuff is here."[1]

Why are we so tempted to belong to the Cult of the Next Thing? It is because our hearts are full of sinful desire. Rather than being satisfied with what we have, we always crave something else. Instead of being content, we covet.

## UNHOLY DESIRE

Coveting is strictly forbidden by the tenth commandment: "You shall not covet your neighbor's house; you shall not covet your neighbor's wife, or his male servant, or his female servant, or his ox, or his donkey, or anything that is your neighbor's" (Exod. 20:17).

What does it mean to covet? To covet is to crave, to yearn for, to hanker after something that belongs to someone else. We covet whenever we set our hearts on anything that is not rightfully ours. John Mackay calls coveting "a consuming desire to possess in a wrong way something belonging to another."[2] It's not simply wanting something we don't have; it's wanting something that someone else has. Since coveting has to do with wanting, it is a sin of desire. The Puritan Thomas Watson defined it as "an insatiable desire of getting the world."[3] By "the world" he meant any of the things that this world has to offer, as opposed to the spiritual things that can only come from God. A more recent commentator has described coveting as "an inordinate, ungoverned, selfish desire for something."[4]

Not all desires are selfish, of course. God made us to be creatures of desire. Our desire for food reminds us to eat. Our desire to do something useful motivates us to work. Our desire for friendship draws us into community. Our desire for intimacy—including sexual intimacy— may drive us to get married. We have many healthy desires, including the deepest of all desires, which is to know God. But like everything else about us, our desires are corrupted by sin. We often want the wrong thing, in the wrong way, at the wrong time, and for the wrong reason, and this is what the tenth commandment rules out. According to the Westminster Shorter Catechism, "The tenth commandment forbiddeth all discontentment with our own estate, envying or grieving at the good of our neighbor, and all inordinate motions and affections to anything that is his" (A. 81).

There is always something envious about coveting. This goes all the way back to the Garden of Eden. Before Eve took the forbidden fruit, she coveted it (Gen. 3:6). This was not because she admired it as a piece of fruit, but because Satan tempted her to envy by telling her that if she ate it, she would be like God. Eve took the fruit to gain something she was not intended to have.

We have been sinning this way ever since. One good place to see it is in a nursery full of toddlers. Nothing arouses a child's interest in a toy like seeing it in the hands of another child, and the transition from coveting to stealing is almost instantaneous. Adults are more subtle, but we are guilty of the same sin. Coveting is what causes that little twinge of disappointment whenever someone else gets what we want. It's how we react when a coworker gets the promotion, when our roommate finds romance and we are still single, or when a friend goes where we can only dream of going for vacation. We are always comparing ourselves to others, and frankly we resent it when we don't get what they have. The apostle James asked, "What causes quarrels and what causes fights among you? Is it not this, that your passions are at war within you? You desire and do not have, so you murder. You covet and cannot obtain, so you fight and quarrel" (James 4:1-2a).

There are all kinds of things to covet. Usually we associate coveting with material possessions, and rightly so. The tenth commandment mentions various forms of property, such as houses, servants, and livestock. Today most people are less interested in donkeys and oxen than they were back then, but the commandment still stands. We covet things like bigger houses, faster cars, and better entertainment. We also covet clothes with designer labels, appliances with more features, gadgets from mail-order catalogs, trinkets from the shopping networks, and a million other trivial products.

Consumption has become our way of life. No matter how much we have, we always want more, and our desire for newer and better things is almost insatiable. This is what makes advertising so successful: our inability to keep the tenth commandment. Has there ever been a more covetous country than the United States of America? The quintessential American writer Ralph Waldo Emerson said, "Things are in the saddle and ride mankind." We usually call it "chasing the American dream," but the Bible calls it coveting.

What else do we covet? The tenth commandment mentions "your neighbor's wife" (Exod. 20:17). This is a reminder that sex can be one of our most unruly desires. Whenever we engage in sexual fantasy, we are guilty of a kind of coveting. We are feeding a sinful desire that soon will demand to be gratified.

To summarize, the tenth commandment lists several things that we are tempted to covet. However, the list is not meant to be complete because it ends by saying, "or anything that is your neighbor's" (Exod. 20:17). This closes any last loophole. The items listed are not exhaustive; they are only suggestive. What we are forbidden to covet is anything at all. We may not covet other people's attributes: age, looks, brains, or talents. We may not covet their situation in life: marriage, singleness, children. We may not covet spiritual attainments, like a more prominent place of ministry in the church or wider recognition of our spiritual gifts. We are not allowed to covet anything at all. God's law rules out every unlawful desire.

## DEADLY DESIRE

Most people think of coveting as a relatively minor sin. Somehow it doesn't seem to be in the same league with the "big" sins like murder and adultery. As one commentator confessed, "It has occurred to me that whoever approved the final order of these commandments didn't have much of a sense of suspense or climax. He put all of those dramatic, intriguing sins like stealing, adultery, and murder first. Then he ended with coveting. It would have seemed more logical to begin with the bland, throw-away sin like coveting, and then work up to the big stuff."[5]

Whenever we are tempted to minimize the evil of coveting, however, we need to remember that God included it in the Ten Commandments. Furthermore, coveting is condemned everywhere else in the Bible. Jesus listed it right up there with theft, murder, and adultery (Mark 7:21-22). The apostle Paul claimed that people who covet will not inherit the kingdom of God (1 Cor. 6:9-10). He also said, "For you may be sure of this, that everyone who is sexually immoral or impure, or who is covetous (that is, an idolater), has no inheritance in the kingdom of Christ and God" (Eph. 5:5; cf. Col. 3:5). The Puritan Thomas Watson gave a vivid illustration. He said, "As a ferryman takes in so many passengers to increase his fare, that he sinks his boat; so a covetous man takes in so much gold to increase his estate, that he drowns himself in perdition."[6] Coveting can sink us down to hell as fast as any other sin.

Another reason coveting is evil is because it causes many other sins. It is such an intense desire that almost inevitably it leads people to break other commandments. The person who covets goes beyond simply wanting something to plotting how to get it. A good example is Achan, the thief we encountered when we studied the eighth commandment. The Bible says that before Achan stole treasure from Jericho, he coveted it (Josh. 7:21). This means something more than that he admired it. It means that he wanted it so badly that he started scheming how to get it. And once he came up with a workable plan, he went ahead and committed the sin. The sinful desire that Achan treasured in his heart took control of his will, until he couldn't keep his hands off someone else's stuff.

This is how sinful deeds always start—with sinful desire. First we see something we want. Then we start thinking about how much we want it, and why. Soon it starts to dominate our thoughts, until finally it becomes an obsession. By the time we reach this point, sin will have its way with us. The apostle James explained that "each person is tempted when he is lured and enticed by his own desire. Then desire when it has conceived gives birth to sin, and sin when it is fully grown brings forth death" (James 1:14-15). Evil desire gives birth to sin and finally to death.

This is why God included coveting in the Ten Commandments:

Unholy desires quickly turn into deadly desires. As the Scripture says, "Those who desire to get rich fall into temptation, into a snare, into many senseless and harmful desires that plunge men into ruin and destruction" (1 Tim. 6:9). Coveting can be just as fatal as any other sin, which should cause us to ask a very practical question: What does my heart desire, and where will that desire lead me in the end?

## THE HEART OF THE MATTER

There is something unusual about the tenth commandment that distinguishes it from the rest of the Decalogue: It goes straight to the heart. The other nine commandments explicitly condemn outward actions like making idols, working on the Sabbath, and killing innocent victims. As we have seen, these commandments also forbid sins of the heart like hatred and lust. According to our "inside/outside rule" (see Chapter 3), each commandment governs inward attitudes as well as outward actions. But the first nine commandments generally start on the outside and then work their way in as we learn how to apply them.

What is different about the tenth commandment is that it starts on the inside. The commandment about coveting is not concerned with what we do, in the first instance, but with what we *want* to do. It governs our internal desires. This has led some commentators to wonder if perhaps the tenth commandment might be superfluous. Isn't coveting really included in the eighth commandment? If God's law against stealing condemns our greedy hearts as well as our thieving hands, then why do we need the tenth commandment?

The answer is that the tenth commandment makes explicit what the other commandments only imply—namely, that God requires inward as well as outward obedience. If God had not given us the tenth commandment, we might be tempted to think that outward obedience is all we need to offer. But the tenth commandment proves that God judges the heart. In case anyone misses the point, the command against coveting shows that God's law is spiritual.

Michael Horton tells of the rabbi who said to him, "You know, one of the greatest differences between our two religions is this idea that you've committed a sin just by desiring or thinking it. We believe you have to actually commit the physical act before it's really sin. Otherwise, we'd be sinning all the time!"[7] The rabbi was right: If God judges us for what is inside as well as for what is outside, then we are all sinning all the time. This is *precisely* what the tenth commandment is intended to teach. Martin Luther said, "This last commandment, then, is addressed not to those whom the world considers wicked rogues, but precisely to the most upright—to people who wish to be commended as honest and virtuous because they have not offended against the preceding commandments."[8] As Luther recognized, this commandment—more than any other—convinces us we are sinners. It does this for the gracious purpose of showing us that we need a Savior.

The tenth commandment seems to have had this effect in the life of the apostle Paul. Paul went through the first part of his life assuming that he could measure up to the perfect standard of God's law. He did not murder; he did not commit adultery; he did not steal; he did not lie—at least not outwardly. Then Paul came to the tenth commandment, and the law exposed his sin. Here is how he described his experience: "If it had not been for the law, I would not have known sin. I would not have known what it is to covet if the law had not said, 'You shall not covet.' But sin, scizing an opportunity through the commandment, produced in me all kinds of covetousness" (Rom. 7:7-8a).

Far from being an anticlimax, therefore, God's law against coveting is what convinces us that we are sinners in need of salvation. The tenth commandment disabuses us of any notion that we are able to keep God's law. As Francis Schaeffer wrote: "'Thou shalt not covet' is the internal commandment which shows the man who thinks himself to be moral that he really needs a Savior. The average such 'moral' man, who has lived comparing himself to other men and comparing himself to a rather easy list of rules, can feel, like Paul, that he is getting along all right. But suddenly, when he is confronted with the inward command not to covet, he is brought to his knees."[9]

## GRAPES OF WRATH

Of all the Bible stories about coveting, the juiciest is the story of Ahab and the grapes of wrath. The Bible calls it "an incident involving a vineyard belonging to Naboth the Jezreelite" (NIV). Then it goes on to explain that the vineyard was "in Jezreel, beside the palace of Ahab king of Samaria" (1 Kings 21:1). This was the perfect setup for a story about coveting: two men, but only one piece of choice property.

The incident began with nothing more than a desire. King Ahab noticed how nice Naboth's vineyard was, and how close it was to the royal palace; and the more he thought about it, the more he wanted it. It was a vineyard fit for a king, or at least that's how it looked to him! Naturally Ahab started thinking about how he would develop the land if he owned it. However nice it was as a vineyard, it would be even nicer as a vegetable garden—especially one that belonged to him. Ahab's mouth started to water; he could practically taste the parsnips and the rutabagas.

So the king decided to make a business proposition: "Ahab said to Naboth, 'Give me your vineyard, that I may have it for a vegetable garden, because it is near my house, and I will give you a better vineyard for it; or, if it seems good to you, I will give you its value in money'" (1 Kings 21:2). It seemed like a fair offer. Ahab would give Naboth a vineyard at least as good as the one near the palace. Or if Naboth preferred to get out of the grape industry altogether, Ahab would pay him whatever the land was worth.

Naboth immediately declined, saying, "The LORD forbid that I should give you the inheritance of my fathers" (1 Kings 21:3). The reason Naboth turned Ahab down was because he knew his Bible. According to the Law of Moses, the children of Israel were not permitted to sell their property. God had said, "The land shall not be sold in perpetuity, for the land is mine. For you are but strangers and sojourners with me" (Lev. 25:23); "every one of the people of Israel shall hold on to the inheritance of the tribe of his fathers" (Num. 36:7). Since the land belonged to God, the vineyard could not be sold. Naboth was the kind of man who served God rather than money. If it meant violating the law of God, he would not sell the family farm, even if it were to his financial advantage. What was merely a luxury to Ahab was a matter of piety to Naboth. God forbid that he should part with the inheritance of his fathers, a vineyard belonging to the Lord!

Naboth is a good example of what Jesus was talking about when he said, "Where your treasure is, there your heart will be also" (Matt. 6:21). Naboth had found his treasure in the promises of God. By contrast, Ahab's heart was in the wrong place altogether. When he saw that his little real estate venture was slipping through his fingers, he did what any little kid does when he doesn't get his way—he pouted. "Ahab went into his house vexed and sullen because of what Naboth the Jezreelite had said to him, for he had said, 'I will not give you the inheritance of my fathers.' And he lay down on his bed and turned away his face and would eat no food" (1 Kings 21:4).

Poor Ahab! What had started as an idle notion had become a sinful obsession. His desire had degenerated into out-and-out coveting. He just *had* to have that vineyard! And when he couldn't get it, he was full of sour grapes. In his commentary on this passage, F. B. Meyer treats the covetous king with delicious sarcasm. He writes:

> In a room of the palace, Ahab, King of Israel, lies upon his couch, his face towards the wall, refusing to eat. What has taken place? Has disaster befallen the royal arms? Have the priests of Baal been again massacred? Is his royal consort dead? No; the soldiers are still flushed with their recent victories over Syria. The worship of Baal has quite recovered [from] the terrible disaster of Carmel; Jezebel—resolute, crafty, cruel, and beautiful—is now standing by his side, anxiously seeking the cause of this sadness.[10]

The portrait of Jezebel's concern is almost touching. She could tell that something was wrong: Her husband wouldn't even come to dinner!

As soon as Jezebel figured out what was eating Ahab, she immediately took charge. She was hardly the kind of woman to let little things like God's law stand in the way of what she wanted. She said to her husband, "Do you now govern Israel? Arise and eat bread and let your heart be cheerful; I will give you the vineyard of Naboth the Jezreelite" (1 Kings 21:7). And so she did. Jezebel bribed some unscrupulous men to accuse Naboth of blasphemy. Since there were two witnesses, the people immediately took Naboth out and stoned him to death, thus clearing the way for Ahab to plant his precious vegetables. This wicked plot proves that "the love of money is a root of all kinds of evils" (1 Tim. 6:10a), for what started out as a covetous desire led to false witness, murder, and stealing.

But God is not mocked, and in the end breaking God's law led to Ahab's destruction. As soon as Jezebel told him that Naboth was dead, Ahab "arose to go down to the vineyard of Naboth the Jezreelite, to take possession of it" (1 Kings 21:16). When the king got there, God's prophet Elijah was waiting to meet him and to speak the words that chilled him right down to his soul: "Have you killed and also taken possession? . . . In the place where dogs licked up the blood of Naboth shall dogs lick up your own blood" (1 Kings 21:19). Ahab's wife received the same sentence. The king and the queen were both thrown to the dogs.

If there is one thing we learn from the stories of the Bible, it is that things do not turn out well for people who break the Ten Commandments. They always get what they deserve in the end.

## If Only . . .

Ahab's downfall started with his discontent. The king had most of the finer things in life, but rather than giving thanks to God for what he had, he became obsessed with the one thing he didn't have: a vegetable garden next to the palace. This is how the whole thing started. Ahab wanted something that didn't belong to him, and then he wanted it more and more badly until finally he coveted it. It all came from not being content.

So much of our frustration in life comes from wanting things that God has not given us. In our covetous desire, we concentrate on what we don't have rather than on what we do have. Ahab said, "If only I had Naboth's vineyard, then I would be happy." All our discontent comes from the same kind of reasoning. If only.

Sometimes we say "if only" about our material possessions: "If only I made a little more money." "If only I had a bigger place to live." Once we start thinking this way, there is no end to our discontent. The story is often told of the reporter who asked the billionaire Nelson Rockefeller how much money it takes to be happy. Rockefeller answered, "Just a little bit more." The Scripture rightly says, "He who loves money will not be satisfied with money, nor he who loves wealth with his income" (Eccles. 5:10). This is true of both the poor and the rich. Coveting is not limited to a particular tax bracket.

Sometimes we are discontented with our physical attributes: "If only I had a different body type, then people would like me better." "If only I didn't have this disability, then I would be able to serve the Lord more effectively." On other occasions we are discontented with our place of service in the church: "If only people would recognize how important my ministry is." "If only they would give me the chance to use my gifts the way they ought to be used."

Then there are all the times when we are discontented with our situation in life. Singles are discontented with their singleness: "If only I could find someone to marry, it would make all the difference." Then we get married, and we are discontented with that too. We say, "If only my spouse would do a better job of meeting my needs." If only.

As long as we base our sense of contentment on anything in the world, we will always find some excuse to make ourselves miserable. Our problem is not on the outside—it's on the inside, and therefore it will never be solved by getting more of what we think we want. If we do not learn to be satisfied right now in our present situation—whatever it is—we will never be satisfied at all. I once heard Charles Swindoll quote the following poem:

> It was Spring, but it was Summer I wanted:
> The warm days and the great outdoors.
>
> It was Summer, but it was Fall I wanted:
> The colorful leaves and the cool, dry air.
>
> It was Fall, but it was Winter I wanted:
> The beautiful snow and the joy of the holiday season.
>
> It was Winter, but it was Spring I wanted:
> The warmth and the blossoming of nature.
>
> I was a child, and it was adulthood I wanted:
> The freedom and the respect.

*I was 20, but it was 30 I wanted:*
*To be mature and sophisticated.*

*I was middle-aged, but it was 20 I wanted:*
*The youth and the free spirit.*

*I was retired, but it was middle-aged I wanted:*
*The presence of mind without limitations.*

*My life was over,*
*and I never got what I wanted.*

## THE SECRET OF BEING CONTENT

The truth is that if God wanted us to have more right now, we would have it. If we needed different gifts to enable us to glorify him, he would provide them. If we were ready for the job or the ministry we want, he would put us into it. If we were supposed to be in a different situation in life, we would be in it. Instead of always saying, "If only this" and "If only that," God calls us to glorify him to the fullest right now, whatever situation we are in.

The word for this is *contentment*. Contentment is the positive side of the last commandment; it is the remedy for covetous desire. The Westminster Shorter Catechism says, "The tenth commandment requireth full contentment with our own condition, with a right and charitable frame of spirit toward our neighbor and all that is his" (A. 80). This emphasis on contentment is thoroughly biblical. "There is great gain in godliness with contentment" (1 Tim. 6:6), the Scripture says. "Keep your life free from love of money, and be content with what you have, for [God] has said, 'I will never leave you nor forsake you'" (Heb. 13:5).

Contentment means wanting what *God* wants for us rather than what *we* want for us. The secret to enjoying this kind of contentment is to be so satisfied with God that we are able to accept whatever he has or has not provided. To put this another way, coveting is a theological issue: Ultimately, it concerns our relationship with God. Therefore, the way to get rid of any covetous desire is to be completely satisfied with God and what he provides. In a wonderful book called *The Rare Jewel of*

*Christian Contentment*, the Puritan Jeremiah Burroughs explained what we ought to say to ourselves whenever we are tempted to be discontented: "I find a sufficiency of satisfaction in my own heart, through the grace of Christ that is in me. Though I have not outward comforts and worldly conveniences to supply my necessities, yet I have a sufficient portion between Christ and my soul abundantly to satisfy me in every condition."[11]

Godly people have always known this secret. Asaph knew it. True, there was a time in his life when Asaph was disappointed with God. He saw wicked men prosper, while he himself had nothing to show for his godliness. It made him angry with God and bitter about what life didn't seem to offer. But then Asaph learned the secret of being content, and he was able to say to the Lord, "Whom have I in heaven but you? And there is nothing on earth that I desire besides you" (Ps. 73:25).

The apostle Paul knew the secret too. He said, "I have learned in whatever situation I am to be content. I know how to be brought low, and I know how to abound. In any and every circumstance, I have learned the secret of facing plenty and hunger, abundance and need" (Phil. 4:11b-12) In other words, Paul had learned that contentment is not circumstantial; it does not depend on our situation in life. So what's the secret? Paul said, "I can do all things through him who strengthens me" (Phil. 4:13).

God is all we need, and therefore all we ought to desire. To be even more specific, all we need is Jesus. God does not offer us his Son as a better way of getting what we want. No, God gives us Jesus and says, "Here, even if you don't realize it, he is all you really need." When we come to Jesus, we receive the forgiveness of our sins through his death and resurrection. We receive the promise of eternal life with God. We receive the promise that he will never leave us or forsake us, that he will help us through all the trials of life. What else do we need?

And as for everything else—all the things that we spend so much time coveting—God says, "Trust me; I will provide everything you truly need." Faith is always the answer to our discontent. Michael Horton writes: "It is not poverty or wealth that leads us to contentment and trust in the Lord, but the confidence that if God provided so richly for our salvation by choosing, redeeming, calling, adopting, and justifying us, and by sending His Spirit to cause us to grow up into Christ's likeness, then surely we can count on Him for the less essential matters of daily existence."[12] Jesus said it even more plainly: "Seek first the kingdom of God and his righteousness, and all these things will be added to you" (Matt. 6:33). The first thing, the main thing, the only thing that really matters is to trust in Jesus. He is enough for us. Really, he is.

## STUDY QUESTIONS

1. If someone gave you twenty thousand dollars, what would you buy?
2. What is the difference between coveting and desiring something?
3. What are the internal and external results of coveting?
4. To what other sins does coveting lead?
5. Some people say that the tenth commandment is superfluous because coveting is included in the eighth commandment. Why is this commandment important in its own right?
6. Read 1 Kings 21:1-29. What words would you use to describe Ahab and Jezebel?
7. What sins did Ahab and Jezebel commit? (It may be helpful to read through the Ten Commandments as you think about this question.)
8. What principles about keeping the tenth commandment can we learn from this passage?
9. What "if onlys" most often float through your mind?
10. What strategies can you use to foster contentment and satisfaction in your heart?

# Epilogue:
# The End of the Law

*Now when all the people saw the thunder and the flashes of light-
ning and the sound of the trumpet and the mountain smoking, the
people were afraid and trembled, and they stood far off and said to
Moses, "You speak to us, and we will listen; but do not let God
speak to us, lest we die."*

EXODUS 20:18-19

John Bunyan's famous book *Pilgrim's Progress* tells of Christian's long
spiritual journey from the City of Destruction to the Celestial City.
The story begins with Christian weighed down by the great burden of
his sin and fearful of the judgment to come. But Evangelist comes to
tell him how to enter the narrow way of salvation, where his burden can
be taken away.

Not long after Christian began his pilgrimage, he met a man who
informed him of a faster way to get rid of his burden. All Christian
needed to do was go and see a gentleman named Legality, who lived in
the village of Morality. To put this in spiritual terms, he could get rid of
his sins simply by keeping God's law. Christian was intrigued by this
possibility. Obviously he didn't want to make his journey any more difficult than necessary. Could Mr. Legality help him get rid of his burden?

When Christian asked the way to Morality, the man answered by
pointing to a high mountain and saying, "By that hill you must go."
Christian followed the man's directions:

[He] turned out of his way to go to Mr. Legality's house for help; but behold, when he was got now hard by the hill, it seemed so high, and also that side of it that was next the wayside did hang so much over that Christian was afraid to venture further, lest the hill should fall on his head. Wherefore there he stood still, and [knew] not what to do. Also his burden, now, seemed heavier to him than while he was in his way. There came also flashes of fire out of the hill that made Christian afraid that he should be burned; here therefore he sweat, and did quake for fear.[1]

John Bunyan did not mention this hill by name, but it is not hard to guess which one he had in mind. It was a hill of fire and smoke—Sinai, the mountain of God's law. Far from removing Christian's burden, that great hill only made him more afraid. This is because the law does not have the power to save, but only to threaten us with judgment, and thus to show us our need of salvation.

## THE TERRORS OF LAW AND OF GOD

When the children of Israel stood at Mount Sinai, they felt the way Christian did. They were terrified. The Bible says, "Now when all the people saw the thunder and the flashes of lightning and the sound of the trumpet and the mountain smoking, the people were afraid and trembled, and they stood far off" (Exod. 20:18). It was an awesome sight. Smoke billowed from the mountain, and great balls of fire blazed from peak to peak. The sounds were awesome, too. There were great claps of thunder and mighty blasts from a trumpet, and the ground shook under Israel's feet. These natural and supernatural phenomena were first mentioned back in chapter 19, where the Scripture explained the reason for such awesome sights and sounds: It was "because the LORD had descended on [Mount Sinai] in fire" (Exod. 19:18). What the Israelites saw were visible manifestations of the glory of the invisible God.

Some scholars have wondered why the description of Mount Sinai is repeated in chapter 20. Why does the Bible describe thunder and lightning both before and after the giving of the Ten Commandments? The answer is that these awesome sights and sounds continued during the whole time that God was giving his law. They are mentioned again in chapter 20 simply to show how the Israelites responded. Back in chapter 19 God set limits around the mountain and warned his people not to break through the boundary; otherwise they would be destroyed. By the time he was finished giving his law, those precautions hardly seemed necessary! The people were trembling with fear; they were shaking in their sandals. The Bible says that "they stood far off" (Exod. 20:18), which implies that they kept well behind the safety perimeter that Moses set around the mountain.

Why were the Israelites so frightened?

One thing the Israelites feared was the law itself. God had just given them his righteous requirements in the form of the Ten Commandments. They could see that God was demanding their total allegiance in every aspect of life. He required them to worship him alone and to love one another in everything they did and said.

The Israelites probably didn't realize the full extent of God's law. Undoubtedly there were some things about the Ten Commandments that they didn't yet understand—how each commandment is both positive and negative, how it governs inward attitudes as well as outward actions, or how it represents a whole category of sin and duty. But surely they understood that God was making an absolute claim on their worship, time, relationships, possessions, bodies, speech, and desires. So the first time they heard the Ten Commandments—even before they learned them all by heart—the Israelites knew that God was giving them one righteous standard for all of life. He wanted all of them, all the time, and this terrified them. Back in chapter 19 they promised that they would do whatever God said (v. 8), but as soon as they found out what was included, they panicked. They were frightened by the total demand of God's law.

The Israelites were also frightened by the threat of God's judgment, and perhaps this was the main reason they were afraid. Fire and smoke, thunder and lightning, the loud blast of a trumpet—whether the Israelites knew it or not, these signs will all reappear at the final judgment. The people had come into the very presence of the great and formidable Judge of all sin. They were guilty sinners before a holy God, and they could sense that this was a life-threatening encounter. Indeed, in the smoke on the mountain they caught a glimpse of the wrath to come. In a sermon on Israel at Sinai, Charles Spurgeon said:

> This terrible grandeur may also have been intended to suggest to the people the condemning force of the law. Not with sweet sound of harp, nor with the song of angels, was the law given; but with an awful voice from amid a terrible burning. . . . [B]y reason of man's sinfulness, the law worketh wrath; and to indicate this, it was made public with accompaniments of fear and death: the battalions of Omnipotence marshaled upon the scene; the dread artillery of God, with awful salvos, adding emphasis to every syllable. The tremendous scene at Sinai was also in some respects a prophecy, if not a rehearsal, of the Day of Judgment.[2]

No wonder the Israelites were terrified! When they looked upon Mount Sinai, they were confronted with the condemning power of a law-giving God who will judge the world on the Last Day.

## Moses the Mediator

One of the first things people do when they get into trouble with the law is to hire a lawyer. This is exactly what the Israelites did at Mount Sinai. As soon as they heard the demands of God's law, they asked Moses to be their legal advocate, their mediator. They said to him, "You speak to us, and we will listen; but do not let God speak to us, lest we die" (Exod. 20:19). The Israelites were afraid to deal with God directly, for obvious reasons. They had heard the commandments of his law, they had seen the fire and the smoke of his glory, and it was all too much for them to bear. So they begged Moses to do the talking: "We don't want to talk to God; *you* talk to him!" And the "you" in verse 19 is emphatic. They said to Moses in effect, "You speak to us yourself."

Many people claim that they want to have an unmediated experience of God. "If only God would speak to me directly," they say. "If only he would show himself to me, then I would believe." People who make such demands really have no idea what they are asking, because anyone who has ever caught even the slightest glimpse of God's true glory has been filled with fear. He is an awesome and all-powerful God whose holiness is a terror to sinners.

This means that the Israelites were right to ask for a mediator. They needed one! A mediator is someone who stands in the gap to bring two parties together. And this is what the Israelites needed: someone to stand between heaven and earth, to bridge the gap between God's deity and their humanity. They needed someone to represent them before God and to represent God before them. They needed someone to be God's spokesman because they could not bear the sound of God's voice. And even if they didn't realize it, what they needed most of all was someone to protect them from God's curse against their sin, the penalty of his law.

When the Israelites asked Moses to be their mediator, they were asking for something that God had already provided. God made Moses the mediator back at the burning bush, and the prophet had been speaking for God ever since. But when God revealed his law, the Israelites finally understood for themselves their need for a mediator. In their fear they begged Moses to be their go-between with God.

No sooner had the Israelites made their request than Moses began to serve as their mediator, doing two things that a mediator is called to do. First, he spoke to them for God: "Moses said to the people, 'Do not fear, for God has come to test you, that the fear of him may be before you, that you may not sin'" (Exod. 20:20). Later, when Moses looked back on this experience, he said, "I stood between the LORD and you at that time, to declare to you the word of the LORD. For you were afraid because of the fire, and you did not go up into the mountain" (Deut. 5:5).

When Moses spoke to the people, it was partly to explain the purpose of God's law. As we saw back in Chapter 2, God's law is a multiuse item. It has three primary purposes. One is to restrain our sin by threatening us with punishment. The law fulfills this function in human society. Its penalties act as a deterrent, keeping people away from sin. Another use of the law is to reveal our sin by proving that we cannot live up to God's perfect standard. Later, after we have been saved by grace, the law shows us how to live in a way that brings glory to God. While continuing to restrain us from sin and to show us our need for grace, it also instructs us in righteousness.

When Moses explained the purpose of God's law, which of its three main uses did he have in mind? At first it may seem that Moses was talking about the civic use of the law, its ability to restrain sin in society. After all, he said to the Israelites, ". . . that the fear of [God] may be before you, that you may not sin" (Exod. 20:20b). Certainly the Israelites were afraid, for they had heard God's voice from the mountain. Thus it would make sense for Moses to say that this experience would help them not to sin. Whenever they were tempted to break any of God's commandments, they would remember his terrible voice, and this would remind them not to break his law. Moses also described Israel's encounter with God as a test. He said, "God has come to test you" (Exod. 20:20a). God's law was a test of Israel's obedience. Did they pass the test? No; they sinned against God. So there is at least a hint here of a second use of the law, in which its function is to show God's people their sin.

God also wanted his people to keep his law, however, and this was a third use of the law. The law was given for their obedience, and it was the mediator's job to encourage them in this. The first thing Moses told them was not to be afraid. It was not God's intention to destroy them, but to save them. So rather than cringing in fear, terrified by God's law, they were called to live for God in joy and obedience. Moses told them that the fear of the Lord would be with them—not fear simply in the sense of abject terror, but also in the sense of reverence and respect. Their experience of God on Mount Sinai would remain with them in order to help them obey. Reverence would lead to obedience.

The point is that the Israelites needed a mediator to tell them all this. They needed a representative from God to tell them not to be afraid and to explain to them what the law was for—its three primary purposes. Moses was the mediator. He spoke to the people for God, so that they could hear and obey.

There was a second thing that Moses did for the Israelites. As their mediator, he went for them to God: "The people stood far off, while Moses drew near to the thick darkness where God was" (Exod. 20:21). "The thick darkness where God was"—this evocative phrase is sometimes taken as a word of comfort for believers in difficult circumstances.

But the darkness Moses approached was not the darkness of personal difficulty; it was the mysterious darkness of God's own being. In the fire and smoke on Mount Sinai, God preserved the infinite mystery of his eternal deity. Who would dare to approach? Who could stand to enter the thick darkness where God was?

Only the mediator. This is what a mediator does: He enters God's presence on behalf of God's people; he draws near to God as their representative. To put it another way, he boldly goes where no one else would dare to go. And Moses did that. While everyone else in Israel was trembling with fear, he alone went up to meet with God, to talk with God and receive the rest of his law. He did this on behalf of God's people so that they would know God's will for their lives. Moses spoke for God to the people and went for the people to God. He was the mediator God chose to lead them in the way of salvation.

## THE LIMITS OF THE LAW

The reason the mediatorial work of Moses matters is because we need a lawyer, too. Earlier I quoted from Charles Spurgeon, who described the giving of the law at Mount Sinai as a dress rehearsal for the Day of Judgment. Spurgeon went on to ask this provocative question: "If the giving of the law, while it was yet unbroken, was attended with such a display of awe-inspiring power, what will that day be when the Lord shall, with flaming fire, take vengeance on those who have willfully broken His law?"[3]

That's a good question: If simply hearing the law was such a frightening experience, then how terrifying will it be to meet God after breaking it? This is an especially good question to ask after studying the Ten Commandments. Many people think that God will accept them because they generally play by the rules. Ironically, most of them would have trouble even naming the Ten Commandments, let alone keeping them. Nevertheless, they assume that because they have never murdered anyone or committed perjury, God will be pleased enough to let them into heaven.

Anyone who thinks that he or she can keep God's law should go ahead and try. But what we soon discover—provided we know what

God's law really requires—is how impossible it is for us to keep the Ten
Commandments. We are sinners by nature, and thus we are unable to
obey God in everything. And if there is one thing we learn from the Ten
Commandments, it is that we are not able to keep them. Frankly, we are
the kind of people who like to serve other gods, use bad language, resist
authority, lust after sexual pleasure, take other people's stuff, and say
things to tear people down. So we know from experience that the
Westminster Shorter Catechism is right when it says, "No mere man,
since the fall, is able in this life perfectly to keep the commandments of
God, but doth daily break them, in thought, word, and deed" (A. 82).

If we cannot keep God's law, then it is a threat to us, a deadly threat.
The famous American missionary David Brainerd remembered a time
in his life when the terrors of the law kept him away from God. The
law made him angry because it was so strict. Brainerd wrote:

> I found it was impossible for me, after my utmost pains, to answer
> its demands. I often made new resolutions, and as often broke them.
> I imputed the whole to carelessness and the want of being more
> watchful, and used to call myself a fool for my negligence. But
> when, upon a stronger resolution, and greater endeavors, and close
> application to fasting and prayer, I found all attempts fail; then I
> quarreled with the law of God, as unreasonably rigid. I thought if it
> extended only to my outward actions and behaviors, I could bear
> with it; but I found it condemned me for my evil thoughts and sins
> of my years, which I could not possibly prevent.[4]

As Brainerd discovered, if we try to keep God's law on our own, we
are doomed to failure and frustration. The Scripture says, "For by works
of the law no human being will be justified in his sight, since through
the law comes knowledge of sin" (Rom. 3:20). It says further that "whoever keeps the whole law but fails in one point has become accountable
for all of it" (Jas. 2:10). The law cannot save us; it can only show us our
sin. John Murray wrote:

> Law can do nothing to justify the person who in any particular has
> violated its sanctity and come under its curse. Law, as law, has no
> expiatory provision; it exercises no forgiving grace; and it has no

power of enablement to the fulfillment of its own demand. It knows no clemency for the remission of guilt; it provides no righteousness to meet our iniquity; it exerts no constraining power to reclaim our waywardness; it knows no mercy to melt our hearts in penitence and new obedience. It can do nothing to relieve the bondage of sin; it accentuates and confirms the bondage.[5]

We know what we have to do—that's not the problem. God has told us what to do in his law. The problem is that we can't do it! If we were able to keep the law, we could be saved by it. But since we cannot keep it, we can only be condemned by it. Like the Israelites, we should be standing at a distance, trembling with fear.

## A Better Mediator

What we need is a good lawyer! And this is how the law leads us to the gospel: It condemns us for our sin so that we start looking for some kind of legal remedy, and then we discover that God has provided one for us in Jesus Christ. Jesus can do what the law cannot do, and that is to save us: "God has done what the law, weakened by the flesh, could not do . . . sending his own Son" (Rom. 8:3a).

The New Testament teaches that the Son of God is our mediator. In fact, he is the only mediator we will ever need. "For there is one God, and one mediator between God and men, the man Christ Jesus, who gave himself as a ransom for all, which is the testimony given at the proper time" (1 Tim. 2:5-6). The book of Hebrews describes Christ's mediatorial work by drawing a comparison with Moses. Moses was a great mediator—the greatest in the Old Testament. But "Jesus has been found worthy of more glory than Moses" (Heb. 3:3a). He is a superior mediator (Heb. 8:6), the mediator of a new and better covenant (Heb. 9:15). Hebrews goes on to assure us that we do not have to go through what the Israelites went through when they met God at Mount Sinai. The Bible says to the Christian: "You have not come to what may be touched, a blazing fire and darkness and gloom and a tempest and the sound of a trumpet and a voice whose words made the hearers beg that no further messages be spoken to them. For they could not endure the order that was given" (Heb. 12:18-20a). In other words, we are not back in Exodus 20. But if we are not at Mount Sinai, then where are we? The Bible says, "You have come . . . to Jesus, the mediator of a new covenant" (Heb. 12:22-24). Things are different for us because we have a better mediator—the Lord Jesus Christ.

Jesus does everything a mediator is supposed to do. He goes to God for us. He is our go-between, the one who approaches the thick darkness where God is and "who speaks to the Father in our defense" (1 John 2:1, NIV). He is able to do this much more effectively than Moses ever did because he is God as well as man. Jesus has both a divine nature and a human nature; therefore, he is uniquely capable to represent us before God. And as he approaches God on our behalf, Jesus does something that Moses could never do: He offers perfect obedience to the law. Whatever mediation Moses offered was limited by the fact that he was a lawbreaker. He was not able to offer perfect obedience to the Ten Commandments. But Jesus could do it. When he presented himself to God, Jesus said, "Behold, I have come to do your will, O God" (Heb. 10:7), and then he did it. Perfectly. Jesus worshiped God alone, honored God's name, kept the Sabbath holy, obeyed his parents, loved his enemies, told the truth, and did everything else God commanded him to do.

This is the kind of mediator we need—someone to keep God's law for us. We are idolaters, rebels, liars, and cheats, and thus we could never be saved by our own obedience. But everything Jesus ever did counts for everyone who trusts in him. By faith in Christ we offer perfect obedience to God's law. Martin Luther said, "[T]he Christ who is grasped by faith and who lives in the heart is the true Christian righteousness, on account of which God counts us righteous and grants us eternal life."[6] All we have to do is trust in Jesus, and this is absolutely necessary because the Day of Judgment is coming. Since we are in trouble with the law, we will need a lawyer. If we don't have one, we will have to face the justice of God's wrath all on our own, and what will happen to us then? But in his mercy God has provided a mediator, and like the Israelites, we should cry out for him to save us.

Once we come to Jesus there is something else that he does as our mediator, and that is to teach us God's law. As the Scripture says, we are "not . . . outside God's law but under the law of Christ" (1 Cor. 9:21).

Earlier we saw how Moses explained the law to the Israelites. Jesus does the same thing for us. First, like Moses, he tells us not to be afraid. This is because the law holds no terror for those who are safe in Christ. Jesus has suffered the penalty that we deserved for our sin, and the law can frighten us no longer: "There is therefore now no condemnation for those who are in Christ Jesus" (Rom. 8:1).

What the law can still do is teach us how to live. As the Puritan Thomas Watson explained, "Though a Christian is not under the condemning power of the law, yet he is under its commanding power."[7] To that end, part of Christ's mediatorial work is to teach us God's law all over again. He does not teach us the ceremonial law, which he fulfilled in his life and through his sacrificial death. Nor does he teach us the civil law, which was especially for the Old Testament nation of Israel. But Jesus does teach us the requirements of the moral law—the eternal standard of God's righteousness. Jesus said, "Do not think that I have come to abolish the Law or the Prophets; I have not come to abolish them but to fulfill them. For truly, I say to you, until heaven and earth pass away, not an iota, not a dot, will pass from the Law until all is accomplished" (Matt. 5:17-18).

More than anyone else, Jesus is the one who teaches us to obey the will of God. He explains God's law and applies it to our hearts so that we can live in a way that is pleasing to him. To put it another way, Jesus takes the law that once drove us to him for salvation and gives it back to us. The Puritan Samuel Bolton put it this way: "The law sends us to the gospel that we may be justified; and the gospel sends us to the law again to inquire what is our duty as those who are justified. . . . The law sends us to the gospel for our justification; the gospel sends us to the law to frame our way of life."[8] So as Christians we now keep the Ten Commandments—not so much because we have to, but because we get to, and because in Christ we are able to! We obey, not to justify ourselves, but to show our gratitude to the Savior who justified us.

Everything we have said about the law and the gospel in relation to Christ has been helpfully summarized by Ernest Reisinger, who says of Jesus, "He explained the law's meaning, He expressed its character, He embodied its duties, and He endured its penalty."[9] When he says "endured its penalty," Reisinger is referring specifically to the cross where Jesus died for our sins, suffering the death that we deserved for breaking God's law. A fuller summary of Christ and the law comes from Thomas Ascol:

> The law was given to teach sinners their sin. When a sinner sees the law in all its strictness and spirituality, he thereby comes to understand the spiritual bankruptcy and grave danger of his condition. The law, able to condemn but unable to save, sends the convicted sinner looking for salvation in the only place it can be found. It sends him to Jesus Christ who, in His perfect law-fulfilling life and perfect law-fulfilling death, gave Himself to redeem helpless sinners. When Christ receives repentant, believing men and women, He forgives them, grants them His righteousness, and gives them His Spirit. He writes His law on their new hearts and empowers them to follow Him in obedient discipleship. As the One who perfectly kept the law Himself, He then leads His disciples to obey the commandments.[10]

And obey the commandments we do. All of them. By the grace of God, we keep what James called "the perfect law, the law of liberty" (James 1:25). We have been liberated from our service to other gods, and now we are free to worship God alone with reverence and joy, taking his name in earnest. We have been justified by faith, not by works, and now we are free to rest in God's grace. We have come to know God the Father through Jesus the Son, and now we are free to give honor where honor is due. By the love of God we have been delivered from murderous hate, and now we are free to forgive. We have found real pleasure in Christ, and now by the purity of his Spirit we are free to be chaste. All our lies have been exposed, and now we are free to tell the truth. And since we have the provision of Christ, there is no longer any need for us to steal or even to covet.

We do not keep God's law in order to be saved. We have been saved by grace alone through faith alone in Christ alone. But why were we saved? To glorify God, which we do by keeping his commandments. Jesus said, "If you love me, you will keep my commandments" (John 14:15).

STUDY QUESTIONS

1. Should people today fear God's law as the Israelites did? Why or why not?

2. Have you ever wished that God would speak to you directly? Has that desire changed after meditating on Exodus 19—20?

3. How does Jesus perform the duties of a mediator—speaking for God and going to God on our behalf? What New Testament passages discuss these roles?

4. In what ways is Jesus a better mediator than Moses?

5. In your experience, what is the relationship between reverence and obedience? Which one comes first? How do they work together?

6. In your own words, explain the relationship between Christ and the law.

7. What is the law's role or function in the lives of seekers today? In the lives of believers?

8. What have you learned about God as a result of studying the Ten Commandments? What have you learned about yourself?

9. What sins (especially ones that formerly you may have overlooked) is the Holy Spirit using the Ten Commandments to bring to your attention? What are you doing to repent of these sins?

10. As a result of studying the Ten Commandments, what new areas are you targeting for future spiritual growth?

# NOTES

## CHAPTER 1: WRITTEN IN STONE

1. James Patterson and Peter Kim, *The Day America Told the Truth* (New York: Plume, 1992), 201.
2. "Religion Is Gaining Ground, but Morality Is Losing Ground," *Emerging Trends*, Vol. 23, No. 7 (September 2001), 1-2.
3. It is also possible to interpret the second person singular as a collective addressing the nation of Israel as a corporate person. But even if the entire nation is in view, the effect of the singular is to personalize the law.
4. The dilemma is posed in *Euthyphro*, where Plato has Socrates ask, "Do the gods love an act because it is pious, or is it pious because the gods love it?" See Samuel Enoch Stumpf, *Socrates to Sartre: A History of Philosophy*, 3rd ed. (New York: McGraw-Hill, 1982), 38.
5. A. W. Pink, *The Ten Commandments* (Swengel, PA: Reiner, 1961), 5.
6. Peter Enns, *Exodus*, NIV Application Commentary (Grand Rapids, MI: Zondervan, 2000), 371.
7. Ted Koppel, quoted in Cal Thomas, *Los Angeles Times* (1994).
8. Ernest C. Reisinger, *The Law and the Gospel* (Phillipsburg, NJ: P&R, 1997), 54.
9. Over against covenant theology, classic dispensational theology believes in the future restoration of Israel as a nation under God, complete with the rebuilding of the temple and the reestablishment of the Old Testament sacrificial system.
10. John Calvin, *Institutes of the Christian Religion,* trans. Ford Lewis Battles, 2 vols., Library of Christian Classics, 20-21 (Philadelphia: Westminster, 1960), IV.XX.14.
11. John Calvin, *John Calvin's Sermons on the Ten Commandments*, ed. and trans. Benjamin W. Farley (Grand Rapids, MI: Baker, 1980), 24.
12. Reisinger, *The Law and the Gospel*, 69.

## CHAPTER 2: A MULTI-USE ITEM

1. These three illustrations come from Randall Grossman, who pastors Grace Bible Fellowship Church in Reading, Pennsylvania.
2. Jochem Douma, *The Ten Commandments: Manual for the Christian Life*, trans. Nelson D. Kloosterman (Phillipsburg, NJ: P&R, 1996), 4.
3. Martin Luther, as recounted in Michael S. Horton, *The Law of Perfect Freedom* (Chicago: Moody, 1993), 263.
4. Thomas Watson, *The Ten Commandments* (1692; repr. Edinburgh: Banner of Truth, 1965), 14.
5. J. C. Ryle, *Holiness* (1879; repr. Durham, England: Evangelical Press, 1979), 26.
6. John Calvin, *Institutes of the Christian Religion*, quoted in R. C. Sproul, *The Soul's Quest for God* (Wheaton, IL: Tyndale, 1992), 111-112.
7. *Stone v. Graham*, quoted by Ronald B. Flowers in *Liberty* (July/August 2000), 4.
8. John Calvin, *Institutes of the Christian Religion*, trans. Ford Lewis Battles, 2 vols., Library of Christian Classics, 20-21 (Philadelphia: Westminster, 1960), II.VII.6.
9. Augustine, in Calvin, *Institutes*, II.VII.9.
10. Martin Luther, *Lectures on Galatians, 1535*, trans. and ed. Jaroslav Pelikan, *Luther's Works* (St. Louis: Concordia, 1963), 26:327.
11. John Calvin, quoted in Ernest C. Reisinger, *The Law and the Gospel* (Phillipsburg, NJ: P&R, 1997), 28.
12. Charles Spurgeon, *Parables and Miracles* (Grand Rapids, MI: Baker, 1993), 3:413.
13. Baloo, *National Review* (October 11, 1999), 51.
14. Luther, *Galatians*, 26:309.
15. Donald Grey Barnhouse, *Exposition of Bible Doctrines, Taking the Epistle to the Romans as a Point

*of Departure; Volume II: God's Wrath, Romans 2:1—3:20* (Grand Rapids, MI: Eerdmans, 1953), 275-276.

16. Archibald Alexander, quoted in David B. Calhoun, *Princeton Seminary, Volume 1: Faith and Learning, 1812-1868* (Edinburgh: Banner of Truth, 1994), 276.

## CHAPTER 3: INTERPRETING GOD'S LAW

1. Baloo, *National Review* (August 28, 2000), 58.
2. John Calvin, *Institutes of the Christian Religion*, trans. Ford Lewis Battles, 2 vols., Library of Christian Classics, 20-21 (Philadelphia: Westminster, 1960), II.VIII.7.
3. Francis Turretin, *Institutes of Elenctic Theology*, trans. George Musgrave Giger, ed. James T. Dennison, Jr., 3 vols. (Phillipsburg, NJ: P&R, 1992-1997), XI.III.9.
4. Thomas Watson, *The Ten Commandments* (1692; repr. Edinburgh: Banner of Truth, 1965), 45.
5. Umberto Cassuto, *A Commentary on the Book of Exodus*, trans. Israel Abrahams (Jerusalem: Magnes Press, 1967), 240.
6. Quoted in Jochem Douma, *The Ten Commandments: Manual for the Christian Life*, trans. Nelson D. Kloosterman (Phillipsburg, NJ: P&R, 1996), 352.
7. Joy Davidman, *Smoke on the Mountain* (Philadelphia: Westminster, 1953), 48.
8. Turretin, *Institutes of Elenctic Theology*, XI.VI.3.
9. Ernest C. Reisinger, *The Law and the Gospel* (Phillipsburg, NJ: P&R, 1997), 74-75.
10. Watson, *The Ten Commandments*, 46-47.
11. See Reisinger, *The Law and the Gospel*, 73-74.
12. J. Gresham Machen, *What Is Faith?* (New York: Macmillan, 1925), 152.

## CHAPTER 4: NO OTHER GODS

1. Jochem Douma, *The Ten Commandments: Manual for the Christian Life*, trans. Nelson D. Kloosterman (Phillipsburg, NJ: P&R, 1996), 16.
2. Godfrey Ashby, *Go Out and Meet God: A Commentary on the Book of Exodus*, International Theological Commentary (Grand Rapids, MI: Eerdmans, 1998), 88.
3. John Calvin, *Institutes of the Christian Religion*, trans. Ford Lewis Battles, 2 vols., Library of Christian Classics, 20-21 (Philadelphia: Westminster, 1960), II.VIII.16.
4. Martin Luther, quoted in Maxie D. Dunnam, *Exodus*, The Communicator's Commentary (Waco, TX: Word, 1987), 253.
5. Thomas Watson, *The Ten Commandments* (1692; repr. Edinburgh: Banner of Truth, 1965), 55.
6. Matthew Henry, *Commentary on the Whole Bible*, 6 vols. (New York: Fleming H. Revell, n.d.), 1:n.p.
7. Robert Bellah, et al., *Habits of the Heart* (New York: Harper & Row, 1985), 221.
8. Oscar Wilde, quoted in Michael S. Horton, *The Law of Perfect Freedom* (Chicago: Moody, 1993), 56.

## CHAPTER 5: THE RIGHT GOD, THE RIGHT WAY

1. Rob Schenck, *The Ten Words That Will Change a Nation: The Ten Commandments* (Tulsa, OK: Albury, 1999), 32.
2. Christopher J. H. Wright, *Deuteronomy*, New International Biblical Commentary (Peabody, MA: Hendrickson, 1996), 71-72.
3. Quoted in John R. W. Stott, *The Message of Acts*, The Bible Speaks Today (Leicester, England: Inter-Varsity, 1990), 277.
4. E. M. Blaiklock, *The Acts of the Apostles: An Historical Commentary*, Tyndale New Testament Commentary (Grand Rapids, MI: Eerdmans, 1959), 137.
5. John Calvin, *Institutes of the Christian Religion*, trans. Ford Lewis Battles, 2 vols., Library of Christian Classics, 20-21 (Philadelphia: Westminster, 1960), I.XI.8.
6. Neil Postman, *Amusing Ourselves to Death: Public Discourse in the Age of Show Business* (New York: Penguin, 1985), 9.
7. Walter Brueggemann, *Theology of the Old Testament: Testimony, Dispute, Advocacy* (Philadelphia: Fortress, 1997), 184-185.

8. Michael S. Horton, *The Law of Perfect Freedom* (Chicago: Moody, 1993), 54.
9. John Calvin, *The Acts of the Apostles*, 2 vols., trans. W. F. G. McDonald and John W. Fraser, Calvin's New Testament Commentaries, eds. David W. Torrance and Thomas F. Torrance (Grand Rapids, MI: Eerdmans, 1973), 2:121-122.
10. Wright, *Deuteronomy*, 71.

## CHAPTER 6: NAME ABOVE ALL NAMES

1. Göran Larsson, *Bound for Freedom: The Book of Exodus in Jewish and Christian Traditions* (Peabody, MA: Hendrickson, 1999), 145.
2. Brevard S. Childs, *The Book of Exodus: A Critical, Theological Commentary* (Louisville: Westminster, 1974), 410.
3. Jochem Douma, *The Ten Commandments: Manual for the Christian Life*, trans. Nelson D. Kloosterman (Phillipsburg, NJ: P&R, 1996), 74-75.
4. Thomas Watson, *The Ten Commandments* (1692; repr. Edinburgh: Banner of Truth, 1965), 91.
5. Gary North, *Chronicles: A Magazine of American Culture* (December 1992), 15.
6. John Calvin, *Institutes of the Christian Religion*, trans. Ford Lewis Battles, 2 vols., Library of Christian Classics, 20-21 (Philadelphia: Westminster, 1960), II.VIII.22.
7. Martin Luther, *The Small Catechism* (1529), in *The Book of Concord: The Confessions of the Evangelical Lutheran Church*, eds. Robert Kolb and Timothy J. Wengert, trans. Charles Arand, et al. (Minneapolis: Fortress, 2000), 345-375 (352).
8. Rob Schenck, *The Ten Words That Will Change a Nation: The Ten Commandments* (Tulsa, OK: Albury, 1999), 53-54.
9. Stephen L. Carter, *Taking God's Name in Vain: The Wrongs and Rights of Religion and Politics* (New York: Basic, 2000), 12-13.
10. David F. Wells, *God in the Wasteland: The Reality of Truth in a World of Fading Dreams* (Grand Rapids, MI: Eerdmans, 1994), 88.
11. Donald W. McCullough, *The Trivialization of God: The Dangerous Illusion of a Manageable Deity* (Colorado Springs: NavPress, 1995).
12. William Shakespeare, *Hamlet, Prince of Denmark*, Act III, Scene IV, lines 100-101.

## CHAPTER 7: WORK AND LEISURE

1. Bill Gates, quoted by Walter Isaacson, "In Search of the Real Bill Gates," *Time* (January 13, 1997), 7.
2. Lance Morrow, quoted in Mark E. Dever, "The Call to Work and Worship," *Regeneration Quarterly* (Spring 1996), 5.
3. Thomas Watson, *The Ten Commandments* (1692; repr. Edinburgh: Banner of Truth, 1965), 93.
4. Umberto Cassuto, *A Commentary on the Book of Exodus*, trans. Israel Abrahams (Jerusalem: Magnes Press, 1967), 244.
5. See James T. Dennison, Jr., *The Market Day of the Soul: The Puritan Doctrine of the Sabbath in England, 1532-1700* (New York: University Press of America, 1983).
6. Watson, *The Ten Commandments*, 97.
7. Ibid., 95.
8. Ibid., 99.
9. Leland Ryken, *Redeeming the Time: A Christian Approach to Work and Leisure* (Grand Rapids, MI: Baker, 1995), 178.
10. Ignatius, *Letter to the Magnesians*, quoted in Jochem Douma, *The Ten Commandments: Manual for the Christian Life*, trans. Nelson D. Kloosterman (Phillipsburg, NJ: P&R, 1996), 139.
11. Benjamin Breckinridge Warfield, *Selected Shorter Writings* (Phillipsburg, NJ: Presbyterian & Reformed, 1970), 319.
12. Watson, *The Ten Commandments*, 101.
13. David C. Searle, *And Then There Were Nine* (Fearn, Ross-Shire, England: Christian Focus, 2000), 67.
14. The best book on this subject is Leland Ryken's *Redeeming the Time*, previously cited.
15. See Dennison, *The Market Day of the Soul*, 94.

16. Robert G. Rayburn, "Should Christians Observe the Sabbath?" quoted in a sermon by George W. Robertson at Covenant Presbyterian Church in St. Louis, Missouri.

CHAPTER 8: RESPECT AUTHORITY
1. Annie Gottlieb, *Do You Believe in Magic?* (New York: Time, 1987), 234-235.
2. John Calvin, *Institutes of the Christian Religion,* trans. Ford Lewis Battles, 2 vols., Library of Christian Classics, 20-21 (Philadelphia: Westminster, 1960), II.VIII.11.
3. John I. Durham, *Exodus,* Word Biblical Commentary (Waco, TX: Word, 1987), 290.
4. Augustine, quoted in *Exodus, Leviticus, Numbers, Deuteronomy,* ed. Joseph T. Lienhard, Ancient Christian Commentary on Scripture (Downers Grove, IL: InterVarsity, 2001), 3:106.
5. Rob Schenck, *The Ten Words That Will Change a Nation: The Ten Commandments* (Tulsa, OK: Albury, 1999), 88.
6. Calvin, *Institutes,* II.VIII.35.
7. Thomas Watson, *The Ten Commandments* (1692; repr. Edinburgh: Banner of Truth, 1965), 130.
8. Ecclesiasticus 3:12-13, in the Apocrypha.
9. Michael S. Horton, *The Law of Perfect Freedom* (Chicago: Moody, 1993), 134.
10. Socrates, quoted in Fran Sciacca, *Generation at Risk,* rev. ed. (Chicago: Moody, 1991), 25.

CHAPTER 9: LIVE AND LET LIVE
1. Dick Wright, *Christianity Today* (March 11, 2002), 15.
2. Jochem Douma, *The Ten Commandments: Manual for the Christian Life,* trans. Nelson D. Kloosterman (Phillipsburg, NJ: P&R, 1996), 216.
3. Stephen L. Carter, *God's Name in Vain: The Wrongs and Rights of Religion and Politics* (New York: Basic, 2000), 126.
4. Quoted in *Christianity Today* (February 4, 2002), 80.
5. Thomas Watson, *The Ten Commandments* (1692; repr. Edinburgh: Banner of Truth, 1965), 141.
6. John Calvin, quoted in Michael S. Horton, *The Law of Perfect Freedom* (Chicago: Moody, 1993), 175.
7. J. L. Koole, *De Tien Geboden,* quoted in Douma, *The Ten Commandments,* 213.
8. Vincent Canby, *New York Times,* quoted in Michael Medved, *Hollywood vs. America* (New York: HarperCollins, 1992), 187.
9. Medved, *Hollywood vs. America,* 188-190.
10. See Parents Television Council, *Special Report: What a Difference a Decade Makes* (March 30, 2000).
11. David Grossman, "Trained to Kill," *Christianity Today* (August 19, 1998), 2-3.
12. Wesley J. Smith, *Culture of Death: The Assault on Medical Ethics in America,* reviewed by Richard M. Doerflinger in *First Things,* No. 115 (August/September 2001), 68-72 (68).
13. Malcolm Potts, quoted in W. Wilson Benton's unpublished sermon "Life Is for Living" (April 18, 1993).
14. John Calvin, *Commentaries on the Four Last Books of Moses,* Calvin's Commentaries (Edinburgh; repr. Grand Rapids, MI: Baker, 1999), 41-42.
15. John Calvin, *Institutes of the Christian Religion,* trans. Ford Lewis Battles, 2 vols., Library of Christian Classics, 20-21 (Philadelphia: Westminster, 1960), II.viii.39.
16. Martin Luther, *Large Catechism,* quoted in Horton, *The Law of Perfect Freedom,* 157-158.
17. John MacArthur, Jr., *The MacArthur New Testament Commentary, Matthew 1-7* (Chicago: Moody, 1985), 293.
18. Calvin, *Institutes of the Christian Religion,* II.VIII.39.

CHAPTER 10: THE JOY OF SEX
1. See Leland Ryken, *Worldly Saints: The Puritans as They Really Were* (Grand Rapids, MI: Zondervan, 1986), 40-41.
2. Ibid., 53.

3.  Douglas Wilson, *Fidelity: What It Means to Be a One-Woman Man* (Moscow, ID: Canon, 1999), 53.
4.  C. S. Lewis, *Mere Christianity* (New York: Macmillan, 1952), 95-96.
5.  David Murray, testimony before the Senate Subcommittee on Oversight of Government Management, Restructuring, and the District of Columbia (May 8, 1997), 2.
6.  Terry Fisher, quoted in Michael Medved, *Hollywood vs. America* (New York: HarperCollins, 1992), 111-112.
7.  Martin Luther, *The Large Catechism*, trans. Robert H. Fischer (Philadelphia: Fortress, 1959), 36.
8.  Wendell Berry, interviewed in *Modern Reformation* (November/December 2001), 40.
9.  These three categories come from a sermon by R. Kent Hughes, "Set Apart to Save: Sexual Conduct," preached at College Church in Wheaton, Illinois (December 2, 2001), 5.
10. Greg Gutfield, "The Sex Drive," *Men's Health* (October 1999), quoted in *Leadership* (Summer 2000), 69.
11. Anonymous, quoted in Hughes, "Set Apart to Save: Sexual Conduct," 5.
12. Thomas Watson, *The Ten Commandments* (1692; repr. Edinburgh: Banner of Truth, 1965), 160.
13. Martyn Lloyd-Jones, *Studies in the Sermon on the Mount* (Grand Rapids, MI: Eerdmans, 1984), 261.

## CHAPTER 11: WHAT'S MINE IS GOD'S

1.  T. Cecil Myers, *Thunder on the Mountain* (Nashville: Abingdon, 1965), 119-120, quoted in Maxie D. Dunnam, *Exodus*, The Communicator's Commentary (Waco, TX: Word, 1987), 251.
2.  Rob Schenck, *The Ten Words That Will Change a Nation: The Ten Commandments* (Tulsa, OK: Albury, 1999), 155.
3.  George W. Robertson, "The Eighth Commandment," *Leader to Leader* (July/August 1997), 3.
4.  Martin Luther, quoted in Michael S. Horton, *The Law of Perfect Freedom* (Chicago: Moody, 1993), 206.
5.  John Calvin, quoted in Peter Lewis, *The Message of the Living God*, The Bible Speaks Today (Downers Grove, IL: InterVarsity, 2000), 158.
6.  John Calvin, *Institutes of the Christian Religion,* trans. Ford Lewis Battles, 2 vols., Library of Christian Classics, 20-21 (Philadelphia: Westminster, 1960), II.VIII.45.
7.  Martin Luther, *The Large Catechism* (Philadelphia: Fortress, 1959), 39.
8.  George Barna, *The Barna Report, 1992-93* (Ventura, CA: Regal, 1992), 117.
9.  Martin Luther, quoted in Horton, *The Law of Perfect Freedom*, 206.
10. Martin Luther, quoted in Dunnam, *Exodus*, 265.
11. John Calvin, *Commentary on Genesis*, quoted in Horton, *The Law of Perfect Freedom*, 204.
12. *Issues and Answers: Gambling*, The Christian Life Commission of the Southern Baptist Convention (November 1993).
13. Jerry Bridges, *The Discipline of Grace: God's Role and Our Role in the Pursuit of Holiness* (Colorado Springs: NavPress, 1994), 88.
14. From a sermon by R. Kent Hughes, "Set Apart to Save: Materialism," preached at College Church in Wheaton, Illinois (November 4, 2001).
15. A. W. Tozer, *Born After Midnight* (Harrisburg, PA: Christian Publications, 1959), 107.
16. John Chrysostom, *On Wealth and Poverty*, trans. Catherine Roth (New York: St. Vladimir's Seminary, 1984), 49-55.
17. Martin Luther, *Luther's Works: Lectures on Galatians, 1535, Chapters 1-4*, ed. Jaroslav Pelikan (Saint Louis: Concordia, 1963), 26:277.
18. Ibid., 277-278.

## CHAPTER 12: TO TELL THE TRUTH

1.  O'Leary's tragic downfall is documented in Gary Smith, "Lying in Wait," *Sports Illustrated* (April 8, 2002), 70-87.
2.  The survey, conducted by Colorado's Avert Inc., is mentioned by Jeffrey Kluger in "Pumping Up Your Past," *Time* (Spring 2002).

3. Paul Gray, in Michael S. Horton, *The Law of Perfect Freedom* (Chicago: Moody, 1993), 225-226.
4. Jochem Douma, *The Ten Commandments: Manual for the Christian Life*, trans. Nelson D. Kloosterman (Phillipsburg, NJ: P&R, 1996), 315-316.
5. Ibid., 316-317.
6. This form of the well-known saying comes from Göran Larsson, *Bound for Freedom: The Book of Exodus in Jewish and Christian Traditions* (Peabody, MA: Hendrickson, 1999), 153.
7. Thomas Watson, *The Ten Commandments* (1692; repr. Edinburgh: Banner of Truth, 1965), 169-170.
8. George Orwell, as seen on a Philadelphia bumper sticker.
9. Paul Gray, quoted in Horton, *The Law of Perfect Freedom*, 225.
10. "Churched Youth Survey," Barna Research Group (1994).
11. Charles Colson, "Post-Truth Society," *Christianity Today* (March 11, 2002), 112.
12. John Calvin, *Institutes of the Christian Religion*, trans. Ford Lewis Battles, 2 vols., Library of Christian Classics, 20-21 (Philadelphia: Westminster, 1960), II.VIII.47.
13. William Barclay, in Maxie D. Dunnam, *Exodus*, The Communicator's Commentary (Waco, TX: Word, 1987), 266.

## CHAPTER 13: BEING CONTENT

1. Mark Buchanan, "Trapped in the Cult of the Next Thing," *Christianity Today* (September 6, 1999), 64.
2. John L. Mackay, *Exodus* (Fern, Ross-shire, England: Christian Focus, 2001), 354.
3. Thomas Watson, *The Ten Commandments* (1692; repr. Edinburgh: Banner of Truth, 1965), 174.
4. John D. Currid, *A Study Commentary on Exodus*, 2 vols. (Auburn, MA: Evangelical Press USA, 2000), 2:49.
5. Anonymous, quoted in Maxie D. Dunnam, *Exodus*, The Communicator's Commentary (Waco, TX: Word, 1987), 267.
6. Watson, *The Ten Commandments*, 178.
7. Recounted in Michael S. Horton, *The Law of Perfect Freedom* (Chicago: Moody, 1993), 167.
8. Martin Luther, *Large Catechism*, quoted in ibid., 241.
9. Francis A. Schaeffer, *True Spirituality* (Wheaton, IL: Tyndale, 1971), 8.
10. F. B. Meyer, *Elijah* (Fort Washington, PA: Christian Literature Crusade, 1992), 135.
11. Jeremiah Burroughs, *The Rare Jewel of Christian Contentment* (1648; repr. Edinburgh: Banner of Truth, 1964), 18.
12. Horton, *The Law of Perfect Freedom*, 247.

## EPILOGUE: THE END OF THE LAW

1. John Bunyan, *The Pilgrim's Progress* (New York: New American Library, 1964), 26-27.
2. Charles H. Spurgeon, "The Mediator—the Interpreter" (No. 2097), *The Metropolitan Tabernacle Pulpit* (1890; repr. London: Banner of Truth, 1970), 35:409.
3. Ibid., 409.
4. David Brainerd, quoted in Ernest C. Reisinger, *The Law and the Gospel* (Phillipsburg, NJ: P&R, 1997), 78.
5. John Murray, *Principles of Conduct: Aspects of Biblical Ethics* (Grand Rapids, MI: Eerdmans, 1957), 185-186.
6. Martin Luther, *Luther's Works: Lectures on Galatians, 1535, Chapters 1-4*, ed. Jaroslav Pelikan (Saint Louis: Concordia, 1963), 26:130.
7. Thomas Watson, *The Ten Commandments* (1692; repr. Edinburgh: Banner of Truth, 1965), 44.
8. Samuel Bolton, *The True Bounds of Christian Freedom* (1645; repr. London: Banner of Truth, 1964), 71-72.
9. Reisinger, *The Law and the Gospel*, 36.
10. Thomas Ascol, in the "Foreword" to ibid., xi.

# SCRIPTURE INDEX

# GENERAL INDEX